CLIMBING THE EQUATOR
ADVENTURES IN THE JUNGLES AND MOUNTAINS OF ECUADOR

NEVILLE SHULMAN

summersdale

CLIMBING THE EQUATOR

Summersdale Publishers Ltd
46 West Street
Chichester
West Sussex
PO19 1RP
UK

www.summersdale.com

Printed and bound in Great Britain

ISBN 1 84024 450 X

Climbing The Equator is dedicated to all the children of South America who need our support and encouragement. All the book royalties are being donated to charities involved in caring for South American children.

CONTENTS

FOREWORD BY JOHN BLASHFORD-SNELL

Colonel John Blashford-Snell, explorer and writer, known as the 'Indiana Jones of Britain', is the Chairman of the Scientific Exploration Society and has led many expeditions including those of the Blue Nile, Zaire rivers, Kota Mama and British Trans-Americas.

Although I have led expeditions in much of South America and explored some of its remotest regions, it is to my great regret that I have never been to Ecuador. However, I hope to remedy this very soon, and then will certainly have Neville Shulman's book to hand.

Having known the author for many years, I admire his enquiring mind and the intelligent way in which he has described this meeting place of the high Sierra, the Amazon rainforest and the fertile Pacific coastal plains, above which towers the snow-covered peak of Mount Chimborazo.

Neville provides a vivid description of the extraordinary wildlife and particularly the fascinating birds. He gives thrilling accounts of his climbs to the high altitude summits of the Andes, facing many dangers and braving challenging, uncertain conditions.

Neville's books are always a great read and this is certainly no exception. He also vividly describes the background and history of Ecuador and we experience the problems of the many indigenous tribes and feel for them, as he obviously does.

Ecuador is a country full of spectacular contrasts and diversity and there are interesting facts and information in every chapter. The author's thought-provoking approach provides us with many insights and opportunities to evaluate the way we think about the rainforest and its inhabitants, whether human, animal or the huge variety of reptiles and insects to be found there. The Galapagos Archipelago is an incredible and special place, full of magical creatures and habitats, and throughout Neville's expedition we encounter enchantment as we accompany him on his colourful journeys. This is an entertaining book with plenty of surprises.

FOREWORD BY CHRIS BONINGTON

Sir Chris Bonington is internationally acknowledged as one of the world's finest mountaineers and is a prolific writer and photojournalist. He has led expeditions throughout the world and was with Colonel Blashford-Snell on the Blue Nile expedition.

This is another intriguing and fascinating book, this time on Ecuador, by Neville Shulman, who as always excels in telling the stories of his adventures and at the same time providing in-depth information and background on the region visited. His approach is from many perspectives and is imaginative and appealing. I have climbed Sangay, the most active of Ecuador's volcanic mountains, and know full well the dangers and difficulties that can be encountered in this small but very attractive South American country. Neville's own mountain struggles clearly illustrate the powerful forces to be encountered and he nobly experiences both failure and success, but feels privileged, as we all do, to be able to climb these high altitude mountains.

This evocative book explores the whole panorama of jungles and rainforests, as well as their indigenous tribes and colourful animals, and their extensive and exotic bird life. Ecuador, like Peru, was the land of the mysterious Incas and of course includes the Galapagos Islands which contain so many extraordinary creatures, such as the giant tortoise and marine and land iguanas, that so greatly influenced the naturalist and writer Charles Darwin. Neville Shulman's book provides compelling insights into the backgrounds of all the animals, birds and marine life of the Galapagos, and it is enthralling stuff.

MAP OF ECUADOR

THE HIGHLANDS

Esmeraldas

NORTHERN ANDES

COLOMBIA

Ibarra

Otavalo

EQUATOR   Pedernales   Mindo   Lago Agrio

Pichincha   QUITO   Cayambe

Ilinizas   Antisana   Reventador

PACIFIC OCEAN   CENTRAL ANDES   Cotopaxi   Sumaco

Latacunga

Manta

Ambato

Baños   AMAZON RAINFOREST

THE COAST   Chimborazo   Tungurahua

Riobamba   Altar

GUAYAQUIL

Salinas   Sangay

CUENCA

Machala   SOUTHERN ANDES

PERU

Loja

PERU

9

MAP OF THE GALAPAGOS ISLANDS

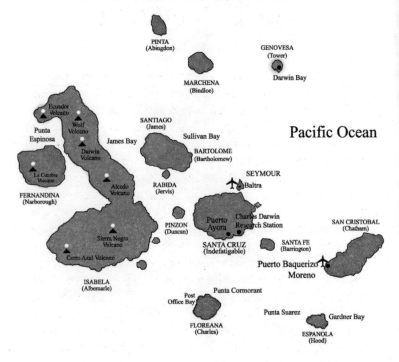

PINTA
(Abingdon)

GENOVESA
(Tower)

Darwin Bay

MARCHENA
(Bindloe)

Ecuador
Volcano

Punta
Espinosa

Wolf
Volcano

SANTIAGO
(James)

Pacific Ocean

James Bay

Sullivan Bay

Darwin
Volcano

BARTOLOME
(Bartholomew)

La Cumbre
Volcano

Alcedo
Volcano

RABIDA
(Jervis)

SEYMOUR

Baltra

FERNANDINA
(Narborough)

PINZON
(Duncan)

Puerto
Ayora

Charles Darwin
Research Station

SAN CRISTOBAL
(Chatham)

Sierra Negra
Volcano

SANTA FE
(Barrington)

SANTA CRUZ
(Indefatigable)

Cerro Azul Volcano

Puerto Baquerizo
Moreno

ISABELA
(Albemarle)

Post
Office Bay

Punta Cormorant

Punta Suarez

Gardner Bay

FLOREANA
(Charles)

ESPANOLA
(Hood)

CHAPTER 1

THE HIGH ROAD TO ECUADOR

The snowstorm swirls furiously around me, its thick flakes dazzling and blinding me from seeing a way ahead as well as preventing me from finding any way back. I feel trapped and isolated, as I lie exposed at full stretch across an unrelenting rock face, which is becoming more slippery and coated in wet ice with every passing moment. Luis is shouting something across to me but whatever he is saying is all too easily swept away by the force of the wind, whipping ferociously around me and threatening to loosen my grip on the one jutting stone on which my safety seems to depend. I strive hard to hear some of his words, not even being certain whether they are spoken in English or Spanish, although I suppose them to be probably a mixture of the two. I try to understand the meaning of the muffled sounds, guessing at the instructions that he is trying to convey; 'jump, *va*, *rápido*, let go, forward, *ahora*.' Am I really hearing Luis's shouts, or merely imagining something fashioned out of the noises created by the frenzied wildness of the wind?

Whatever his words are I know it has to be my choice. I can't remain as I am for much longer and it is time for a fast – and urgent – decision. I need to go for it, somehow, some way. I remember the Russian proverb I have carried as a mantra on many mountains before, '*Doveryai no proveryai*' – 'Trust but verify'. There's no chance of that now. Here

11

I will have to trust without knowing. I prepare myself mentally to let go and to slide forward, hoping to find another secure hold to prevent myself falling further down the rocks. How many times in the past have I experienced moments such as this and how many more would there be to encounter on these high Ecuadorian mountains? This now - or - never moment feels as if it has locked me into its own space. High up on a mountain the thin atmosphere can play very strange tricks on the mind. Time has no real meaning in the ordinary sense and can stretch in any direction, creating its own dimension. My body is refusing to let me move and my mind starts to flash backwards.

I am again feeling the call of the wild, and it is time to plan a journey to another remote part of the world. Many friends working for charities I've supported in the past are also asking when and where I will go next, and if I would consider fundraising for them. It's the extra spur I need. But where should I go?

As always, needing some inspiration, I begin by looking through my maps and atlases, searching for a place, a name even, which will pull me in a certain direction and help me to decide. I always strive to find a unique corner of the world, some intriguing spot in which to attempt another challenge that might again persuade friends and colleagues to support my efforts, whilst also providing me with opportunities to expand my understanding and gain some personal insights. I always cover the cost of the entire expedition myself, so at least they can be confident that the entirety of any donations will go directly to the particular charity, and that has usually encouraged them to give more. Having already climbed a number of mountains on several continents, trekked through many remote jungles and rainforests and even travelled to the Arctic and Antarctic

Poles, finding a fresh challenge that is equally inspiring won't be easy.

I spend a great deal of time considering possibilities but it is proving very difficult to come up with something really interesting, hopefully spectacular and worthy of supporting. I even consider re-visiting Mont Blanc, my first major conquest, and adding on some other Alpine peaks. I can't work up enough enthusiasm for that as an expedition formula however, as I need each adventure to be unique and individual.

Browsing through my collections of antiques and artefacts gathered from so many different parts of the world, I come across a small Incan musical instrument. It is a simple, coloured, clay carving in the shape of a seated musician playing his pipes, with two tiny holes, one on the back and one in the base, used jointly to obtain a breathy, low - pitched single note. Or at least that's all I have ever managed to create from it. Probably the Incan musician to whom it had originally belonged had been able to produce some wonderfully melodic sounds from it. Holding this tiny, beautiful object created over 500 years ago, I start to feel that it holds the key to deciding my next expedition destination. The Incas were a mystical race who mysteriously vanished, shortly after being vanquished by the invading Spanish in the sixteenth century. Theirs is an intriguing story and their legacies still influence the contemporary peoples of their regions in so many ways. Many of them undoubtedly carry Incan blood and it's easy to see that some still have their facial characteristics.

The two countries of the ancient Incas were Peru and Ecuador and from previous travels through both of them I know that they are saturated with interesting places that would provide numerous opportunities for further exploration. My further research however, reveals Ecuador in particular to have some special and appealing features.

Of particular significance to me is the fact that Ecuador is home to a beautiful, challenging and very high mountain, Chimborazo. Chimborazo is, in fact, considered to be 'the tallest' in the world, due to its location on the 'bulge' that occurs on the earth's surface around the equator and runs through the centre of Ecuador.

Of further interest to me in Ecuador are the remote and fabled Pacific islands known as the Galapagos Archipelago. These islands contain many endemic and amazing creatures that were the primary influence on Charles Darwin in creating his evolutionary theory of natural selection. Darwin, the noted naturalist, geographer and philosopher is one of a handful of men who have always been an inspiration to me and it has been a lifelong ambition of mine to follow in his footsteps to the Galapagos Islands. This decides it. Ecuador will be my own 'natural selection', the destination of my next expedition. During my travels through this tiny country, my prime goals will be attempting to scale the 'tallest' mountain, Chimborazo, and encountering the descendants of some of the creatures that inspired Darwin all those years ago.

I immediately start to commit myself mentally and physically to the expedition, announcing my intentions to my friends, training hard, making my plans and research as well as selecting the charities for which I will fundraise this time. As with my previous expeditions, I always find it important before going to learn more about the country of my choice, its history and background, its different peoples and the habitats of the creatures I hope to encounter. I now start to feel the surge of adrenalin and emotion that I always experience before any expedition, the contemplation of the unknown, and of who and what I might expect to discover.

The sub-continent of South America consists of some 12 countries of extraordinarily diverse cultures, backgrounds and ways of life. I have been exceptionally fortunate to travel in and through most of these fascinating countries and experience their enchantments first hand. The whole region is very exciting and full of wonderful sights, interesting sounds and strong flavours. Ecuador, although one of South America's smallest countries is, for a number of reasons which I will endeavour to make apparent, one of the most magical and in many ways epitomises all that is so interesting and special about this vibrant continent. At the same time Ecuador sadly also symbolises the many economical and sociological difficulties of South America. This has primarily occurred as a result of successive, sometimes corrupt, governments giving insufficient attention to the nurturing of the magnificent flora and fauna with which this country has been so richly blessed.

Ecuador has it all: wild and impenetrable jungles and rainforests, high Andean, snow-capped mountains, wide curving valleys, sweeping rivers, indigenous tribes of countless cultures and traditions, and so many exotic creatures and flora that provide an illustration of the vast spectrum of Nature's gifts. We can consider Ecuador as a microcosm of the whole world, as a way of examining the immense problems created by so many generations failing to address extensive global warming and its myriad consequences. In its continuing misuse and reckless over-exploitation of its land and natural resources, Ecuador has inherited many of the environmental problems which so many countries need to address in order to attempt to overcome the enormous and continuing dangers that lie ahead for all of us. A Zen question expresses the predicament that we all find so difficult to resolve. 'Who can untangle the tangle of this world?' Who indeed, but certainly we must all try.

Although Charles Darwin only visited the Galapagos once, for an intensive five weeks in September 1835, his amazing encounters and experiences there allowed him to prepare and publish his ground-breaking theories on evolution, and in so doing turn many previous theories upside down. I believe that upside down is often a good way, and it is particularly a Zen way, to approach and consider anything. As Roald Dahl, the famous writer, stated, 'A little nonsense now and then is cherished by the wisest of men and women.' Ecuador is full of nonsenses and surprises and is certainly a place to inspire contemplation about the nature of life. This book endeavours to express the knowledge and impressions – as imperfect and painfully acquired as they were – of my Ecuadorian travels and adventures.

An important caveat is always to remember that Ecuador is a country of *mañana*, where something will often only take place tomorrow or indeed very many days later. If you can, take your time – it's not a place to hurry through but one in which to linger and slowly and gently enjoy its many delights. Moreover, everything may not be as it first seems, and Ecuador is certainly a country of contrasts and contradictions. Not least, it is important to remember that there are several spellings of the indigenous names and also a number of confusing interpretations of their meanings. There are also often differing calculations of the heights of some of its mountains, as well as the distances between places, even the area measurements of the National Parks. The Ecuadorians are not at all fazed by this and hopefully you won't be either. It's always a matter of trying to feel and understand the soul and spirit of this gorgeous country.

The heart of the country actually relates back to many of the indigenous tribal traditions, established well before even the Incas invaded and certainly long before the Spanish conquistadors were on the scene. Unfortunately the rights of these indigenous tribes have been abused over many centuries and this has stirred enmities and suspicions that remain to the present day. A number of those who came seeking New World riches found in Ecuador a country whose people were all too easy to exploit and whose traditional ways they could ignore or reject without any recourse. Or so they thought. These indigenous tribes, previously known erroneously as 'Indian' by those invading their territories, have primarily lived within the jungle and the rainforest and they know and respect its mysterious habitats as well as the wild animals and creatures they contain. Any further use of 'Indian' other than the proper term 'indigenous tribe' has been restricted and has only been used where considered necessary in the context.

Unfortunately, commercial interests have for far too long now been allowed to take precedence and to dictate how the land should be used, so indeed it is often misused. We all should care about the past, as it helps to shape the future. The often oppressive and uncaring intrusion by loggers, prospectors and so many others into the rainforest causes immense damage.

Climbing in the mountains should allow me time for contemplation, for reflection, and I hope to learn a great deal. I can only hope the spirit of the indigenous peoples of Ecuador will always be present during my expedition and help to guide me through the dangers that I will face.

CHAPTER 2

RUNNING THE JUNGLE

He has run his heart out and there is nowhere left to run. They are too close and he knows his only chance is to vanish, if he is to survive. The rain has stopped but the wetness remains. He presses his face into the damp earth and tries to still his senses. If he can't see them, hear them, feel them, then perhaps they won't find him. First he had turned into a powerful, fighting jaguar, then a slithering, twisting anaconda, now finally he becomes a small, burrowing beetle. His colour also gradually changes. The monkey's body is still warm and for a moment he thinks it might still be alive and might exact its revenge and shout out a cry. He listens intently but there is no heart murmur, no sound, nothing at all. Slowly, gently and carefully he pushes it away further into the decaying vegetation covering it with a thin layer of leaves.

The monkey's life had ended some time back, when he had finally spotted it in the canopy and lifted Moonbeam to his lips, to send the dart speeding towards it; now his life might also be forfeit. He hadn't hesitated to bring it down, even though he knew its life was precious, for it was the law of the jungle. Although he knew he had been wrong to follow it into another tribe's territory he had felt he had no choice. His family needs food and he has to provide for them. He had been tracking it carefully for some time, following it deeper into the rainforest, ever since he had spotted it swinging leisurely between the giant cedars, seemingly unaware it was being observed. Within the jungle he knew how to make himself invisible then and hopes he can do the same now.

They must have been close by and heard the sounds of the monkey falling but probably wouldn't have known what it was. But they are also hunters and would need to investigate. He is well outside his own territory and inside theirs and that makes him an enemy and they will be determined not to allow him to leave. He had quickly gathered up the monkey from the foliage, sliding it into his net but even then he had worried that there had been too much noise, although the jungle is always filled with many strange movements. Immediately he starts to move faster although not running, as that could also attract attention, but making his way back as fast as he can, knowing how pleased everyone would be with his kill. At first he doesn't hear them but then there are too many similar sounds behind him and suddenly he realises that he is being followed. He guesses there are perhaps four or five of them pursuing him. He can't fight them all and his only chance of survival will be to outrun them or to hide.

He steps up his pace listening intently to all the sounds of the rainforest, as he knows they will as well. Previously he had allowed his quiver with the remaining darts to fall, it could easily be replaced, but he is still finding it difficult carrying both the monkey and Moonbeam, and together they are slowing him down too much. He can't leave the monkey as that would mean it had all been for nothing. So, as soon as he can without slowing his pace, almost within just a heartbeat, quickly finding a partly-broken, hollowed-out tree, he slides Moonbeam inside and hides it behind some loose, green and yellow vines. The broken tree is next to a larger kapok tree and three thin, chonta palms, so he hopes to be able to come back within a few days and recover it. Since a child he has known how to read the forest and understand the way of the trees and he should easily find it again. Now the most important thing is to escape.

He lengthens and quickens his stride, breaking and cutting his way through the dense foliage and bushes and twisted lianas which try to impede him. There is no need to be quiet now, speed is everything. He is strong, completely determined and he thinks he can make it. Their following, echoing sounds had at first intensified but now they gradually start to fade and he feels he is faster. His heart is pounding so hard that it feels as if it might burst through his chest, but he knows they will be the same and that encourages him to keep going. The hunter is himself being hunted but he has no fear, feeling only the necessity of survival. He starts to think he is winning the contest and to feel confident he can make it through as he hugs the monkey to his body. Its warmth seems to be willing him to continue.

Now he is sure he is losing them and he runs harder, his lungs almost bursting with the effort. Suddenly there are foreign sounds from his left, then also from the right, closer than before. He realises that they have started to circle around him. They know the jungle better, this is their territory. He now recognises, although again without fear, that he isn't going to out run them – they would know how to take advantage of the shortcuts. He must use all his cunning to outwit them. That will be his only chance. It is time to vanish. Where is the right place? Not here, nor over there but he must do it soon, before they come too close.

This seems the ideal spot, a gentle banking slope that is covered with low bushes and full of decaying vegetation that should hide his smell and even more importantly, the smell of the monkey. He slows, listens and then allows himself to sink softly to his knees before rolling, so quietly that they won't hear, into and underneath the vegetation. It takes only moments and he is out of sight.

He stills his breathing and becomes a creature of the rainforest; gradually changing to one of the smallest. Now he can hear nothing of them and soon he feels convinced they have no knowledge of what he's done and have lost him. It becomes so quiet that he can hear the silence of every leaf that falls. The jungle and the rainforest are magical places and even now, in the midst of danger, he can appreciate what raw, potent beauty exists here for those who understand it. He keeps his eyes closed, partly in the belief that if he can't see them, just as if he can't hear them, they won't see or hear him. Gradually, it takes several long seconds, he opens his left eye, his instinct telling him there is something to know, although at first he can't see anything. Then very close, just over a hand length away, a long line of the fierce soldier ants marches into his vision. Their proximity makes them seem even larger than usual and he hopes they haven't been attracted by the smell of the monkey. Many times previously he has used them, mostly when out hunting, to bind a wound as their pincers are incredibly strong and they will never let go. If any were to grip him now he wouldn't cry out, he would take any pain without a murmur. His very life depends on it and he understands only too well the lore of the jungle. It seems almost an eternity, it is a very long column but eventually the ants pass by and disappear into the undergrowth and he is alone once again.

There are still no sounds of his pursuers and he gradually starts to relax. Hopefully they have also passed and lost him. He thinks he could soon be safe and then tonight he would provide his family with a feast and a story. The forest is slowly drying out and there are all kinds of rustlings as it starts to spring slowly back into life. The sun is still trying to fight its way through, as always without much success, attempting to pierce the thick, overhead canopy that binds most of the trees together. They are all in a constant life struggle to reach upwards to the light and the essence it provides. Overhead a solitary bird flutters its wings as it also struggles its way through the intensely intermingled branches. He doesn't need to see it to know it is a macaw, just as he knows when a caiman is close by, hiding and waiting in the river shallows, even though he can't see it.

It has suddenly become very quiet, too quiet, and he feels instinctively uneasy. He guesses they are near, very near, and he tries to go deeper inside himself in order to avoid attracting their attention. They are good, very good, possibly better than he is and so after all he hasn't fooled them. This is their territory and they would probably know every part of it, as he knows his. They had never given up looking for him and have continued to use all their senses to track him. It is much too late to run now, even without the monkey, they could be anywhere around him. Probably they had split into several groups, one or more of them staying behind, at least another one circling in front. They may be closing in. He asks the jaguar and the anaconda to save him although he realises it is probably too late, perhaps it was a curse from the dying monkey. He dare not move in any way, he must know nothing of what is around him, he is ceasing to exist.

Until the vine is looped through his ankles he doesn't feel their approach but as it tightens he then hears their soft battle whoop of victory, signalling his capture. He makes no sound. It is not his way and it is not the way of his tribe. They start to pull him upwards, with harsh, unrelenting force, his bound feet making it difficult for him to stand but he won't allow himself to fall. Without their asking he knows what is required, it is the rule of the jungle and he pulls out his treasured knife and passes it over. It had been given to him by his father, only one long blade but honed extremely sharp, the way he was always taught to keep it. The knife could slice through anything but now it will be used against him. His sadness is that he won't be able to give it to his son. He doesn't close his eyes but stops seeing, focusing his mind on a distant high mountain, in the way he had learned as a child. Now his running is over.

CHAPTER 3

TOUGH TIMES ON EL NORTE

I am anxious to climb and ready to test myself again, and Luis, my guide, thinks I should have a good chance of climbing Iliniza Norte to the summit. Previously I had been expecting to climb with Domingo, who had been highly recommended by another climbing colleague. Dom and I had built up a good understanding through our e-mails but he unfortunately became unavailable due to a family problem in another part of the country. I met Luis at one of the climbing schools and he agreed to climb with me in Dom's place. Subsequently discussing our plans, it turns out that Luis is more hesitant in making climbing decisions, which I find somewhat worrying. I always prefer a guide who is as determined as I am, somebody with strengths to balance my lack of greater experience, but who takes into account my commitment and enthusiasm. I've climbed with many different types of guides over the years, but usually only on the mountain and in adverse conditions does real character show through. Time will undoubtedly tell. I have to focus intently on the mountain.

Now we're close to setting off and Luis suddenly reveals a few concerns. The current weather forecasts are not favourable on most mountains and there have been several recent reports of mishaps involving climbers who experienced severe difficulties in constantly changing conditions and only just escaped in time. Norte is not usually snow capped but there have been some worrying reports of sudden snow storms around the summit that are creating difficulties for climbers. Despite these worries, Luis knows I am keen to attempt a climb and this one has such a reputation, we agree to proceed. We both know that it's rare for there to ever be an ideal time to climb, as high mountains carry their own weather which can always change rapidly. Anyhow, Iliniza will be good practice for my later attempt on Chimborazo, which I am planning to climb towards the end of the expedition.

Luis is a thin, wiry climber, supposedly well experienced in the mountains but rather taciturn and doesn't express his emotions easily. In that way he is certainly not the typical South American or Ecuadorian whose loud and excitable voices can invariably be heard throughout this region expressing diverse opinions on every subject under the sun. In fact, the hot Equatorial sun usually adds on several degrees of noise and volatility to any 'discussion'.

'We'll go if you want to. I'll leave the decision to you.' Those aren't exactly the words I want to hear, but I am prepared to climb.

The Ilinizas are, in fact, twin summits comprising Iliniza Norte (North) and Iliniza Sur (South). Norte is 5,126 metres (16,818 feet) and Sur is 5,248 metres (17,218 feet). Iliniza was originally one volcano but now there are two peaks, which were separated by a huge eruption many years ago and are now joined by a low rock saddle and set approximately one kilometre apart from each other. It was a favourite mountain of the Incas and often used for sacrificial purposes. There can be found the remains of a number of Incan fortresses (*pucaras*) here on the lower slopes, as well as on other high hills or ridges. They always tend to blend in with the rock background however, so you need to be eagle-eyed, or even condor-eyed, to spot them. Its name comes from Quichua, the language of most of the indigenous tribes, and apparently means, 'The Supposedly Sick One', probably deriving from the knowledge of the volcano in the distant past splitting into two. There is also the mythical story that the peaks are two lovers that were forcibly separated and then eventually changed into female and male mountains by a powerful wizard.

To reach the area of the mountain we drive away from the hustle of the city of Quito for several hours across very bumpy terrain, passing herds of grazing cows and sheep that don't even bother to look up as we pass by. I start becoming more excited the closer we come to the mountain and start bouncing up and down in the front seat. That could of course be caused by the shaking of the car which hardly appears to have any suspension, and Luis seems to be deliberately seeking out the parts of the track which are the most uneven. He can obviously see my excitement but doesn't enquire why the approach to the mountain is having such an effect on me. Initially I try to explain, telling him about some of my past adventures on European mountains and in the Himalayas, particularly climbing in Tibet. However I am just not getting through to him, so after a while I give up and decide to keep my thoughts and emotions to myself. Anyway there's so much to see, to observe and to feel.

Finally we reach the village of El Chaupi, travel quickly around it and then arrive at a gently sloping area called La Virgen. It is a grassy, relatively open area, often used for parking and is not positioned too far from the Ilinizas mountains. We will be able to trek in from there early the next morning and then start the actual climb of Norte. Our parking has brought us within striking and viewing distance of the twin peaks of the mountains and I'm almost brimming over with anticipation, although as Luis is nonchalant as ever I try to keep my feelings to myself. We agree to set up our tents with a cook tent in between, along the narrow trail leading towards the initial stony and rocky slopes. Luis puts up his tent near to the car but I pitch my tent much further towards the upper sections of the trail, closer to the mountains, as I want to have a clear view of our proposed ascent route as soon as possible. We seem to be blocking the way for other vehicles to pass by, but Luis assures me that this is unlikely to occur at this time and anyhow there aren't really any other flat areas we could use safely. Driving in this region is always hazardous to say the least and I guess that if any other drivers want to pass by our tents they will undoubtedly do so, even if it means them driving initially down the steeper slope just below us, in order to pass around our vehicle and our tents.

As it's already late in the afternoon and therefore too late to climb to any real extent today, Luis suggests we rest and have an early night after preparing dinner. I am feeling too excited about what lies ahead however and don't want to wait, so I decide to trek off on my own in order to climb for a while on the lower slopes. I want to get a feel of what it will be like tomorrow and test out how the terrain feels before we commence our actual ascent. Luis is happy about it and I leave him at the tents preparing our evening meal while I quickly set off alone up the main trail. 'Don't get lost. If you do, head downwards and shout. Otherwise I'll eat your dinner as well.' His remark sends me off with a smile and after several minutes I turn around to wave but there's only the tents gently moving in the breeze to reply.

There are springy tussock areas just ahead and I decide to climb through them, reasoning that this will be much easier on my feet. In fact I find the first sections rather wearing, although still manageable, and very soon get into a rhythm which feels comfortable. Initially I climb through a rather woody area before then reaching a high moraine ridge which allows me to look back and see our faraway camp, already microscopic in the distance. However, shortly after that I enter onto a hard rock section and from then on the going becomes very much tougher. My legs are starting to feel heavy, probably because of the high altitude and I worry as I am obviously still not sufficiently acclimatised. However I won't give up too soon and continue climbing for about a further hour before deciding it's time to head back down. It feels reasonably cool with only a slight warm breeze, so I feel the concerns about storms and unsettled weather are a false alarm and we will be able to climb tomorrow without that worry. Going back down feels good and easy and I manage a fast pace and return within an hour.

Back at our camp we share in a basic dinner of meat and potatoes in the cook tent and after clearing up together I return to my own tent to catch up on some reading. It's warmer than I expected so I undress totally and then get into my sleeping bag, which is more than adequately insulated to cope with the colder mountain night air which tries unsuccessfully to intimidate me. After completing only two chapters of a Gabriel García Marquez novel, I try to fall to sleep, wanting to be fresh for the early morning start. I find it difficult, as I am still keyed up by the thought of what tomorrow will bring.

After about half an hour I am finally dozing off when I am suddenly wakened by some very loud bellowing and see large, menacing, shadowy shapes clearly visible through the thin tent fabric. They seem to be passing extremely close and I feel, whatever they are, that they will invade my tent at any moment. I'm pretty certain they are cows, although certainly more energetic than the ones we passed on the way up, but the loud aggressive noises, now circling all around me, make me feel that one at least could be a bull. Initially I shout out, trying to warn them away, but to no avail and eventually I am forced to dress and step outside the tent to investigate. It seems we have tented along the pathway of a herd of cows that are returning, without any herder, to their evening pastures and they probably, quite rightly, resent anything and anyone being in their way. Fortunately for me, there is no bull. I wave my arms about in a mad fashion in order to try to frighten them off, even bellowing at them in a similar manner and eventually, after looking at me with seeming disbelief, the cows slowly take the hint and move off further down the hillside, looking to graze in quieter pastures.

In fact I now realise that my disturbance by the cows was a blessing in disguise, because now that I am outside the tent I discover there is an amazing sight to be seen, as if just waiting patiently for me to wake up and view it. Gazing skywards I witness what must be thousands or perhaps millions of intensely bright stars twinkling with all the energy they possess, as if desperately trying to attract the attention of all Earth's creatures. They have certainly captured mine. The entire sky is crammed with light and brilliance. I realise it's another wonderful benefit of my being at the Equator and at such a high altitude: We are so far removed from the bright lights of the cities and so way above the many layers of pollution. Every politician from every part of the world, who doesn't live within a clear atmosphere, should be brought, forcibly if necessary, to experience such places as this. They should be made to witness at first hand what Nature provides and what Mankind so very often takes away, losing so much by not being more aware of the continuing damage to environment and to the Planet's future.

After drinking in the starry, starry night for a very long time, I finally return to my tent and its peaceful seclusion and this time, totally relaxed, I fall quickly asleep. Not for long however, as the cows return again, although, as cows mostly look alike, they might be different ones returning from elsewhere. At any rate the aggressive bellowing has recommenced and once more I go outside and resume my imitation cow noises until the animals reluctantly traipse off. Spellbound by what I see I wonder how many of the stars are really still alive and how many may have died countless light years ago with only their light still visible and travelling through space to reach Earth. Light travels at around 300,000 kilometres (186,000 miles) per second so the distances covered are truly colossal or 'out of this world'. It seems as if I am actually looking back in time, thousands of years into the past. It's quite a thought.

Reluctantly I drag myself away from this celestial brilliance and unearthly stargazing and return once more to my tent to try and sleep, otherwise I won't get enough rest before our early start. Of course, the cows then come back again. This comical see-saw process continues until I finally give up and leave the cows in control. Eventually I am able to fall asleep, although mostly by counting cows instead of sheep. In the morning the large amount of cow dung around proves that it was no dream. I accept that the cows have the right of way and will undoubtedly be there this evening and probably every evening. The sight reminds me of the expedition leader who goes off scouting the way ahead and after some while returns with his report. 'I've got good news and bad news. The bad news is we are lost and all that there is to eat is cow dung. The good news is that there is plenty of it.' Well, there is certainly a lot of it around my tent but I am not that hungry, not yet anyway.

After our very early breakfast we empty the tents, although leaving them standing, and pack everything not needed on the climb into the boot of the car, then quickly start out on our trek towards Iliniza Norte. It's already slowly beginning to get light so we don't need torches, and there's a cooling, brisk wind flowing all around me that helps me not to overheat, particularly with all the equipment and extra clothing, carried in case of mountain emergencies. My backpack is much heavier than I would like and I regret not leaving more behind. Trekking in silence we soon reach the point that I had climbed to yesterday, and I feel pleased with the faster pace Luis is now setting which at this stage is very comfortable for me. The weather is fine, only slightly overcast, and it looks like any fears of difficult weather problems were unfounded. I am enjoying the slow transition into daylight, watching the shadowy shapes around me spring into being, feeling life re-asserting itself. Then stupidly I step into a hidden hole, wrenching my right ankle and foot, and I crash over heavily. Luckily the pain is only momentary and I quickly manage to get myself up and catch up with Luis who is climbing steadily, just a metre or two ahead. He obviously knows the way well and I'm very content to follow in his footsteps and just experience the wildness of the rolling landscape and the stone terrain which stretches far into the distance. We are soon climbing amongst steeper rocks, which are testing but I manage well. The actual two mountains of Illinizas are still far off, and as always at the early stages of any climb, they never seem to get any nearer.

There is now more wind but I put that down to our traversing through rather open country and being more exposed to the elements. Then I feel some wet spots on my face, thinking at first they are from my own sweat or perhaps thrown up by my boots from the foliage underneath. However, they persist and I have to admit that they are not man-made when they become more rapid and frequent and then are followed by a small snow flurry. I can only hope it will pass and won't develop into something larger. Luis hasn't stopped but I assume that he is also aware of the changing conditions and that this is usual or he also expects it will cease shortly. I couldn't be more wrong. Soon the snow starts falling with a vengeance and it's being driven hard into my face. I pull my hood down to my sunglasses (in these circumstances that is certainly a misnomer) and button up tightly. That makes the climbing more difficult and it becomes a far greater struggle than I expected, with increasingly strong but intermittent snow storms coupled with fierce biting winds attacking from all sides.

At times it becomes impossible to see literally a hand in front of my face and the rocks are now so slippery that I can't help but fall several times. Luis doesn't fall once of course, but each time I do he waits patiently until I've righted myself and have recommenced climbing. He makes no comment nor offers any advice and I prefer it that way. Luckily we soon see the Refugio Nuevos Horizontes some distance ahead of us, and Luis alters our route so that we climb directly to reach it. Although I'm anxious and certainly willing to press on, he decides we should stop at the Refuge for some tea to warm us before continuing on any further. Several guides and their climbers have been using this as a staging post to stay overnight, in order to make it easier to climb to the summits the next day. Some are still horizontal in their bunks and look as if they haven't moved for days. I feel we would also have benefited considerably, particularly in these bad weather conditions, from staying there overnight rather than sleeping in our tents and climbing up from such a long way below. I don't mention this to Luis but wonder if he is possibly less experienced than the other guides, not to have at least made some contingency plans to arrange to move us into the Refuge should the weather deteriorate in the way it has. We stay only a short while to gulp down the tea as I am nervous about remaining there too long, and quickly decide to set off even though the weather continues to worsen. We rope up together to provide greater safety against any falls, although this is often a hindrance to the climbing itself and we sometimes have to unrope to climb the steeper rock sections.

A short while after leaving the refuge, I find myself stretched across a rock face, seemingly unable to move up or back down or even go sideways. Luis is some way behind me and he is trying to shout some instructions over to me. In the wind and the storm it's almost impossible to understand his words and at first they seem to be in English and at other times in Spanish although all are mostly incomprehensible. He obviously can't reach me or it's too precarious to try, so I know I must make my own decision. In Zen the wrong way to do something is known as *muri* but you may not realise it's the wrong way until afterwards. The extension of that thought in Zen is just letting go, believing, and being prepared to fail. That is in fact the only way for me to proceed, to let go and slide and allow myself to fall further down the rock face. That requires a great leap of faith but eventually there's no choice and I throw my ski sticks ahead into the gully to my right, let go of my handhold and roll myself after them. I actually slide down for a very short distance, although it feels like an eternity, before I fortunately manage to grab another jutting rock and pull myself to a more secure position. I have made it somehow but cannot yet feel any relief as there's still a long way to go.

I gingerly reclaim my sticks and Luis expertly skirts around that rock section to rejoin me and we continue our ascent. Neither of us says anything to the other but there are several arguments going on inside me, discussing over and over what occurred and whether I should have dealt with it differently. I don't resolve the argument.

After some arduous further climbing we eventually reach the saddle between the two Ilinizas and now set off to head towards El Norte. There are several small cairns piled up helpfully to indicate its summit route. We then climb up the flank of the south-east ridge, avoiding the looser scree and keep climbing on the hard rock sections, which provide more support to the feet, although in the wetness the rocks are still terribly slippery. Gradually and slowly we work our way to the pyramid rock, also known as the false summit, although I don't want necessarily to accept that initially, in case we cannot climb any further to reach the final summit. 'Do you want to continue?' I nod vigorously at the question for emphasis as it's difficult to find the words. We have reached 5,000 metres and I am feeling happier for having at least made it to that height in these tough conditions. We drop down the ridge to climb around a stone tower. Then it's time for the climbing of 'Death Pass' (El Paso de la Muerte); the snow and sleet make it much more difficult than it would be usually and it requires all my strength and effort to make it across. Fortunately the pass doesn't live up to its ominous name and I finally struggle through successfully.

After more strenuous climbing, with lots of precarious slipping, we eventually reach the summit block and take a rest for a few moments to try and gather strength for the final push. It's not much help, however, due to the atrocious weather conditions which never abate, even for a few minutes. We then make a final, hard push up some stone gullies and loose rocks, a number of which decide to tumble down around us, so that we both have to dodge sideways a couple of times to avoid being struck. A few metres more climbing and scrambling and we finally accomplish our goal and breathlessly reach the summit of Iliniza Norte. Unfortunately, the weather makes it almost impossible to see anything, but I gain a certain satisfaction from touching the iron cross that indicates the highest point on the mountain. With visibility extremely poor, the only thing now is to return as fast as safety will allow.

The way down seems more hazardous than the climbing up, as we are in constant danger from falling rocks. We edge downwards trying not to slip and, if and when we do, not too far. Even Luis is slipping quite a lot now and we support each other as best we can, remaining on a very tight, short rope for safety. We are also being forced down by a constant barrage of snow flurries and it's so wet everywhere that I am drenched through. My clothes are also coated in heavy clay from my earlier scrambles across the rocks, and I try to scrape some off by rubbing the back as well as the front of my jacket against the rocks, although mostly in vain. My strange antics must appear rather funny, but there's no one or nothing around to watch me except Luis and he pays little attention. The soles of my boots in particular are covered in clay, preventing me from getting much of a grip on the very wet rocks and stones and causing me considerable problems in descending, and I try not to overbalance Luis.

Eventually we make our way down from the mountain itself and then must start the long trek back to tent civilisation. At least now we can unrope which provides more freedom, and Luis moves further ahead. The sleeting snow is relentless and constantly tries to find its way inside my jacket and gloves, often with considerable success. The weather conditions do not improve, indicating that the planned second stage attempt of Iliniza Sur, definitely not possible at this time, is going to be a real challenge that will test me to the limits. When I finally reach my tent I first have to partly crawl in on my hands and knees, then slowly turn around and back gingerly inside whilst attempting to divest myself of my jacket, boots and trousers to avoid bringing the clay and mud inside with me. My efforts are only partly successful, and I know I will have a heavy cleaning job in the morning. At least the bad weather keeps the cows away during the night, but sadly there are no stars visible. I think I hear one solitary, plaintive bellow, presumably from a lost cow.

Over dinner Luis tells me he didn't expect me to make it in those atrocious conditions and, although he doesn't use the actual word, I take it as a form of congratulations. He suggests I take a few days off to recover and explore more of Ecuador before we climb again which sounds an ideal suggestion to me. I know there is still so much to see and a great deal more to learn about this country and its people. The meal is a hurried affair as I'm extremely tired and I turn in quickly, soon falling fast asleep. It feels like the sleep of the dead and my dreams take me back to the mountain, where I slide again down the rock face, although this time I don't have anything to hold on to stop myself, and I keep on falling all the way. I'm so tired that I actually welcome this slide into oblivion. I doubt very much if any of the cows could wake me tonight even if they were to bellow at the top of their lungs, although in the continuing storm they are probably huddling somewhere for safety and warmth and saving their voices for another time. It feels as if I have hardly been asleep before it becomes morning and the light wakes me to another day.

CHAPTER 4

THE CENTRE OF THE WORLD

D uring my planning for the expedition I am very intrigued to learn that in Ecuador, along the Equator Line, a place has been established and accepted as the Centre of the World. This is fascinating information and I quickly make it one of my expedition goals to journey to Ecuador's Centre of the World. It will certainly add another exciting dimension to the expedition. Explorers, travellers and writers alike have often conjectured about what it would be like to venture deep down through to the Earth's core. Of course the immense heat, as well as the incredibly powerful centrifugal forces generated, would be too intense for any known living thing to travel there – let alone survive. Jules Verne, the famous French storyteller and visionary, a master writer in creating a fictional reality from the impossible, wrote his novel *A Journey to the Centre of the Earth* in 1864. I re-read this extraordinary tale, of an eccentric professor and his friends descending through a dormant Icelandic crater, which is absolutely thrilling in its imaginative invention and the many adventures it relates.

Through my Fellowships of the Explorers Club and the Royal Geographical Society, I very often meet up with other explorers who are prepared to risk all trying to reach remote and inaccessible places, in order to make scientific and geographic discoveries to bring back and share with other Fellows. The 'discovery' of Ecuador's Centre of the World, like so many other discoveries, came about through chance and, as often happens, as a result of an expedition established for entirely different purposes. After the arduous and aggressive arguments were finally resolved in establishing that the World really was 'round', it subsequently became important to determine its actual shape. Differing theories were propounded by various scientists, particularly as to whether there was a flattening at both the North and South Poles. This theory was proposed and argued vehemently by some scientists, whilst others expressed opposing views and insisted that the *centre* of the Earth bulges outwards. The arguments on these and related propositions became extremely heated but went unresolved for many years. Eventually, to settle the position and establish the truth once and for all, two expeditions were organised by the French Académie des Sciences. Initially it organised an expedition to the Arctic region and then, as part of its parallel research, in 1736 it also sent a group of French and Spanish scientists to Ecuador, led by the French aristocrat, Charles-Marie de La Condamine. Once they arrived they were assisted by a very able Ecuadorian scientist who was able to contribute to their eventually successful findings by providing specialist local knowledge of the tribal people and their territories through which the scientists had to travel. During their several years there, whilst conducting various experiments, the scientists also spent time trying to establish the exact location of the Centre of the World, assumed to be sited somewhere along the Equator Latitude Line. After making a series of mathematical observations and taking various calculations, they were finally, in 1743, able to determine that the centre was at a place just north of the Ecuadorian capital city of Quito. However, as it wasn't part of their original remit, apart from recording the fact, nothing was actually done to commemorate these findings for nearly two hundred years. As I mentioned, this is certainly a country of *mañana*!

Eventually in 1936, in the same year that the Galapagos Archipelago was declared a National Park, having realised the importance and benefits that both of these places could bring to the country, the Ecuadorian Government decided to build a special monument to celebrate the Centre of the World (called *La Mitad del Mundo*). For political and prestige reasons of the day, in particular the site's close proximity to Quito, the monument was actually erected at the town of San Antonio de Pichincha. Over the years, a complex of buildings and shops as well as a museum were built around this obelisk-shaped monument. Since that time, Quito has always treated this monument and the museum as being primarily under its control. For many years this monument was taken as being the actual site of the Centre of the World and it is where all visitors and travellers were directed so that they could have their photographs taken next to the monument.

Subsequently however, it was established (although not to everyone's liking or agreement) that this site for the Centre of the World was incorrect and therefore the monument should be moved. It was suggested that it should now be placed in the smaller and more northern town of Calacali. This was hotly (after all it is the equator) discussed and argued about for some years, but eventually there was nothing else to do but to move it. So in 1979 the original monument was carefully dismantled and transported several kilometres north, to be rebuilt in Calacali. However, the authorities couldn't (or wouldn't) move the museum and the other monument buildings, so as part of the compromise it was agreed that a replica monument, three times the size of the original, would be built on the original site at San Antonio de Pichincha. This second monument was completed in 1982. Now the two towns both have similar equatorial monuments, both known as *La Mitad del Mundo*, although most visitors still travel to the first site to have their photographs taken there. Nobody usually tells them otherwise, but it doesn't matter too much as it is largely symbolic. However, in a manner reminiscent of a scenario from a Mel Brooks film or a Monty Python television sketch, it was subsequently decided that neither monument was geographically correct and that a place some 250 metres north of the original site was accurate. No one wants a third monument built, so the real Centre of the World remains in 'the eye of the beholder', which seems to me like a pretty good place for it. To be on the safe side, I recommend everyone interested to travel to both monuments, as you are bound to cross over the actual place of the real centre, wherever it should be. Of course it's the spirit of the thing that really matters, and certainly if you cross the Equator Line enough times you're bound to hit the exact spot, the mysterious C spot that everyone seems to be always searching for.

You are of course able to 'circle' the world by crossing over the centre from the Northern Hemisphere to the Southern Hemisphere and back again, or vice versa. The Centre of the World also has the unique distinction of being set at 0 degrees latitude. To be even more precise, it is at 0 degrees, 0 minutes, 0 seconds and this is also listed in the shorter and more evocative form, as 0-0-0. The Ecuadorians are rightly very proud of it. And close to or across the Equator Line there are a number of other interesting and special places worth visiting, including the coastal shrimp fishing town of Pedernales within the coastal region, the exotic birders' village of Mindo in the northern lowlands, the third highest mountain in Ecuador, Cayambe in the mountains of the Sierra Volcano, and in the jungles of the Northern Oriente the newly-created oil town of Lago Agrio (Sour Lake). Unfortunately, because of the way the environment has been misused around it, the Lago Agrio inhabitants have plenty to be sour about and no amount of oil will create a bridge over those troubled waters.

Latitude positions have always been relatively easy to establish, but the extreme difficulty for travellers, explorers and primarily sailors, was always in agreeing the longitude of any place. Many seafaring nations used their own prime meridians of longitude, so that charts and maps were drawn up differently in many countries, creating considerable confusion and conflict and sadly resulting in a large number of shipwrecks. Finally in Washington in 1884, the International Meridian Conference was organised specifically to consider the issue, and resolved the Meridian point of the city of Greenwich, England, already world famous for its first class astronomical observatory, to be the universal Prime Meridian of Longitude.

The story of how longitude was finally established is a fascinating one and told brilliantly in Dava Sobel's book, *Longitude*. From 1884 the longitude positions of every point on the Earth's surface have been described as either east or west of Greenwich, which itself therefore is given the privilege of having its own unique zero longitude position and listed as being 0 degrees. Like the latitude bearing at the Equator, it is also recorded on maps as 0 degrees, 0 minutes, 0 seconds and often listed in the exact short form as 0-0-0. It is therefore very simple for anyone at Greenwich, similar to straddling the Northern and Southern Hemispheres at the Equator, to stand across the Western and Eastern Hemispheres, with one foot in each.

The longitude lines or meridians connecting the points of the same longitude originate from the North Pole to the South Pole, radiating out from Greenwich to east and west. The latitude lines or parallels measure out from the Equator, to the North or to the South. At the exact opposite position of Greenwich, 180 degrees east or west of it on the world map, more easily shown on a globe, is where the International Date Line (IDL) is sited, a point also confirmed in the same 1884 international conference. In 1879 Sandford Fleming, also responsible for inventing the 24-hour clock and designing Canada's first postage stamp, had come up with the concept of Standard Time. Fleming proposed that 24 equal time zones should be created, each representing 15 degrees of longitude, therefore equating to the total 360 degrees circumference of the Earth. Fleming also proposed that the time within each zone would be exactly the same, one hour. Before then recorded time had varied from place to place somewhat arbitrarily and indeed the United States had around 300 different and confusing local times. In fact it was the US railways that were the first to realise how much this regularised and simplified rail timetables and they quickly adopted the system. By 1890 all countries had also adopted it. At the 1884 conference the British, who in those days had more influence on world decisions than most others, were able to persuade the other European countries that it served all their interests to site the IDL on the other side of the world from Greenwich at its 0 degrees longitude and sited at the measurement of 180 degrees longitude. This decision has caused some interesting consequences and effects. By crossing it, depending in which direction you are travelling, you are able to gain or lose one complete day of time. If you travel west across the IDL you move gradually into the next day and if you travel east you gradually move back into the previous day.

In another classic tale by Jules Verne, *Around the World in 80 Days*, Phileas Fogg thinks initially that he has arrived back in London too late to win his race and bet to circle the world in 80 days. Fortunately at the eleventh hour his quick-witted manservant, Passepartout, realises they had previously crossed the International Date Line to the east and Fogg had forgotten to adjust his otherwise accurate watch timepiece by 24 hours. There are then some thrilling, suspenseful moments while the two of them race across London in a hansom cab (a fast two-wheeled carriage drawn by one or two horses), before managing to reach the Reform Club in Pall Mall with literally a split second to spare.

The same situation and confusion actually occurred in real travel history with Magellan's circumnavigation of the Globe in 1519, although as he was travelling in the opposite direction to the west, he had actually lost a day. Magellan couldn't believe at first that he was a day adrift and it took him some time to accept he hadn't been robbed of one day. The imaginary IDL line does not always follow exactly the 180 degrees longitude line as it should, because then it would divide certain areas where it wouldn't make sense for there to be different time zones. So the line is deflected eastwards through the Bering Straits (part of Russia) and westwards of the Aleutians and also eastwards of Tonga, Fiji and New Zealand. One of the oddities created with these slight changes, is that the neighbouring islands of Tonga and Samoa run on different times and jointly have two consecutive Sundays. It probably provides an excuse to work less. Newfoundland is actually divided down the centre by a time zone and therefore made the interesting decision to adjust its time overall by only half an hour, which means it is always half an hour later in Newfoundland than those places having Atlantic Standard Time.

The meridians of longitude and the parallels of latitude, obviously invisible in themselves, are drawn onto most maps to form a grid, circling the earth. This allows every place to have its unique measurement designation, thus enabling all of us to know where we are, or perhaps more importantly, where we are going to. The astronomer, Sir Patrick Moore, Fellow of the Royal Society, lists his personal bearings on his notepaper, as being at Latitude 50, 43, 49.25 N and Longitude 00, 41, 41.25 W. Moore, who is always being asked to give his comments on space-related events, explains this with some celestial witticism: 'It's so everyone will know my position'.

Due to the Earth having this physical 'bulge' at the Equator, it is a fact that if one were to measure from the Earth's core to the summit of Ecuador's highest mountain, Chimborazo, they would find that this mountain reaches further into the Earth's atmosphere than any other mountain in the world. It is therefore correctly considered the 'tallest' mountain in the world. Of course it is not the highest, which is the magnificent Everest, measuring from sea level, the normal basis of calculating the heights of mountains, 8,848 metres (29,028 feet). However, now knowing this special aspect of Chimborazo and the zero positions of longitude and latitude, I am now able to formulate an expedition itinerary which has never been undertaken before.

My decision, simplistic and even minimalistic in concept, when undertaking the plans for my trip, is to commence my expedition from the city of Greenwich, London, starting out at 0-0-0 longitude, to arrive to the Equator point north of Quito in Ecuador at 0-0-0 latitude and cross the Centre of the World. Whilst in Ecuador I will climb in the country's high mountains and endeavour to reach the summit of Chimborazo, the 'tallest' in the world. This is in addition to my hopes to see what Darwin discovered.

To commence any journey you only need to begin. However it's always important to learn more about where you are going and what you can hope and expect to find there. There was so much to explore before I even reached Ecuador.

CHAPTER 5

THE BUMPY RIDE
OF INDEPENDENCE

O ne of the important screen goddesses, although from many light years ago, was Bette Davis, and one of her most memorable roles was in a film called *All About Eve*. In one of the central scenes, in a clipped, staccato voice, she utters the famous words, always afterwards associated with her and the persona she created as an imperious Hollywood film star, 'Fasten your seatbelts, it's going to be a bumpy night!' Those words have become part of film lore and are always listed in the top ten of quoted movie lines. Ecuador as a country has had many 'bumpy nights' and indeed 'bumpy days' for several centuries, and unfortunately in many ways they are still continuing. Its story is also one of passion, power and greed.

It's a digression, but at one time I worked in Hollywood and owned a duplex apartment off Sunset Boulevard. Bette Davis, by then retired, although not by her own choice, owned the apartment directly above mine and hers had a narrow balcony, always filled with potted plants, built over my living room. Every once in a while water would run down from her balcony and stain my main living room wall. Whenever I discovered this, I would quickly rush upstairs, ring her apartment bell and when she opened her front door, would gently, apologetically, say something along the lines of, "Miss Davis, there's water coming down my wall again." She would just arch one eyebrow and declare, with

45

much emotion and a great deal of artistry, I being after all a captive audience, 'Neville, it can't be me, certainly not me, I never water the plants.' The fact that she might be holding a watering can in one hand, as if daring me to refute her statement, was of no consequence of course. Naturally, I never would contradict her; how can you argue with one of the great film legends? And so each time I would just arrange to re-paint the wall again. I think that wall ended up with more coats of paint than a vintage Rolls Royce.

But back to Ecuador, and specifically my research into its history.

The first inhabitants of the region now known as Ecuador were hunters and fishermen who lived in and around the Andes, possibly up to 50,000 years ago. Traces of early inhabitants have been discovered dating back to at least 10,000 BC. They gradually turned to farming of a kind, harvesting the wild crops before learning how to grow their own. Pottery and other objects have been found and dated back to the Valdivia Culture, to approximately 3,000 BC. Sites of their many small towns and villages containing earthenware figures have been excavated throughout this area and are some of the oldest in the whole of South America. The figures or figurines are often found broken – thought to have been destroyed deliberately – and it is assumed that this occurred as part of fertility and healing rites. There were also carvings of pregnant women (the so-called Venus figures) and again these seem to be part of fertility rituals and historic stylisations. The tribes living in the region were thought to have traded with other tribes living in areas that are now known as Peru and Brazil, as well as with some of the more remote Amazonian tribes within the rainforests. Most of the tribes developed metalworking skills, lived in harmony with each other and in peaceful surroundings, until the most well known of all of the tribes of those regions, the Incas living to the south from what is now Peru, decided to expand forcibly their own territory.

The Inca kingdom existed from at least the eleventh century, initially being situated around Lake Titicaca in the area of southern Peru. The Incas believed their sun god, Pachacamac, had created the moon, the stars, the planets and everything else, himself rising out of Lake Titicaca after a terrible flood had destroyed the people living on earth as punishment for their great sins. He was also known as Viracocha, the creator. Pachacamac's son was the first Inca Emperor. The Incas started to explore northwards in the early fifteenth century under the leadership of Yupanquil and his son Tupac-Yupanquil and initially made peace treaties with their northern neighbours and a certain amount of open trading took place. Soon, however, Tupac-Yupanquil wanted to conquer this territory as well and began to push aggressively northwards with his armies. There was of course strong resistance from the two main tribal groupings, the Quitucaras and the Cañaris but they were not capable of defeating the Incas who were ferocious warriors. The Incas soon destroyed the Cañari city – which they subsequently renamed as Ingapirca – taking the Cañaris living there as prisoners and building a sun temple and an astronomical observatory. The Cañaris, like the Quitucaras, were moon worshippers and as part of their humiliation they were now forced to worship the sun as the Incas did. The Incan king, Huayna-Capac, the son of Tupac-Yupanquil, was born in Tomebamba and his mother was a princess from the Cañaris. She was reputed to sing as sweetly as any bird.

Once Huayna-Capac had extended his Inca kingdom by adding parts of north-west Argentina and northern Chile, he decided he would finally conquer all the Quitucaras as well. They were then led by a woman, Quiloga, and she was induced with false promises by Huyana-Capac to come to his camp and discuss peace terms. Entering his tent she immediately fell into a concealed pit and was impaled on spears and knives fixed into the ground. Her killing had a very dispiriting effect on her followers but they still continued to struggle on for some time and to try and resist the more powerful Incas. The Laguna de Yaguarcoche (the Lake of Blood) is named to commemorate the massacres suffered by many of the Quitucaras in that region. After some fierce fighting, eventually in 1492, one of Huayana-Capac's generals captured the city of Quitus, eventually re-named as Quito. The Quitucaras still continued to resist fiercely and it took another twenty years before the Incas were totally triumphant throughout the territory. As part of their domination they made everyone use their Quechua language.

Huayna-Capac made Quitus his residence and married Paccha, the daughter of Carchi, the captured Quitu leader. Their son, Atahualpa, was to become the Incan king, remembered in Ecuador even to this day, and many places and areas have been named after him. Huayna-Capac died in 1526 of an epidemic which was sweeping the country, probably brought in by the Spanish adventurers and conquistadors. Before he died he arranged to divide his empire into two, allowing his son Atahualpa to rule the northern region from Tombebamba and Quitus, with his other son, Huáscar, ruling from the south, from Cuzco in Peru. Huáscar's mother was an Incan princess and the two half-brothers, sharing only the blood of their father, were always quarrelling bitterly. You could say there was definitely bad blood between them.

Eventually Atahualpa decided to march against his half-brother, and after defeating him in battle arranged for his murder together with the murder of his whole family. That was the Inca way. Atahualpa immediately became the ruler of the whole region but this fighting amongst the Incas weakened his hold over the kingdom which left the country more susceptible to defeat by the Spanish. In 1532, the Spanish adventurer Francisco Pizarro, landed on the coast and started his trek inland from Tumbez. Pizarro had been greatly influenced by Bartolmé Ruiz, a noted Spanish explorer, into believing there were considerable gold treasures just waiting to be gathered throughout the Inca kingdom. The Incas were in awe of the bearded Spaniards with their 'rods of fire', regarding them almost as gods. They were not able to put up much resistance.

The conquistadors easily entrapped Atahualpa, imprisoned him and then held him for ransom, demanding gold and silver sufficient to fill a cell. The Incas, who worshipped the Sun and only used gold as a reflection of the Sun's power, didn't think that highly of it, quickly collected the huge amount required and paid it over. It proved of no avail as despite receiving this enormous ransom, in July 1533 the Spaniards decided anyhow to murder him, actually by strangling, certainly a very unpleasant, long-drawn out way of dying. That was the Spanish way. First, however, by threatening to burn him alive, which he believed would prevent his journeying into the afterlife, they forced him to become baptised. I suppose it was lucky they didn't believe in circumcision.

Atahualpa's followers then had his body secretly dug up and transported it away to bury it in a special place near Quitus. The burial site has never been found and is still waiting to be re-discovered, possibly containing all the many Incan gold and precious objects that would have been placed alongside the Incan Emperor's body. Meanwhile, the Guatemalan Governor, Pédro de Alvarado, had also decided to invade and with his army landed on the coast at Manta and set off to conquer Quito. He badly misjudged the situation, however, by attempting to head across the high mountain passes near to the mountain of Chimborazo, not realising how difficult that would be. Consequently he lost many of his men and his forces were severely delayed, meaning that he was unable to mount his attack in time.

In 1534, the Spanish adventurer Sebastián de Benalcázar, hearing of the planned assault by Alvarado decided to set off from Cajamarca, head north and capture Quitus. Quitus was at that time being ruled over by Rumiñahui, one of Atahualpa's generals, who eventually decided to destroy the city himself rather than allow it to fall into the hands of the Spaniards. After defeating Rumiñahui, Benalcázar founded the city of San Francisco de Quito built over the Incan ruins, to form the basis of the present capital city of Ecuador. Within fifteen years the Spaniards had captured the remainder of what now makes up Ecuador, and their conquest was complete. The country from the middle sixteenth century had become known as 'Audiencia de Quito', a title that naturally helped to fuel the continuing disputes between Quito, Guayaqul and several other cities. The Audiencia was considered from 1718, although with some breaks of a few years in between, as part of the greater Vice-Royalty of New Granada (Vice-Royalty of Nueva Granada), whose capital was based in Bogota in Colombia.

The Spanish conquest and the stories of fabulous Inca riches gave rise to a frenetic gold rush and it was believed there were huge deposits of gold to the east, especially in the Amazonas region. There were endless stories of this *pais dorado* (land of gold) and many expeditions were organised to find it. General Francisco de Orellana, the Spanish conquistador, set off in 1541 with several hundred soldiers and several thousand Indians to find the fabled gold in the Amazonas. His men, however, being totally unprepared for the tropical climate suffered horrifically in the jungle and the rainforest and most died of disease. A much greater claim to historic fame was to be granted to him however, in that he became the first European to cross South America from west to east and to 'discover' and navigate the mighty

Amazon River. The tremendous importance of this can be more clearly understood when it's remembered that the Amazon is the second longest river in the world after the Nile. It actually runs from the mountains of the Andes to discharge into the Atlantic every minute some 15.5 million litres of water (3.4 million gallons), 14 times more than the Mississippi.

Orellana's epic journey has given rise to claims and counter-claims between the Ecuadorians and the Peruvians over the centuries and has caused a tremendous loss of life, as well as, unfortunately for the Ecuadorians, a considerable loss of territory. Because Francisco de Orellana opened up the Amazonas starting out from the city of Quito, Ecuador claims that it should have total and free access to the Amazon River. They have even coined a phrase, *'Ecuador, Pais Amazonian'*, ('Ecuador, country of the Amazon'), which is blazoned and expressed in many ways, particularly at festivals and at other celebrations. Peru expressly states in return that Orellana actually started out initially from Cuzco in Peru, before then entering the Amazonas from Loja and Cuenca and therefore Ecuador's claim is not valid. It is an issue that is not likely to be resolved, as too much is at stake and there would never be any solution acceptable to both countries.

The Spaniards continued to consolidate their hold and control over the country and the indigenous populations, and many tribal 'Indians' died from a variety of European illnesses and diseases. Much of the land of the indigenous people was confiscated, and they were forced to work for the Spanish landowners who called them *huasipungueros*. This name was derived from the word *huasipungo*, meaning 'at the door of the house', to indicate that they had been allotted a piece of land set near to the main house. This land however, was usually infertile or in need of extensive and difficult work to create any soil worth tilling or using for growing crops. The further injustice was that if it then subsequently became of value then the land would be confiscated. Ecuador was governed initially from Lima in Peru, then from Bogotá in Colombia, although some would rightly say that it was in fact *mis*governed, with many injustices against the indigenous people taking place.

Spaniards born in Ecuador were called *criollos* and in turn they also felt discriminated against because those coming from Spain (the *peninsulares*) were always allotted the best positions and generally treated as superior due to their more immediate European connections. The *criollos* started to demand equal rights, and many an heroic protest was organised, though these were met with considerable repression and resulted in the imprisonment of several protestors and the deaths of others. One of the heroes of the movement, although coming from a mixed and humble background, was the doctor, lawyer and writer Eugenio de Santa Cruz y Espejo, who espoused the cause of the freedom movement brilliantly but still ended up dying in prison. He is always acknowledged as the one who really started the freedom process.

Once the fight for independence started in earnest, it would not cease. It was a time for brave men to stand up and be counted. Following the invasion of Spain in 1808 by Napoleon and the overthrow of King Ferdinand V11, which caused shock and disarray throughout the colonies, a group of *criollos* seized power in Quito in August 1809 and demanded the cessation of the Spanish trade monopolies. They announced that they were supporting the restoration of rule under King Ferdinand. Whether that was a ploy or not, it didn't result in rallying sufficient support to their cause, and the *criollos* were quickly ousted by the Spanish troops sent from Peru and Colombia, imprisoned, and sentenced to death. A year later the jail was stormed in an effort to free them before the death sentences were to be carried out, but the rescue attempt was badly organised and the imprisoned leaders were immediately killed by their guards.

Further protests and small uprisings took place and even the independence of the Audencia de Quito was proclaimed. Brave but foolish attacks then took place against the stronger and well-trained Spanish troops, who were easily able to quash the rebellion at Ibarra in 1812. After further years of simmering resentment and continuing protests, a new intensive uprising was planned which came to fruition in the trading city of Guayaquil, and was led by José Joaquin de Olmedo. Olmedo was first and foremost a politician, and knew that alone they couldn't succeed. Urgent appeals were therefore made to the two great South American liberators, Simon Bolivar of Venezuela and José de San Martin of Argentina, to lend their support both morally and physically with troops. They swiftly received the backing and encouragement that they sought, and so Olmedo and his supporters seized power and proclaimed independence on October 9 1820.

A series of inspiring, though unresolved, conflicts followed, and one of Simon Bolivar's youngest generals, the 26-year-old José de Sucre, arrived with strong forces to support the cause. He was victorious at Guayquil, though unsuccessful at Ambato. The decisive and historic battle was shortly about to occur however. On 24 May 1822, near to the slopes of the mountain of Pichincha, Sucre fought an inspired campaign and decisively overcame the Spanish army. This finally resulted in the settlement that the *criollos* had been longing for. It was certainly a very sweet moment in Ecuador's history, and Sucre is always venerated for his supreme role in helping to achieve Ecuador's independence. The Ecuadorian currency subsequently was named the sucre in his honour and remained in common usage until recent times, although the US dollar took over as the official currency in 1999.

Simon Bolivar immediately took charge and set up the borders between the new countries. He founded the Federation of Gran Colombia (a title that would not particularly endear itself to the other member countries), which comprised Ecuador, Colombia, Venezuela and Panama. The Federation started to fall apart within a very short space of time, and in 1830 Ecuador was the first to leave with the other countries withdrawing shortly afterwards.

Another Venezuelan General, Juan José Flores, founded the state of Ecuador, taking the name from the scientists and explorers who had decided on the exact place of the Equator and who in their report had used the words, *'las tierras del Ecuador'*, the lands of the Equator. The colours yellow, blue and red had been used in the flag of the Federation of the Gran Colombia, and after 1830 Ecuador decided to appropriate them for its own flag. It is understood the yellow represents the sun as well as corn and wealth, the blue stands for sea and sky and the red represents the blood of those who died in the struggle for Ecuador's freedom.

From the outset, there were border disputes with Peru, Ecuador's neighbour to the south and east. These disputes continued up to present times and have never been resolved satisfactorily, at least from Ecuador's point of view. Peru at the time, and ever since, has refused to accept the original borders that were set when Ecuador was formerly called Audiencia de Quito. Since it was renamed as Ecuador, Peru insisted that it was a new country and should be defined by the new borders as stipulated within the Gran Colombia which enclosed considerably less land than those previously held. Both World Wars caused uncertainty and reduced trading opportunities, and thereby resulted in territory disputes being 'settled' in ways which were detrimental to Ecuador. The country also suffered considerably as a result of bad decisions and a lack of foresight by its leaders and governments. In 1916 the border dispute with Colombia, its neighbour to the north, was settled by conceding part of the Amazonian rainforest of Ecuador to it, part of which it then promptly transferred to Peru, in order for Colombia to be allowed free access to the Amazon River. This extra territory emboldened Peru to launch an invasion into Ecuador in 1941, which was only resolved by the intervention of several other South American countries as well as the United States. They all forced Ecuador to accept the loss of considerably more territory in order to ensure that Peru would discontinue the fighting and withdraw.

Further territorial disputes and conflicts leading to more fighting have regularly taken place, even as recently as 1995, although there is now a holding truce between the two countries. No one knows what the future holds for both countries, as continuing political and economic crises and a lack of government stability have also dogged Peru. The size of Ecuador is small compared to most South American countries, and its territory is only slightly larger than the size of Britain, or either of the states of Colorado or Nevada, or about half the size of France.

The *criollos* had initially won power, but there were further conflicts to follow between the conservative and liberal ideologies represented within the country. These continuing disputes were particularly centred on the three main cities, Quito, Guayaquil and Cuenca. Fighting, and even civil war, took place periodically within the country, although the nineteenth century saw truces, albeit uneasy ones, between the different factions. In 1861 the ultra conservative and devout Catholic Gabriel García Moreno seized power for a while, even going as far as to change the country's name to the Republic of the Sacred Heart of Jesus. This was only temporarily tolerated, however. Moreno was vehemently opposed by the liberals and one of the most influential opponents was the journalist, Juan Montalvo. There was bitter hatred between the two men and, when Moreno was suddenly assassinated in 1875, Montalvo triumphantly declared, 'My pen has killed him.'

The late nineteenth century was also a period of greatly increased international trade, due to the increasing demand for cocoa and coffee, and this led to the city port of Guayanquil becoming more powerful. The Liberal dominance lasted until 1912 and during that period many considerable economic reforms occurred. A railway line was created between Quito and Guayaquil, which greatly reduced the journey time to only 12 hours by rail, as opposed to the 12 days by road that it had previously taken. The First World War however brought this progress to an abrupt halt, as trade diminished and further internal conflicts occurred. From then on, through the subsequent decades and the Second World War, there were periods of economic chaos with intermittent short periods of economic stability, with regular military takeovers 'to restore order'. Along with much of South America there were a number of these military coups and this all contributed to greater uncertainty. The only mitigating circumstance of all these military occupations was that each was what is described as a *dictablande* (a soft dictatorship) rather than a *dictadura* (a hard or harsh dictatorship).

Only in 1979 did Ecuador finally achieve a democratically elected government. The new President, with full democratic authority, Jaime Roldós Aguileras, was very well thought of and showed great promise as a leader but was tragically killed in a plane crash in 1981 before he could make any real progress. Unfortunately this meant there was still no economic stability and in all subsequent periods, no matter who was president, the country did not prosper. As an indication of the considerable turmoil continuing to take place, Ecuador had 18 presidents between 1897 and 1934 and 25 presidents between 1934 and 1988. A truly bumpy ride indeed!

CHAPTER 6

EL SUR TAKES ME TO THE LIMIT

I am now determined to attempt my second of the two Ilinizas. Although they can be attempted in either sequence, usually it is the slightly lower Norte that is climbed first and then afterwards the more challenging Sur. I arrange to climb this time with another guide, normally known as Marcos Jean-Louis to differentiate him from several others similarly named. He wants me to call him only Marcos however, and besides, anything else on the mountain would be too much of a mouthful.

'Call me Marc if you prefer, or M even, although I'm not a James Bond fan and anyhow she's a lady. I'm certainly not, and not even a gentleman!'

His English is excellent, certainly good enough to allow him to make jokes in it. In fact I think of him more as Marcus Aurelius from *Gladiator*, as he is very broad-chested, with a muscular body that would certainly look good in a toga and he has arms thicker than my thighs.

I met Marcos at the mountaineers' club in Quito, and after talking to him for a while I feel that he would be more likely to take me through some of the more difficult stages of the mountain than some of the other guides that I had previously met. We agree to start out the next morning after breakfast and we are on the road by ten, with Marcos driving another beat-up jeep – it's the preferred choice – which shudders over every bump it encounters. Vehicles in Ecuador seem mostly to be on their last legs, or should I say on their last wheels? As before, we travel across the countryside to arrive at La Virgen in the afternoon and Marcos parks his jeep along the trail more or less at the same place as Luis had parked. At present, the trail is empty of cows but there are the usual signs they were there recently, and I am sure they will return that evening.

Although Sur is a more technical and difficult climb than Norte, once you have climbed the latter you feel that you are halfway there, and weather permitting, it must always be worth trying to achieve the second. Whether to treat it as a direct add-on to Norte or starting it afresh as I am now, it is obviously advantageous to climb Sur in two stages, staying overnight at the Refugio Nuevos Horizontes and starting the major climb from there. Doing it that way makes the second stage of the climb less of a rush and allows you to tackle any potential difficulties, particularly those relating to changing weather elements, in a more relaxed and balanced fashion. There are two main ways to climb to the Sur summit, and Marcos and I decide we will take what is usually known as the Direct Route.

To begin with, the weather appears much more favourable than when I climbed Norte, but to the north-east the sky looks dark and overcast, and there's a strong head wind. There's no going back for anything we might need later so we load our back packs to the brim, knowing we can leave some things at the Refuge. Marcos starts off more slowly than Luis did which makes me impatient, and after a while I suggest that we quicken our pace. Marcos instead stops, takes off his pack, sits down and stretches out his long legs. He gestures for me to sit down next to him and, surprised by his action, I comply but still keep my backpack on.

'My friend, what's the rush? Have you another appointment or are you planning to meet someone?'

I shake my head, uncertain how to respond. Marcos continues, his broad face beaming out at me.

'Well then, think about it, when will you come this way again? Look around you, enjoy, there's a lot to see. Often at high altitude the slower we go, the more likely we are to make the summit. Anyhow there's no reason to hurry, wait til you see where you're sleeping tonight.'

He's right, of course. I don't reply but get slowly to my feet and hold out one hand to help him up too. He sees I understand, grabs my hand and in one bound is back on his feet. He pats my shoulder gently and puts on his backpack so we can continue, at his pace. I breathe the mountain air in deeply and take a long look around me; there are two kestrels circling and swooping downwards to look for anything that might provide lunch. We continue to climb silently together but every time I see something special I point it out to him and he smiles a response and points out many things I miss. He has learned how much I dislike climbing on loose scree and tries to avoid it as much as he can, so we head mostly into the rock sections even though it's a longer, more circuitous route.

Our climb up to the Refuge without the pressure of having to continue to either peak the same day now seems relatively straightforward, and although it's taken us longer than did the climb to Norte, I arrive feeling fresh and very relaxed. Marcos had already phoned to arrange our stay there overnight and book our two bunks. Mine, looking dank and very uninviting, is not one you'd relish the thought of spending more than one night in, but I'll be using my sleeping bag to keep out any unwanted visitors. I understand more the remark about not rushing to get here now – the less time we spend here the better. The Refuge provides extremely basic accommodation, with absolutely nothing to do inside, so there's plenty of time to catch up on my reading and writing. There are two other guides, fortunately neither of whom I've climbed with previously, and four climbers, of which three are to attempt Norte and one is going for Sur like myself. Every climber is from a different country and no one seems anxious to chat, all spending their time mostly reading. Marcos and the other guides know each other well and are soon engrossed in deep conversations from which huge peals of laughter break out every so often, echoing noisily in the narrow confines of the hut. I have my food and water with me but also make tea for Marcos and myself. I offer to make tea for the others but they seem to want to look after themselves. As soon as it gets dark it becomes more difficult to read with a torch, so soon I turn in and try to get some rest. It's not easy to sleep as the roars of laughter continue well into the night.

I set my alarm and pull my sleeping bag tighter, and before I know it I hear the insistent beeping next to my head signalling a new day. I quickly switch it off to avoid disturbing anyone. I can also hear some rushing noises and it takes a while before I realise it's the sound of rain on the roof. It appears quite light and I hope will not be too much of a hindrance but it means I'll have to put on my waterproofs from the outset. Soon further alarms go off and everyone starts dressing by torchlight and packing, ready for their individual climbs. Marcos and the guides step outside to check the weather situation and are gone for a while. I drink some tea, start on my packed meal, and wish everyone good luck. I receive their good wishes in several languages in return. I put the items I'm not taking with me on the climb into a sack provided by the hut manager, to collect on the way down. Then Marcos comes back in and takes me to one side.

'The weather's really bad, it's sleeting down hard and could get worse. Are you sure you still want to go? Perhaps we should wait an hour and see if it improves. It's going to be a difficult climb in these conditions and may become quite dangerous. But it's up to you.'

I immediately get a queasy feeling in my stomach and almost want to shout out, 'No!' But my determination not to give up prevents me and I reply quietly,

'I think we should try it and see how it goes. If it becomes impossible we'll have to give up and return.'

Marcos nods, as if he'd expected my answer. He tells me to get ready to leave, and that we will rope up together inside the hut, whilst our fingers can still fasten the carabiners. The others confer with their guides and it seems two will try for Norte but the others, including the climber for Iliniza Sur, are going to wait and see if it eases off and the weather improves. I wish them good luck again in whatever they decide and step outside the hut. Immediately I want to step back inside. Marcos said it was sleeting hard but this is torrential. I can't see anything through it. But I'm not going to give up at the outset.

'Let's go.' Perhaps they were my words or perhaps I only thought them, perhaps they were from Marcos. Now it is the mountain's turn to speak.

We are starting out from the Refuge before daylight but even if it was light it wouldn't make any difference in this weather. There's just no visibility. 'Take it real slow.' These were his only words of instruction but I was grateful to receive them. Marcos is just one step ahead of me and I am almost shuffling forward as I edge behind him. I feel weighed down by my backpack and my waterproofs are soaked within seconds, with the water cascading off them. We are making very slow progress and I don't see how we will have any chance of climbing all the way to the summit. It's so bad that in a strange way the climbing isn't a problem and we get into some kind of steady rhythm which allows us to move gradually upwards. As planned we are heading up to the saddle between the two mountains and are now on a steep moraine, which is very slippery yet manageable at our slow pace.

The climbing is slow and laborious and after about an hour, although I can't risk trying to get to my watch to check, we reach a terrace and Marcos motions me to stop. He huddles into me and shouts into my right ear – although it sounds more like a whisper:

'OK?' I nod, although I'm not sure if that's right. 'Do you want to turn back?' I shake my head although again I'm not sure if that's the right answer. 'Drink something and we'll go on.'

I do as I'm told, although the procedure is more tiring than the benefit, but I know he's right and I must keep drinking as I ascend.

'This is the Hourglass Pass.' Marcos waves his arm around and I nod again although I can't see anything that looks like an hourglass.

'We're doing well.'

You could have fooled me but if he says so, then it must be. I drink some more and can see some large rocks ahead. I wonder what they are and then realise that the fact I can see them means the weather's improved. Indeed it's almost stopped sleeting and snowing, although it's still raining but not as hard. I point upwards to Marcos but he doesn't seem to understand and takes it as a sign to continue so I hastily stuff the bottle inside and start after him as the rope yanks me forward. We are below some large rock outcrops and the way up is not apparent. It appears to be very steep. We are in a broad couloir that according to Marcos' shouts is called La Rampa, and it's a tiring struggle to the top. We pause for a breather and then head to the left to climb through a series of snowfields into which my boots sink deeper and deeper. The effort to extract them each time is so tiring that my movements are getting slower and slower. It feels as if we've been climbing for hours, and perhaps we have. I am more than dog tired and would love to sit down in the snow, but know that would be fatal.

We are now traversing through a huge crevasse and the snow is ramped around us not looking too stable. I stick close to Marcos and am very glad when we leave it behind. The weather is getting bad again – it's sleeting harder and visibility is again dropping all the time. The climbing is not proving at all easy – that's probably a major understatement – but we are taking it slowly and I am determined to get through it, or rather up and over it. There is another very lengthy, steep ice wall to overcome, and at one stage I slip backwards but quickly jam in my ice axe to prevent myself sliding too far. Marcos holds the rope steady until I've righted myself but if we weren't roped I might have easily slid down a considerable way and doubt I would have had the energy to climb back up. I'm grateful for those huge arms of his, which took my weight when my feet left the rocks and there was nothing but air supporting me for a few terrible moments. Finally we are able to leave that section, climbing over to the left, and then we cross through an area of crevasses full of nasty surprises. It's the ones you don't see rather than the ones you do which create the problems.

There's a further rock band to overcome but Marcos tells me we are nearly there. Once we have clambered over that we need to climb across to the right and, on reaching a long rock ridge, head left to reach Ambato Peak. We're still not there however and it seems that Marcos had meant the dreaded mountaineer's version of the word 'nearly'. We follow the ridge along from Ambato, going around 'El Hongo' (the mushroom) but don't stop to eat and soon Maximum Peak is in front of us, all ready for the climbing. Marcos graciously allows me to lead this final stretch and I feel I manage it well, as the summit is urging me on. Finally we reach it. The summit of Iliniza Sur. The weather's still bad which means that we have little time to enjoy the lack of a view before we must descend. In the words of the Lakota wise man, known as Lame Deer, 'What you see with your eyes closed is what really counts.' My eyes are not closed although outwardly I can see very little. Inside, however, I can sense a great deal, and lock in some precious moments.

Going down is a piece of cake – that's if you like your cake broken into bits with each bit squashed all over. Only kidding of course, but the way down is potentially very treacherous and there's need to take extreme care if we want to arrive in one piece and walking rather than crawling. The wind continues to be very fierce and all the time the snow dances aggressively around me. I would easily lose any sense of direction if Marcos wasn't there to guide me. We reach the Refuge, which is steeped with snow banking up to the walls and door, and the hut looks abandoned. Inside it's practically the same scene as when we left all those hours before. No one made it outside for more than a few metres before being forced to return. Marcos tells them that we made it and how it was, and they generously crowd around to congratulate us both on our achievement, although I know I owe it mostly to him. They tell us they have all decided to remain another night in the Refuge, and I hope that the weather improves tomorrow so they can try again.

The thought of another night in the hut is not in any way appealing and it makes me even more pleased with my own struggles on the mountain, because I am in a position to leave now. After trying to warm myself up with a few cups of tea which only partly work, we pack up, say our final farewells and set out to retrace our steps down to La Virgen. I only hope the jeep is still there and wonder whether the cows have commandeered it for shelter. The way down is no joy, even with the successful ascent fresh in my memory to spur me on. By the time we reach terra firma and the sanctuary of the jeep, which actually has one cow slumped across the right front wheel, I feel more like a zombie than a mountaineer. Possibly that's why the rock band called themselves the Grateful Dead – perhaps they were climbers in another life.

Marcos, after all this 'excitement', thinks I should take a short break from the mountains and suggests I see more of the main cities of Ecuador. He recommends the port city of Guayaquil, beautiful Cuenca and Quito. Sounds good to me, and I'm certainly in need of time for reflection. Marcos Aurelius, I salute you.

CHAPTER 7

A TALE OF FOUR CITIES AND A MOUNTAIN

My journey to Ecuador starts out from one historic city, London, and during my expedition I will travel through three great Ecuadorian cities, Quito, Guayaquil and Cuenca. Many scientists, writers, historians and philosophers have visited these cities and have found the architectural, historical and scientific treasures in each of enormous interest and importance. I am certainly very keen to experience and gain something from them as well.

Officially the start of my expedition occurs when I travel by boat east along the River Thames from Westminster Bridge, passing some of the great sights of London, including the London Eye, St Paul's Cathedral, and the Tower of London, until an hour later I arrive at the Greenwich Docks. After disembarking, looking rather incongruous in my mountain gear, I can't resist the urge to board the famous and exquisitely designed three-masted sailing ship, the *Cutty Sark*, built as a tea clipper and moored at Greenwich in a dry dock next to the Thames. The *Cutty Sark* was built in Scotland in 1869 and was able to out-run all other sailing ships of that period. It's still kept in fighting condition, featuring many nautical treasures, including some excellent ship figureheads and is open to the public, even to mountaineers.

I then trek my way slowly through Greenwich Park and up its small central hill to reach the Royal Observatory, originally built by Sir Christopher Wren in 1675. From here, I am able to achieve my first expedition goal and stand at 0-0-0 longitude, then astride the Prime Meridian Line; one foot in the Western Hemisphere, the other in the Eastern Hemisphere. This Prime Meridian Line in the Royal Observatory Courtyard is now known to be slightly inaccurately sited and the true Line is actually a few metres away next to the imposing statue of General Wolfe, presented by the people of Canada in 1930. My travels in Ecuador will lead me eventually to the Centre of the World, to reach 0-0-0 latitude where I intend to straddle the Equator Line, with one foot then in the Southern Hemisphere and the other in the Northern Hemisphere. There are several rooms in the Observatory full of clocks, chronometers, compasses, astrolabes, sextants and other measuring instruments used on land and sea. In homage to those who created these ingenious measuring instruments housed in the Observatory, I wait till it is exactly 12 noon before departing Greenwich for the South Americas, where the time is 7 am. It allows me some special moments for inner reflection and tranquility before commencing my travels. God speed.

Amongst the major influences on my life are two men with very similar names, both of whom lived in England within the same century. One is the social commentator and writer Charles Dickens (1812–1870) and the other the naturalist and writer Charles Darwin (1809–1882). I will later have cause to say more about Charles Darwin and his travels to the Galapagos Islands, but now here I'm reminded of Charles Dickens who wrote passionately about the evils of poverty and social injustice and the need always to battle on against the odds.

One of my favourite Dickens novels, *A Tale of Two Cities* (first published in 1859) is set between London and Paris, at the time of the French Revolution. My expedition is also a story of several cities and the ways in which they connect. The memorable opening line of his wonderful story is one which immediately draws us in: 'It was the best of times, it was the worst of times.' These words have been used in plays, musicals and films, and express the inner conflicts and thoughts we all experience in whatever we attempt to achieve. Sometimes facing great difficulties on a powerful mountain, whether climbing up or down, that opening line has often come to my mind and I'm sure many mountaineers have also expressed similar sentiments, as they too have struggled against the raw elements.

Within Ecuador, the three most important cities are undoubtedly the political capital, Quito, Guayquil the major commercial port, and Cuenca the southern stronghold. Apart from the massive country of Brazil (30 times larger than Ecuador), which would naturally be expected to have more than one major city, Ecuador is the only other South American country to have two equally important cities, Quito and Guayaquil. The intense rivalry between these two cities has continued unabated for centuries and at times has almost led to open warfare. Cuenca is a much smaller city and doesn't try to compete in size but only in providing a very special quality of life, and in that it certainly succeeds. Cuenca is a place where the old adage, size doesn't matter, is never more true.

Cuenca is actually Ecuador's third largest city, and because it is probably the most beautiful has been named a UNESCO World Heritage Site. It is in the valley of Guapondelig flanked by mountains, and is surrounded by four rivers, the Tarqui, the Yanuncay, the Tomebamba and the Machangara. The city was founded in 1577 and is full of quaint cobblestone streets, pristine, whitewashed haciendas and relaxing plazas. It is the cultural centre of Ecuador and many of the country's writers and artists continue to live there.

I have been recommended by a theatre friend from Santiago, capital of Chile, to visit Fernando's bar near the cathedral and make that my first call. I'm in luck. Fernando's is no hideaway and his welcoming bear-like embrace makes my bones rattle. He wants to know all about me and how it is on the mountains and why 'a crazy Englishman travels all this way just to climb a few rocks'. Fernando has never climbed anything in his life, unless he has to, 'other than the stairs of my *casa*' and believes in expending as little energy as possible. His voluptuous stomach bears testimony to that belief but because he towers over me, with a huge frame, somehow it all fits well together. It is already after breakfast but he insists we sit down and eat together and summons his favourite waitress Lola to serve us several enormous dishes, until my stomach seems to be bursting. Coupling that with *mucho vino* means that my planned sightseeing today goes quickly onto the back burner and I become Fernando's guest to stay above the bar for that night. I enjoy several larger meals with him and some other guests over the rest of the day and although he doesn't have the energy to come along, he makes Lola take me the next morning to see some city sights.

The Cathedral (La Catedral Nueva) is rather special and its sky-blue domes dominate the city. Lola takes me inside to look at the exquisite stained glass windows and gold leaf altar, and she suggests we light candles 'to atone for our sins'. Her English is strangely accented, and it sounds more like 'scenes' – perhaps that is what she really means. In any case, she lights an extra large candle but I don't ask why.

She tells me the original cathedral was destroyed by fire and this one is only just over one hundred years old. To make up for that she also takes me to the Convent of La Concepcion dating from 1599 where there's a special room full of nineteenth-century dolls and toys. There's usually an entrance fee but a wink from Lola to the young guy in charge got us easily waved through. She says that the most colourful of the *paso del niño* (passing of the child) festivals takes place in Cuenca at Christmas time and it's great fun. The figure of Jesus, represented by a small antique figurine, is passed from one family to another and the person who ends up holding the figurine is appointed *prioste*, becoming the person responsible for organising the festival at that time.

Ecuador is a predominantly Catholic country (some put the percentage as high as 95 per cent) but there are still connections going back to the past and traditional beliefs in other gods and deities. There remains amongst the indigenous population, as well as amongst many others, the acceptance of the powers of the animal kingdom and the powerful spirit of the nature found within this country that is filled with such a rich diversity.

It is a country full of wonderful churches and ecclesiastical buildings and indeed Simon Bolivar initially called Quito 'the Monastery'. There are colourful and exciting celebrations of all the main religious festivals, and many others that possibly are pure inventions, created just for the fun of the event. Ecuadorians love a sense of occasion and the opportunity to dress up, so any excuse for a party is always seized upon. There are many shrines throughout the country for pilgrims to worship, and they will journey from distant parts just to participate in a special ceremony.

All Saints Day (also known as All Souls Day) is when those who have had a death in the family can receive visitors who wish to express their sympathy. The family traditionally opens their doors to anyone and offers a meal of the deceased's favourite food, with the visitors saying, '*Angeles somos, pan queromos*' – 'We are angels and we want bread'. The guests are then supposed to drink three glasses of the deceased's favourite wine (spirits might be considered inappropriate) and take a bag of bread with them when they leave. I wonder if the visitors decide to pay their respects to more than one family, and drink three glasses of wine in each home, there is the likelihood that they may soon forget where they are going and even who they are and may end up saying, '*Diablos somos, vino queromos*'!

There are actually two cathedrals, and Lola also shows me the very old one (Catedral Vieja). It was intended to be the largest in South America but there was a miscalculation by the architect, Juan Stylis, about the weight the building could hold, so the towers that were meant to be put on top of the cathedral had to be placed alongside. These towers are believed to have been used by Charles-Marie La Condamine in his original meridian measuring to confirm the 'bulge' at the Equator. I much prefer this cathedral, although it smells somewhat musty, so I don't spend too long inside.

The city of Cuenca has an expanding colony of artists and every two years it holds the Bienal Internacional de Pintura Festibal, in which artists from all over the world participate. Lola seems to know many of the local artists and each one we meet tries to insist we celebrate, although I'm not sure what we are celebrating. It quickly turns into a series of intense artistic and philosophical discussions where my Spanish seems to improve rapidly, although I'm not sure if anyone understands what I am saying, despite the vigorous nodding on all sides. Cuenca has always had a close association with the United States and many of its citizens emigrate to live there, so there's a love of all things American. I am able to talk about my work in Hollywood with film directors, which goes down a treat, and we toast each one. In my honour a number start wearing their cowboy hats and insist on showing me their cowboy boots and other American clothing. The city motto is '*Primero Dios, Despues Vos*' (First God, Then You) and this is the toast made several times during our ambling from one *casa* to another. I discover that Cuencas is also a city where I can drink the local tap water with impunity. In South America that can't be a bad thing, and is an additional recommendation of the virtues of this great city.

Cuenca unfortunately suffers from a commercial and image injustice, which seems to be impossible to correct. In collaboration with the manufacturers from the city of Montecristi it markets the straw hat which is universally admired but is known internationally under the name 'Panama'. It seems as though this came about because, many years back, the manufacturers sold their straw hats to the construction workers on the Panama Canal and somehow the name 'Panama Straw Hat' stuck. Cuenca Straw Hat or Montecristi Straw Hat just doesn't have the same ring to it. The hat makers have since rather belatedly put a label inside each hat they manufacture, reading, 'Made In Ecuador' but it is likely the damage has been done, as 'Panama Straw Hat' has a certain cachet about it and is likely to remain the accepted name. Even a factory producing the hats is locally referred to as the 'Panama Hat Factory'. I suggest to my new friends they need to create another catchphrase and put forward two possibilities, 'If you want to get ahead, get a hat,' or 'Which ever straw you pick, with our hats you always pick a winner.' They are very impressed by that, although it might be the *vino* talking, and I am ceremoniously presented with my own straw hat and more toasts follow. We are in no fit state to make our way safely to Fernando's on our own so are given a raucous escort through the city. Late the next morning, Fernando very reluctantly lets me leave.

Guayaquil is the capital city of the southern Guayas Province and is the most important port city of Ecuador. I like ports and this one has great vibes so I enjoy my strolls amongst the loading docks, which are bustling with itinerant traders from all over South America. The city has suffered somewhat from having lost many of its historic buildings compared to many other major cities and therefore tremendous efforts are being made to restore many of its original features, particularly from an architectural point of view. It is trying to become known as 'the Pacific Pearl' and a few years back created the very impressive riverside development known as Malecon 2000. This is a two-and-a-half-kilometre waterfront walk, and feeling the need for some exercise to burn off the effects of too many paellas, I run the whole length and most of the way back. It's flanked by all kinds of interesting buildings, shopping parades, markets, entertainment complexes, as well as gardens and trees, and is the largest architectural development in the last century of Guayaquil's history.

This is the most populated of all the Ecuadorian cities, with roughly double the number of citizens of Quito, and therefore has almost double the number of city problems to deal with, many that can unfortunately be described as rough and tough. Crime previously soared to enormous and uncontrollable levels but stringent measures seem to have got it mostly under control. However, as in every city, you have to watch your back and should never backpocket your wallet. It is definitely a pulsing city, full of commercial activity and the trading and nightlife continue hand in hand all round the clock. I manage to keep going until the early hours before needing to rest for a few hours, and it looks as if Guayaquil is another city that never sleeps.

It is of course a river port and there is a constant flow of river cargo boats coming down the Daule and Babahoyo Rivers, joining to the Guayas River, that bring produce from all parts to be loaded onto the large container ships and sent all over the world. I find it fascinating to watch the boats being unloaded, and there's a constant activity of container trucks and lorries dropping off and picking up. I see some things being loaded onto trucks that don't seem to be part of the normal commercial activity, but perhaps it is just my suspicious mind. The police, however, are definitely looking the other way.

The city is named after the Huancavilcan indigenous chief Guayas and his wife Quil, who both chose to die rather than be captured by the invading Spaniards. The adventurer and explorer, Francisco de Orellana, founded the present city as Santiago de Guayaquil in July 1535. The first steam boat ever, the *Guayas*, was constructed in its shipyards and the first trials of any submarine, which was known as the *Hippopotamus*, also took place here. There is plenty of steam here, as the city swelters in its exposed coastal position just north of Peru, whose government has made several unsuccessful attempts to move the border. I myself am sweltering in the heat and need to use my new 'Panama–Ecuador' straw hat both as a shield and a fan. Although it's quite a challenge, I cannot resist the temptation to walk (not run this time) the length of the bridge, the Puente de Unidad Nacioanal, which is the largest in Ecuador and indeed of the whole Pacific Coast of South America. It's a distance of three kilometres but I confess to making my return journey in a cruising taxi.

Guayaquil, like Cuenca, has a blue-domed cathedral in Calle Diez de Agosto and its main altar is built of marble actually produced in Cuenca. I don't have a Lola to take me around but everyone in the cathedral seems anxious to talk to me, try out their English and find out what I think

74

of their city, as well as recommend where I should go next. Most suggest the Clock Tower in Avenida Diez de Agosto y Malecon so I decide to clock a quick visit. It's designed in a Moorish style and is 23 metres in height. The tradition is that every day someone has to climb the steep stairs to wind the clock. It seems to be closed but, after I've been banging on the heavy wooden door for some time, the keeper of the Clock Tower finally appears and tells me it's closed. But Juan's another friendly soul and we talk for a while, exchanging stories. When he hears I'm in Ecuador climbing mountains, he relents and agrees to treat me as a special visitor, allowing me to climb on my own to the top. The view is spectacular but I don't know how to wind the clock and hope that it's already been done for the day. Juan proudly tells me the clock was originally bought in England and was inaugurated in October 1842 in remembrance of the victims of a yellow fever epidemic that had occurred a few years earlier.

Juan's recommendation is La Rotonda. This is considered a very important part of South American as well as Ecuadorian history, and was built by the Spanish sculptor José Antonio Homs. It was the site of the famous meeting in July 1822 between the two acknowledged liberators of South America, the Venezuelan General Simon Bolivar and the Argentine General José de San Martin. There they agreed that Guayaquil would be annexed to Gran Colombia rather than to Peru, which meant that, when Ecuador subsequently left the Gran Colombia, it was able to take Guayaquil with it, thus circumventing further conflict between the two countries. If someone whispers on one side of the monument the words can be heard on the other side, and lovers go there to whisper their secrets to each other. I try a whisper and then a shout but no one is there to respond to my call. Still I can dream.

A 'must see', for me at least, is a visit to the Guayaquil Municipal Museum to view the shrunken heads exhibited there. This is the only museum in Ecuador to house such an exhibition, and after hearing about the shrunken heads before setting out on my journey, I have been waiting for an opportunity to visit the museum. They were created by the Jivaro Indians many years ago, and still scientists are baffled as to how the severed heads could have been reduced so dramatically in size, to not much bigger than a fist, without losing the original features of the person. They certainly appear to be perfectly normal in shape, but on a much smaller scale; they make an extraordinary sight. The indigenous name for these shrunken heads is *Tzantzas* and as I stare at them in utter amazement, they seem to stare back. I can only conjecture what it must have been like for captives of the Jivaros. The horror experienced by their victims who would undoubtedly have seen what was in store for them must have been overwhelming.

One used to be able to take an incredible 450 kilometres (280 miles) railway journey between Guayaquil and Quito that enabled the hardy (or foolhardy) traveller to arrive at either city after only 12 hours, as opposed to the 12 days that this journey would previously have taken by road. Sadly the El Niño of 1982/1983 destroyed most of the railway, but some 100 kilometres of track have been restored and it must be the most exciting ride in the whole of South America. I can't resist the opportunity to take the ride but my stomach wishes I had, as I have to hang on for all I am worth once the train starts its ascent of 'Nariz del Diablo' or 'Devil's Nose'. The exceptionally steep gradients reach 45 degrees, 1:18 at times, zigzag switchbacks are hewn into the rock of the mountain and at the Urbina Pass the train rises to nearly 3,700 metres (12,000 feet) above sea level.

The route takes me from the old trading city of Riobamba (known as the Sultan of the Andes because of its closeness to

Chimborazo), through Capabamba and the Colta lagoons and the Guamote village, finally reaching Alausi. Along the way I experience nearly every kind of habitat: jungle, forest, plantation, volcano, mountain and river. On the way down the train actually goes backwards. I'm allowed, and very hesitantly agree, to climb onto the roof for the last section. Slightly wary due to the continuous screams from those who've travelled like that all the way I only dare climb up because I can use my mountain gloves for a firmer grip and can tie myself on with a very tight rope connection. It's like hitting one's head against a brick wall; it feels so great when it's over. At the end I stagger off with the other white-faced railroaders and have to sit by the roadside for some minutes before sufficient blood flows in the right direction to enable me to stand. Hopefully one day the whole Guayaquil to Quito route will re-open and I'd like to volunteer to be on the inaugural journey, though I certainly wouldn't eat anything for many hours before commencing and probably couldn't for some time afterwards.

Quito, set at a height of 2,850 metres (over 9,000 feet) is the second highest city in Latin America (after La Paz in Bolivia), and is the third highest in the world (the highest being Lhasa in Tibet). There is just a three hour drive north along the Pan American Highway to reach the border with Colombia. It is 22 kilometres (14 miles) south from the Equator and was built over Incan and even older Indian tribal ruins. Its full name is San Francisco de Quito and it was founded by General Sebastian Benalcazar on 6 December 1534. Simon Bolivar the Liberator wasn't initially very enamoured with the city and dismissed it somewhat derisorily as 'a Monastery', but eventually he also grew to admire its beauty and very considerable charms. As it is the capital city, distances to most places in Ecuador are usually calculated as being so many kilometres (or miles) from Quito. The quite spectacular backdrop to Quito is the volcanic mountain of Pichincha, 4,794 metres (15,729 feet) high, and the two have always been inextricably linked. The city has started to spread upwards towards its lower slopes, but unfortunately sometimes the volcano also spreads downward towards the city. Wherever I am in Quito, I always see or sense Pichincha and feel it is waiting for me and expecting my return.

Quito is a wonderful city to wander around, with its wealth of decorative churches and ecclesiastical buildings, many dating from the sixteenth, seventeenth and eighteenth centuries. The fact it went through a severe economic decline in the eighteenth and nineteenth centuries has actually worked in favour of the city from an architectural point of view. Unlike many other major South American cities such as Lima and Caracas, it was too impoverished to be able to demolish its old buildings and replace them with new constructions. Quito has fortunately since realised the intrinsic value of retaining its ancient architecture and is now trying to preserve it for future generations, as part of its colonial history. Many of the churches and buildings are impressively decorative in their gold leaf glories and the city's wealth of colonial architecture fortunately impressed UNESCO sufficiently for it to declare it a World Heritage Site in 1978, the first city to receive that honour.

There are many contenders but in my opinion I think the most glorious church in Quito (some have described it as the best in the whole of South America) is La Compania de Jesus. The church façade is sculpted in a kind of finely etched, lace lattice of stonework and it feels great just to run my fingers along it. Some of its columns are copies of those built in the Vatican by Bernini, one of the greatest Italian sculptors. There's a vaulted interior ceiling and the interior walls are covered with extremely decorative Moorish style designs. The altar however, is the absolute masterpiece, with etchings of birds, fruits and plants all covered in exquisite gold leaf. There are also many gorgeous paintings by important Spanish and Ecuadorian artists as well as several wonderful sculptures by the famous Bernardo de Legarda, who also has his sculptures in many other churches and religious organisations in Quito.

I walk through the main Plaza Indepencia, also known as the Plaza Grande, and stop to admire the Palaces of the President and the Archbishop which compete with one another in grandeur (although they would never admit to it). If you are lucky, you might even get to see one of the men appearing, dressed in all his finery, prepared to wave benevolently at us lesser mortals. For my money though, once you've seen one archbishop you've seen them all and as presidents change so fast in Ecuador you might even be standing next to one of the previous ones in the street without knowing it. This reminds me of the eccentric British Government minister, George Brown, whom I knew well, a very loveable character, although he had an eye for the ladies, liked his liquor too much and in the evenings was usually the worst for wear. Surprisingly he was appointed Foreign Secretary and was attending some diplomatic reception when he spied what he thought was a vision of loveliness dressed in a flamboyant scarlet gown. As the orchestra was playing, he impulsively went over and asked for a dance. The affronted reply was, 'Certainly not sir, in fact on three accounts; first you are drunk, secondly they are playing our national anthem and thirdly I am the Archbishop of Montevideo.' George seemed to specialise in creating international incidents.

I am particularly impressed by the imposing Metropolitan Cathedral (La Catedral), which is also in this Plaza and has several architectural styles, mostly baroque and Moorish. Inside I look around for a priest to guide me round, and someone with double the girth of Friar Tuck offers his services. He initially takes me to the small altar where the remains of Antonio José de Sucre, the general who liberated Quito from the Spanish royalists, are buried and then relishes telling me about the deaths and murders that have taken place within these hallowed walls. He has been eating onions or garlic, or both, in such great quantities that I am quickly forced to make my excuses and escape outside or it's likely that another corpse will soon be added to the list.

In the smaller Plaza San Francisco I naturally find the exquisite church of San Francisco and leave a little part of my heart there. It's said that Friar Jodoco Rique sowed the first grain of wheat in Ecuador here. It is the oldest religious building in South America (1535) and rather surprisingly set within the highly decorative Moorish ceiling are several Incan sun god symbols. Whenever I come across a pagan symbol in a religious building, I wonder whether it was simply put there in error or whether it was a way of covering all possibilities, just in case. Perhaps there's an opportunity for another *Da Vinci Code*-type mystery to be written on the meanings of the pagan carvings in these churches. Although Catholicism is dominant in this country, the indigenous and Incan influences are surprisingly still very much in evidence everywhere.

At the Plaza Santo Domingo I pensively position myself beneath the statue of the revered warrior, José de Sucre, pointing directly to the slopes of the Pichincha Mountain, near to where he defeated the Spanish army. Sucre seems to be actually encouraging me towards the mountain and suddenly I feel compelled to attempt it. Marcos unfortunately is not available so I make contact with Luis and ask him if he's free to take me there to climb the next morning. He's surprised at my request and tries to persuade me to go a few days later, but eventually agrees to pick me up the next morning at 6 a.m. Luis advises me to get some rest in the meantime but I feel too keyed up to relax, and there's a lot still to see and explore in the city and its surrounding area.

I make another long visit to Libri Mundi (Books of the World), the bookshop I would recommend to anyone coming to Quito who wants extensive information on any aspect of Ecuador. The manager, as before, is very welcoming and, after helping me find the books I need, introduces me to Axel, a climber from Germany, whose name intrigues me and who is looking for another mountaineer to climb Chimborazo with. At first I am wary of teaming up with anyone I don't know, but over coffee we find we have shared similar climbing situations in many parts of the world, so it seems a good idea to combine forces at some stage.

I discover that Axel trains horses and works on a farm outside Dusseldorf. I guess he certainly must know something about balance and therefore should be good on the mountain as a climbing companion. He's also had problems with a previous climbing guide, so we visit the Explorers Club on the corner of Jorge Washington (I tell you no lie) and are luckily introduced to two new guides, Jorge and Enrique. Both are very knowledgeable and they agree to accompany us when finally attempting Chimborazo. Two guides will provide us with more back up in case of any emergencies occurring high on the mountain. Axel has many other trips planned in the meantime, so we all agree to make contact later, to arrange and attempt this final climb together.

Although I know I should be taking it easier, I feel too excited at the prospect of soon being on the mountains, so I decide to fit in a fast taxi trip to the Cochasqui Archaeological Complex, just north of Quito. This is a wonderful and peaceful area where 15 pyramids are situated, along with a number of dome-shaped burial tombs all dating pre-Inca. The indigenous people take considerable pride in these structures, as they comsider their history to be the oldest in Ecuador and confirm that they were here before all the others. They rightfully claim that they have been totally mistreated within their country, initially by the Incas, then by the Spanish invaders and conquerors and even now by the Ecuadorian authorities. They feel that they are owed justice and they are no longer prepared to wait for it. This understandable demand is the cornerstone cry of many repressed populations throughout the world, who often feel laws and regulations discriminate against them and are unjust, or are not morally acceptable and therefore should not be automatically followed. It's absolutely essential that everyone's legitimate rights are recognised by all others and, where there is continuing conflict, it's resolved by fairness coupled with understanding.

At the Cochasqui Centre there is a superb herb garden with some species of herbs dating back to pre-Colombian times, and research is being carried out there to investigate their special healing powers. Perhaps they may yet discover one which helps people to be more tolerant and caring to one another and less bloodthirsty; an interesting term that refers back to the times when it was acceptable to drink the blood of your enemies, in order to take in their strengths. A special time to visit Cochasqui is on and around 21 June when they celebrate the festival of the solstice, the Inti-Raymi Festival, although you must be prepared to share this spectacular event with many indigenous tribal people who travel in from all over the country, and should be aware that one of the traditions at Inti-Raymi is to throw stones at each other. Only small ones though!

I don't need my alarm call and am awake very early, soon waiting impatiently. Luis, however, is punctual to the minute, and we set off very early. Pichincha is a volcanic mountain in the western range. Its history is very much bound up with the history of Quito, and the famous battle of Pichincha between the victorious Sucre and the defeated Spaniards was the deciding one, resulting in Quito being freed, and subsequently Ecuador itself. Pichincha has several peaks and heights to aspire to: Guagua Pichincha, El Padre Encantado, Ladrillos, as well as Rucu Pichincha. Guagua Pichincha as a volcano is not considered very active although it did erupt as recently as 1999. The one before that however was over 300 hundred years earlier in 1660. I think the folks in Quito can perhaps relax and rest easily for another century or so, although you never know!

I am really looking forward to climbing this mountain as its historical connections to the freeing of Ecuador marks it out in a very special way. All Ecuadorians think of it as their own mountain and for me, it is one mountain that must be accomplished. One of my knees has started playing up, so although it's not a tough climb I carry out some extensive stretching exercises before I leave the hotel, in an attempt to limber up. Luis tells me the weather is improving so we shouldn't encounter any problems this time. 'No problema.' He is as short on conversation and comment as ever, and prefers to rely mainly on gestures. But we share some chocolate and he seems happy.

Together we decide to climb the main summit initially, Guagua Pichincha, reaching nearly 4,800 metres. Guagua is usually known as 'the mountain that boils' but hopefully today the 'kettle' will not be operating. Luis and I set off to drive to the mountain slopes in his jeep, which is looking even more battered than I remember. We initially pass the village of Lloa, before starting to wind slowly up the foothills approaching the mountain. We have loaded the jeep up with plenty of equipment just in case, but it's unlikely that we will need it today. As Luis indicated the weather seems fine, with a bright sun and very little wind. The road is more a dusty trail and the journey is bone-shattering as the

83

vehicle bumps its way over hardened earth, stone and rocky outcrops, slowly but steadily climbing upwards. Half-way up, I have had enough of this and tell Luis it would be preferable and more of an interesting test if I trek the rest of the way, climbing from this earlier point rather than waiting till we reach the mountain itself. Luis agrees and stops the jeep, parking it to one side so others can easily pass, and we quickly put on day packs to continue.

My knees are still feeling stiff so I take it easy until I can get a decent rhythm going. We soon reach approximately 3,500 metres and, remembering Marcos' advice, I start to relax and to feel in tune with the surroundings. The air is so clear that I can see far into the distance, and am able to admire the view of the rolling plains stretching in every direction and the small herds of deer dotted over several hillsides. I see a huge bird circling slowly over to my left, and Luis confirms it's a condor. There is a group of trekkers ahead and I feel confident enough to catch up and pass them. They are going quite slowly anyway, and are possibly worried about acclimatising. They wave me on and a few take the opportunity to stop and drink some water, indicating in gesture that the height and the heat are getting to them already. I only hope I am not being overconfident and will not pay for it later.

We start following a winding path, which is stony and tough on the feet, but I probably need the pressure to help get me into better shape for the much higher and more difficult mountains later on. My knees are less sore and I want to feel the hardness of the ground underneath as it strengthens my hamstrings. The *páramo* grasslands on either side are covered in a tussock grass, which is very springy underfoot and seems to stretch forever. We continue to climb, trekking for about three hours until we finally reach the Ministry Refuge. We make a joint decision not to pause here, and we continue to push on and head for the summit.

We are soon trekking over volcanic outcrops and the terrain becomes barren and desolate. It's a long, hard, but manageable slog and all one needs is a good pair of lungs, two strong legs, and totally focused determination. At least I have the determination. There's a huge slab of rock to our left and I nonchalantly ask Luis whether it's the route to follow and if we will need to climb it. I know really it's not necessary, but something gets lost in the translation as he shrugs and seems to indicate it's up to me. I decide I must take the challenge and burn up a huge amount of energy and effort in struggling my way over it, whilst Luis stands bemusedly watching me and then walks easily around it to join me on the other side. I collapse momentarily and need to drink a whole bottle of water to replenish some of what has poured from me.

It takes a while longer trekking upwards, but we finally reach the crater of the volcano. I peer inside to watch the misty lines of smoke spiralling upwards, and vanishing mysteriously into the pale sunlight. There are several lava domes inside, strangely shaped and almost looking as if they were recently created. I know that most are from several hundred years ago, although some could have been created in the 1999 eruption. I don't ask Luis whether I should climb down as he might shrug again and I don't fancy 'going on the boil'.

We walk along the crater rim for about half an hour before reaching an old metal cross that signals that we have achieved the summit of Guagua (baby) Pichincha. The summit height is actually 4,794 metres (15,727 feet). It isn't a difficult climb overall, apart from feeling a little reaction to the altitude, but is well worth all the effort to arrive at the top. Standing there, able to see so much in all directions but in particular the sprawling city of Quito far below, I feel a sense of contentment on top of this Ecuadorian summit. I wonder how I'll feel if I manage to reach the summit of Chimborazo, a further hefty 1,700 metres (5,000 feet) higher. That's for the future, however, now it's time to enjoy the present. The sun's very hot and I wish I had brought my straw hat with me, but a baseball cap suffices. We still have time and energy to spend on more climbing and so decide to travel to the other main summit, Ruca (old) Pichincha, also known as Virgen del Cinto. This means that we must trek down towards the Refuge again but this time head north and then trek around to the east, where we are also able to climb to another summit, El Padre Encantado at 4,500 metres (14,764 feet). From there it's a climb up a rock basin that becomes a continuous stumble over areas of loose scree and rock, which as always I find unpleasant. It's worth it at the end, however, when we reach the summit of Rucu Pichincha at 4,698 metres (15,413 feet), the peak again marked by another cross. Although not high peaks by Ecuadorian standards, I know that the three summits achieved today are certainly good training for the really big ones. That night I sleep well.

CHAPTER 8

ADVENTURERS, EXPLORERS, MOUNTAINEERS

One of the many benefits of climbing in foreign countries is that it always provides considerable thinking time and opportunities to learn more about where you are, and the people and events that have helped to shape the country's destiny. When in a tent or a mountain hut I spend my free time reading more about the county's history, and those who have left their mark on it. Ecuador has always been of very considerable interest to many explorers, travellers and of course mountaineers, as within its borders there is such a vast diversity of extraordinary ecological and geographical features. It's also a country where much blood has been spilled, as some have sought to conquer and to restrict its traditions, whilst others have only wanted freedom and an open society. Despite the conflicts occurring over many centuries and the bitterness caused throughout its history, Ecuador has always also been a place of joy and fascination to many, partly because of the magnificent fauna and flora to be found in wonderful and extraordinary locales.

There is little doubt that General Simon Bolivar must be judged as the foremost person who influenced the destiny of Ecuador. His vision and determination created the opportunity to free Ecuador, as well as many other

South American countries, from the domination of Spain. Because of his heroic and ultimately successful efforts, Bolivar became known as the Great Liberator. He also was a great opponent of slavery and was responsible for freeing slaves in many places where his soldiers fought for freedom and against tyranny. Although he was of Venezuelan birth, his dreams were for the whole of South America and his greatest desire was to see it unified into one Federation, with all its peoples helping and supporting each other. That wasn't to be, but it certainly wasn't for his lack of trying. Bolivar was an intellectual who dared to comprehend 'the big picture', using his military and political skills to advance the cause of freedom everywhere and to oppose those dictatorships which ignored the needs of the people.

In 1815, whilst biding his time in the West Indies, Bolivar produced his famous 'Jamaica Letter', in which he reviewed and analysed the prospects for the whole South American sub-continent. Six years later, after several battles along the eastern coast, Bolivar was finally able to overcome all resistance successfully and established the independence of Venezuela. Bolivar then turned his attention to Ecuador and financed two armies with the intention of liberating its capital, Quito. Simon Bolivar was in charge of the army invading from the north and General Antonio José de Sucre led an army from the south, starting out from Guayaquil. The initial attacks by Bolivar weakened the resistance of the Spanish and, buoyed by his success, Sucre fought courageously and tenaciously on the plains of Pichincha, finally capturing Quito from the Spanish. This victory, which took place on 24 May 1822, proved to be the key battle in Ecuador's fight for freedom and together Bolivar and Sucre were finally able to free it from Spain's dominance.

Bolivar had created the Republic of Gran Colombia, comprising Venezuela, Colombia, Panama and Ecuador and he became its President in the hope of creating greater opportunities for all its citizens. His dream of establishing a viable South American Federation seemed about to be realised. In an historic meeting, Bolivar met in Guayaquil with General José de San Martin, the other main creator of South American liberation who had arrived from Peru. San Martin initially wished to negotiate a takeover of Guayaquil, although Bolivar could not agree to this as he had already incorporated the city into his Gran Columbian Republic. San Martin graciously accepted this, recognising the greater importance of solidarity in South American countries. The meeting proved the measure of the qualities of both men, these two great heroes of nineteenth-century South America, in each recognising and respecting the role of the other and agreeing to part in friendship, without animosity. They will always be remembered in history as the two Great Liberators.

Charles-Marie de la Condamine was a French aristocrat with impeccable credentials in the fields of science and one further special qualification: he was very rich. When the prestigious French Académie des Sciences were looking for someone to lead and partly fund a scientific expedition to Ecuador, La Condamine was an ideal choice. For some time there had been a conflict between two scientific theories concerning the shape of the Earth, one propounded by Isaac Newton, Britain's eminent mathematician, physicist and astronomer and one by the Astronomer Royal of France, Jacques Cassini. The French Académie decided to resolve the conflict (naturally hoping the French theory would win out) by sending one expedition to the Arctic region (actually Lapland) and another headed by La Condamine to Quito, the capital of Ecuador close to the Equator. Both teams would undertake research and carry out scientific measurements to resolve the issue.

La Condamine, a mathematician and geodesist, took with him the astronomer Pierre Bouguer, the mathematician Louis Godin, the botanist Joseph de Jussieu and several other French notables. To obtain the King of Spain's permission and approval for the expedition, it was agreed that two Spanish scholars would participate, Jorge Juan y Santacilia and Antonio de Uloa. The group of scientists, once they had arrived in Ecuador, divided into separate groups and travelled by different routes, in order to make stops along the way to map and measure the coastlines as well as to take other territorial and mountain measurements. The party led by Bouguer eventually arrived in Quito from Guayaquil in May 1736 and La Condamine and his party arrived there from the north coming through the province of Esmeraldas. There is still controversy as which of them arrived first but it doesn't really matter, as they immediately put their rivalry and personal feelings to one side and agreed to collaborate on their scientific observations and share their findings.

On his way La Condamine was joined by the noted Ecuadorian mathematician and explorer, Pedro Vicente Maldonaldo y Sotomayor, a Creole by birth, who became part of the expeditionary team and was therefore able to uphold the interests and honour of Ecuador. Maldonaldo introduced la Condamine to the properties of rubber (*caoutchouc* or *jebe*) and instantly realising the tremendous potential of this product, he was the first to bring back samples to Europe. He actually fashioned a rubber pouch to house his instruments in order to keep them dry. On his journey along the Esmeraldas River he had also come across an interesting metal, neither gold nor silver, which was locally called *platino*, which we know as platinum. Maldonaldo also introduced La Condamine, for expedition purposes, to the naked Colorado 'Indians' painted in bright red dye, who were happy to treat him as a friend and agreed to escort the party through the jungle. During their arduous journey they had to climb through the Andes before finally reaching the city of Quito.

Once in Quito, La Condamine met up with Bouguer and the other scientists, and they immediately began the work for which they had all travelled so far and with such difficulty; calculating the measurements of the Earth. They chose as their initial site the level, semi-desert plain of Yarqui to the north-east of Quito, constructing several brick pyramids as markers and measuring points, in many different locations, as well as taking positions on several mountain peaks in order to send measuring signals to each other. Their work continued over several years, however with considerable problems occurring to interrupt it. Sometimes these were because of conflicts between the interests of the countries represented as well as other countries of the region, and at other times due to difficult and dangerous local conditions, often resulting in the sickness and fatalities of some of the scientists. Their camps were unsanitary in the extreme and their provisions were constantly being invaded by cockroaches, flies, ants and insects of all kinds. Their feet and other extremities were bitten by fleas and worse, and some of the team argued that they should abandon their work and head back to Europe.

La Condamine wouldn't, however, be deterred and stuck with it until finally in 1743 all their findings and measurements were complete. Their prime finding was to confirm that Newton's theory on the shape of the world was correct, rather than Cassini's, and the expedition to the Arctic and Lapland confirmed this same finding. It was testament to the scientific integrity of La Condamine that he wasn't swayed by any nationalistic loyalty in arriving at this conclusion. As previously mentioned, La Condamine and his colleagues were also able to determine and record the exact place of *Mitad del Mundo* (Centre of the World).

They didn't mark the actual site with anything however, thus leading to the subsequent claims and counterclaims two hundred years later of where exactly it was. They also made the calculation of the distance from the Equator to the North Pole, based on the Paris Meridian, which in 1791 would become the basis for calculating the metric system; one metre being taken as being one ten-millionth of the distance between the Equator and the North Pole.

Members of his team, adventurous and foolhardy in equal part, were also the first to climb Pichincha at 4,794 metres (15,728 feet) and El Corazon at 4,788 metres (15,708 feet) and also determined that Chimborazo was the 'highest mountain in the world'. Amazingly they actually measured it as being the 6,310 metres (20,702 feet), a measurement which is still accepted today. This belief of it being 'the highest' persisted until around 1820, after which the Ecuadorians had to settle for it being only 'the tallest'. The team also measured many of the other high mountains but unfortunately these measurements weren't as successful, and controversies still continue today as to the actual heights of certain mountains. Several important mountaineers have come up with differing measurements for various mountains and, very surprisingly in this time of high technology, the exact and accurate agreed heights still have to be resolved. A prime example is Cotopaxi itself, as La Condamine's team measured it as 5,751 metres, Humboldt at 5,753 metres and Whymper at 5,978 metres.

After their work was completed, this brilliant and diverse group of scientists dispersed to many different parts and posts, with some choosing to stay in South America. La Condamine himself as the leader had to return to France with his findings but returned via the Amazon in order to map this massive river. His adventures and misadventures down the Amazon and elsewhere, in travelling back to France, are almost unbelievable and he narrowly escaped death on several occasions. He eventually returned to Paris in February 1745 in order to present his report to the Académie, nearly ten years since he had left on his historic journey.

Baron Friedrich Heinrich Alexander von Humboldt, was a German (although more aptly in those times described as Prussian) scientist and explorer who first visited Ecuador in 1802, reaching Quito in January. The city was still recovering from the earlier massive Pichincha eruption and the earthquake that killed over 40,000 people, with volcanic rumbling still occurring to warn of the power the mountain was always ready to unleash. One of the results of that eruption was to affect the local climate for a considerable time, so it was much cooler than it had been in previous periods. Travelling through the mountains, Humboldt coined the name 'Avenue of the Volcanoes', which has been used ever since to describe the area closed in between the two great mountain ranges of the Cordilleras.

Humboldt loved being in Ecuador and journeyed throughout the country, making extensive notes of his travels and observations. His pioneering work was such that he is often referred to as the father of modern geography. Even Charles Darwin called him 'the greatest scientific traveller who ever lived'. Following on from his studies and investigative work of the oceanic currents and the effects they produced, he was honoured by having named after him the cold Humboldt Current flowing from the South Pacific, always powerfully affecting the climate of the Galapagos Archipelago, as well as the mainland coastal regions. The following words help to sum up his depth of feeling for this jewel of a country and the impact it had on him: 'A trip across Ecuador can only be compared with a trip from the Equatorial Line to almost as far as the South Pole.' Having travelled to both fascinating areas myself, I can well understand what he meant. Although vastly different in every conceivable way, the tropics and both polar regions exemplify the enormous wealth and beauty of every kind to be found within Nature, as well as the geographical and natural treasures that are readily available to everyone who is prepared to seek them out.

Humboldt was even described by Simon Bolivar, as 'the true discoverer of America'. He was born in Berlin and studied botany, mineralogy, chemistry and astronomy. At a very early age he became keen on travel and exploration and decided to dedicate his life to the furtherance of scientific knowledge and studies. In Ecuador, Humboldt commenced his preparations for his subsequent pioneering essays on the 'Geography of Plants' and his connecting the relationship of the local flora with its region's geography. He was probably responsible for the growth of the worldwide guano industry, as he provided the initial samples for analysis to colleagues in Europe. Humboldt invented the term 'magnetic storms', so encouraging the establishment by the Royal Society of more observatories, set up initially to study sun spot activity and his work on isotherms and isobars was the basis for the creation of the science of climatology. He was always a man of the people and totally opposed to slavery, calling it 'the greatest evil', no easy position to take in those Spanish colonial times. On one occasion, his shoes having disintegrated, he was forced to travel barefoot as he would not contemplate the unfairness of being carried by an indigenous 'Indian'. His friends included Goethe the German writer and philosopher and of course Darwin, who undoubtedly himself was greatly influenced in his own works by the writings and thoughts of Humboldt.

Although not a real mountaineer, Humboldt loved the mountains and was the first to establish from his personal experiences whilst climbing on Chimborazo that there was a connection between someone suffering from altitude sickness and experiencing lack of oxygen. He actually weighed the air at altitude to determine the differences occurring. Above all he wanted to achieve the summit and possibly succeeded to reach over nearly 6,000 metres (over 19,000 feet), although some thought he might have 'miscalculated' by some 300 metres (1,000 feet). For many years afterwards he always thought he had managed to climb higher than anyone else in the world had, and was bitterly disappointed later in his life to discover that others had climbed higher elsewhere. Perhaps in his mind's eye however, in so many ways, he had 'climbed' the highest of all. He actually also climbed many of Ecuador's other mountains, including Guagua Pichincha as it started to erupt. The inhabitants of Quito who suffered the ill effects of the eruption were highly suspicious of him, his being a 'German' and also a 'scientist', and accused him of throwing gunpowder into the volcano crater, without regard for the consequences. Fortunately for us, and more fortunately for him, they didn't throw him into the crater.

Humboldt didn't climb Cayambe, Ecuador's third highest, but he thought it to be exceptionally special and described it as 'one of the most beautiful to be ever seen… it can be considered one of the eternal monuments with which Nature has marked the great divisions of the globe.' Humboldt attempted on three occasions to climb Chimborazo, but unfortunately didn't make it to the summit. Yet the fact that he attempted it at all, reaching 'a great height', made him very famous in Europe, at the time becoming the most famous person after Napoleon Bonaparte.

He was a true romantic, and one of his main desires in climbing high was to be able to see across to the Pacific Ocean. His comments on achieving that goal bear repeating: 'We now for the first time commanded a view of the Pacific.

We saw it distinctly, reflecting along the line of the coast an immense mass of light and rising in immeasurable expanse until bounded by the clearly-defined horizon.' Due to his desire for knowledge he would more readily than most believe the stories told to him by the indigenous tribes, and one very fanciful story is always associated with Humboldt who even wrote a detailed paper to confirm it. He was told by some tribespeople that several volcanoes would emit thousands of fish into the air when they erupted, and that the fish would fall to the ground still alive, where they could be easily gathered and eaten. His paper was called *Dissertation on a new species of pimelodid, thrown out by the volcanoes of the Kingdom of Quito* (*Mémoire sur une nouvelle espèce de Pimelode, Jetée par les volcans du royaume de Quito*). This story would haunt Humboldt forever, as he just couldn't find it in himself to admit that he had been fooled.

Despite his gullible nature, Humboldt made many interesting observations, one of which was that in crossing a swaying rope bridge travellers should only cross one at a time and always lean forward, as well as not look down to avoid becoming afraid. Travelling further south, he arrived at the ancient pre-Inca Canari kingdom where he was to investigate the fortress ruins located there and with his writings on them so became the first archaeologist of South America. Using the improved techniques and instruments now available, Humboldt also re-drew many of La Condamine's maps and this proved of considerable value to many explorers coming after him. Above all he was not afraid to be a man of vision and his ideas and dedication to looking for eternal truths possibly helped to inspire the young Simon Bolivar who declared, 'Baron de Humboldt did more for the Americas than all the conquistadors.' A name also very worthy of mention and associated with Humboldt's is the French botanist Aimé Bonland, a doctor by profession whose medical skill would prove invaluable on many of their journeys. He accompanied Humboldt on most of his travels and explorations as well as his mountain climbing, and Humboldt owed a great deal to him. Bonland was, however, always content to remain in the background and in his shadow, provided he had his plants to collect and study. Humboldt eventually died at the great age of 90 in 1859, the year Darwin's extraordinary *The Origin of Species* was published.

Edward Whymper, a wood engraver by profession, was definitely a mountaineer, the most successful of all those who have climbed in Ecuador. Some years after his masterful but tragic first ascent of the 'unclimbable' Matterhorn in the Alps in 1865 (four of his companions died on the way down), he travelled to Ecuador in 1879 where he accomplished a string of high peak successes. First of all he was astounded to learn that Chimborazo had two or more summits whereas Humboldt and Bonland had only mentioned one.

He also had theories on why it seemed easier to climb high mountains in Europe and wanted to see whether it was something to do with the vegetation they did or didn't possess. He was therefore surprised to find that the Pacific slopes of the Andes were wooded up to great heights, whereas the eastern slopes were almost devoid of vegetation. Although not the first to accomplish the feat, he climbed Cotopaxi at 5,897 metres in 1880 and in the same year was the first to climb Chimborazo at 6,310 metres. He climbed these mountains with two Italians, the very experienced Jean-Antoine Carrel, age 52, his competitor on the Matterhorn, and his nephew, Louis Carrel, age 26. Whymper was now 40, a more sober character since the Matterhorn tragedy, and throughout his subsequent illustrious climbing career felt he had to atone in some way. At first his tremendous feat was not believed, so incredibly he proved it by climbing Chimborazo a second time in the same year again with the Carrels, but this time also with two Ecuadorian climbers, David Beltran and Francisco Campana. His personally descriptive and painful words about that first triumph, though, standing on the summit of Chimborazo, tell the mountain story for many of us, even with the exhilaration we can often feel on a successful ascent of a mountain. 'We were hungry, wet, numbed and wretched.' He, unselfishly and in true scientific manner, carried both aneroid and mercury barometers with him in order to try and establish the mountain's correct height.

Whymper then went on to climb Cayambe, the third highest mountain at 5,790 metres and Antisana, the fourth highest at 5,704 metres. Whymper's book, *Travels Amongst the Great Andes of the Equator* was published in 1892. In it he sets out some of his thoughtful ideas on altitude survival, saying 'It has long been debated whether human life can be sustained at great altitudes above the level of the sea in such a manner as will permit of the accomplishment of useful work.' Following on from some of the observations of Humboldt on the breathing problems caused at high altitude, Whymper also referred to 'the rarity of air', and was only too aware of the tremendous difficulties experienced by those climbing high mountains, particularly carrying heavy weight.

Whymper also recorded the reaction on the human body of being at high altitude and, with some ironic pleasure at being able to experience and record the symptoms at first hand, he suffered the mountain sickness (*soroche*). In all these mountain attempts he climbed with the two Carrels and they then went on together to climb a further five first peaks, Iliniza Sur (5,248 metres), Carihuairazo (5,020 metres), Sincholagua (4,898 metres), Cotacachi (4,944 metres) and Saa Urco (4,676 metres). The only one he failed at was El Atar. Although a more lowly 5,319 metres, this mountain is a serious technical climb and wasn't fully climbed until 1963. Whymper didn't attempt Sangay, the most active volcano, but was very aware of it and watched it from his camp three on Chimborazo, later writing, 'There were snow-filled beds near its summit, but the spur of the cone was black and was doubtless covered in fine volcanic ash. The saying is current that eruptions of Sangay are to be apprehended when Cotopaxi becomes tranquil and the opinion seemed to prevail that the two mountains act as safety valves to each other.'

Whymper was a mountaineer but was also much more than that. He was a collector of insects, moths and butterflies as well as crustaceans and other creatures. He even found earthworms at 4,800 metres. Whymper was the one to debunk the Humboldt fanciful story that the volcanoes would periodically shoot a certain type of fish from their craters and they would land in the plains far below still alive, to be caught and eaten by the local tribespeople. Whymper was fascinated by the power and unpredictability of the volcanoes, and studied them whenever he had the opportunity. On his second Chimboarazo ascent, he allowed the others to climb ahead whilst he stopped to watch an eruption on Cotopaxi. 'I lingered behind and saw the commencement of an eruption. At 5.40 a.m. two puffs of steam were emitted. At 5.45 a column of inky blackness began to issue, and went up straight in the air with such prodigious velocity that in less than a minute it had risen 20,000 feet (6,000 metres) above the rim of the crater. The top of the column was therefore nearly 40,000 feet (12,000 metres) above the level of the sea.'

Whymper was conscious of the need to collate and impart information for future generations of mountaineers, and was always making and comparing measurements to that end. He produced a table of snow line data showing from various sides of the individual mountains where each snow line approximately began. He would be absolutely horrified at learning that just over a hundred years later all the snow lines have leaped upwards and are continuing to retreat at a very fast pace. The problems of unchecked global warming will leave so many mountains eventually devoid of all their snow coverings and we are all the losers for that, whether mountaineers or not.

In 1872 the German mountaineer Wilhelm Reiss with the Colombian Angel Escobar were the first to climb to the summit of Cotopaxi's Summit from the south-eastern side. Another German climber, Alfonso Stubel, in 1873 followed the same route up the mountain but was accompanied by four Ecuadorians, the first time Ecuadorians had climbed any major mountain; Rafael Jantui, Eusebio Rodriguez, Melchor Paez and Vicente Ramon. Reiss and Stubel in that year together made the first ascent of Tungurhua at 5,023 metres. Now Ecuadorians are firmly established as first class mountaineers in their own right and climb in all parts of the world.

The Ecuadorian climber who gained the highest reputation in mountaineering was undoubtedly Nicolas Martinez, who is considered to be the foremost Ecuadorian climber of his day and an inspiration to all the Ecuadorian mountaineers who have followed after him. He made the first Ecuadorian ascents of many mountains and in fact was the very first climber to climb Iliniza Norte at 5,126 metres in 1912. Martinez also climbed Tunguruhua in 1900, Antizana in 1904 and Cotopaxi and Chimborazo in 1906. The first ascent of the Sangay volcanic mountain at 5,230 metres was by an American Robert Moore in 1929 during a period when Sangay, usually the most active of all Latin American volcanoes, was relatively inactive. Marino Tremonti, who led an Italian Alpine team in 1963, finally climbed El Atar, the last remaining of the unclimbed mountains, at 5,319 metres.

The less high mountains were by then also being climbed, notably Cerro Hermosa at 4,571 metres by a German team and Quilindana at 4,877 metres by a team of Ecuadorians. New routes were constantly being undertaken and achieved on all the mountains, particularly by Ecuadorians who were finally coming into their own as a strong climbing fraternity. In December 1984 even the north face summit of El Atar was achieved from inside its crater by two Ecuadorians, Oswaldo Morales and Gilles de Lataillade, and in that same month the Canonigo peak of El Atar was also summated from inside the crater by Luis Naranjo and Maurice Reinoso. Truly a golden period of Ecuadorian climbing had arrived and was certainly going to remain as even more ambitious routes were being achieved.

It is only right to include here a mention of the historic hotel and hostelry known as La Cienega that has been used by many international travellers and mountaineers over several hundred years, particularly by those contemplating an attempt on Cotopaxi. Many mountaineers coming into Ecuador from around the world have stayed in this famous hacienda, either before attempting Cotopaxi or after climbing it, the latter usually either as a reward or for consolation. It is known as a mountaineer's sanctuary. La Cienega is actually a large country mansion with several acres of land surrounding it and dates right back to the seventeenth century. It has many original cobbled-stone pathways and Moorish-styled fountains and is full of interesting features.

La Cienega was built originally as a colonial hacienda for the Marquis de Maenza, and his descendants lived there for over 300 years. This family was predominant in the plotting that took place amongst many established aristocrats, who considered their allegiance to Ecuador was far greater than their ties to old Spain. They met in secret to plan the ways in which to remove the authority of Spain and to claim independence. Undoubtedly many of the clandestine meetings took place in La Cienega. As part of its historic connections in the region, a bell was installed in the stone chapel in 1768 (and is still rung on special occasions), to give thanks for the ending of the Cotopaxi volcanic eruptions, which had then been occurring continuously over a 20 year period.

Many of the important statesmen, travellers and mountaineers coming to Ecuador stayed at La Cienega, including both Alexander Von Humboldt and Edward Whymper. The three French and two Spanish academicians primarily responsible for determining the place of *Mitad del Mundo* (Centre of the World) also worked on their calculations in the main house. Two of the Frenchmen, Charles-Marie de La Condamine and Pierre Bouguer, journeyed from La Cienega to climb Pichincha during the time they were there preparing their calculations and measurements.

I mentioned previously two of the major influences on my thoughts and understanding of the mysteries of this extraordinary world and referred to Charles Dickens. Now I want to refer to Charles Darwin. Just as Simon Bolivar totally changed the history of Ecuador through his military planning and actions, so Darwin through his initial field research in the Galapagos Archipelago of Ecuador, coupled with his findings elsewhere, changed the natural history outlook of the world. Darwin arrived in the Galapagos in September 1835 and was utterly astonished by what he found there. He first stepped ashore on Chatham Island (now known as San Cristobal) and was initially shocked by the sight of the black volcanic lava fields, which seemed to have destroyed everything. He soon realised however how much more there was to understand and research, and the sight of the extraordinary creatures he found in the islands thrilled him beyond measure.

They moved onto Charles Island (Santa Cruz) and the giant tortoises on so many of the islands gave him great cause for concern. How did they get there if they can't swim? Why are there different kinds on several islands? He began to ponder these mysteries, and some kind of realisation started to form in his mind, as he questioned more and more, these 'islands formed of precisely the same rocks, similar in climate, rising to similar heights, yet so differently tenanted'. He then spent his whole time feverishly exploring many of the islands, collecting his specimens, making his notes and couldn't wait to get back to England to continue his research. Paradoxically, it was only when he was an older man in his forties, after realising that Alfred Russell Wallace had arrived at similar conclusions, that he finally set down his full findings and theories on natural selection in his ground breaking book, *The Origin of Species*. Wallace was living in the Malay Archipelago and had generously sent Darwin his own manuscript entitled, *On the Tendency of Varieties to Depart Indefinitely from the Original Type*. Darwin finally woke from his 'reverie' as if from a trance, realising there was no time to lose and was immediately spurred on to publish. The rest is history – natural history.

The theory of evolution by natural selection of course has wider and more immense implications than initially conceived, explicitly implying that life is about 'the survival of the fittest'. This broadly means that Nature will decide which specimens of any kind will survive and that the weaker ones will perish, with those characteristics needed to survive being passed on or adapted to future generations. In this way new species are or were being constantly created, with related species having sometimes very important differences because of environmental effects or necessities.

These revolutionary findings were first published in November 1859 and immediately they caused enormous controversy in those more puritanical and religious times. This controversy continued intensely for at least a hundred years or more, and in many ways still continues to this day. In fact in the 'Bible Belt' States of the USA, such as Kansas and Arkansas, many people still believe that the world was actually created 6,000 years ago. It's a somewhat strange irony that Darwin's propositions should cause such considerable disharmony with many religious leaders, as in fact his original intention had been to take up holy orders when he finished at university where he was actually studying divinity. Darwin's theories were an enormous influence then, and have still continued to be a huge influence on, amongst many others, scholars, scientists, philosophers and religious leaders.

Darwin also recorded his extensive sea travels in his earlier book, *The Voyage of the Beagle*, still a great read to this day. In it, he refers to the Galapagos and states that, 'It seems to be a little world within itself; the greater number of its inhabitants, both vegetable and animal, being found nowhere else.' It was the differing characteristics of the many species of finches in particular that started Charles Darwin on his own voyage of discovery of the theory of evolution, although he was actually prompted to publish his findings by the learned taxonomist John Gould. Together they examined the thirteen species of stuffed finches they had brought back, and particularly observed the different sizes between their beaks which helped to define their varying characteristics. As a few examples of the amazing range of finches discovered, there is the large ground finch which uses its huge beak to crush seeds and nuts, the tiny warbler finch which will only eat insects, and then the strangest finch of all, the one that feeds by drawing blood from nesting sea birds.

After returning to England Darwin never again travelled abroad; as if what he had seen and learned was more than sufficient for his lifetime. One of the odd habits picked up from his years at sea, in common with many sailors, was that Charles Darwin enjoyed taking snuff. On board the *Beagle* sailing ship he had indulged himself to such a degree that, on his return to England, he found it impossible to give it up. He decided his only way to cut down, for he would never give it up totally, was to keep the snuff locked in the basement of his house and put the key in the attic. Although it made it difficult to access and certainly slowed down his taking it, perhaps the exercise of constantly climbing up and down the stairs contributed to keeping him fitter than otherwise he might have been. (Enough on snuff, any more might get up your nose.)

Darwin was a man of vision and brilliance, but was also an extremely modest and gentle man who hated to hurt anyone. He possibly delayed publishing his work for so many years in part at least to avoid offending his more religious father and wife who were extremely disturbed by his radical views. Of course his many opponents, seizing on the concept that Darwin seemed to be saying we were all descended from apes, used every opportunity to decry his work and ferocious debates and violent arguments occurred throughout the world. The genie, however, was out of the bottle and could never be locked in again. Darwin died in 1882 and was buried in Westminster Abbey, next to the great thinker, Sir Isaac Newton. I think this choice of resting place and the position given to him was an appropriate way to honour this most remarkable man.

CHAPTER 9

THE HUAORANIS ON THE RUN

S ome came to Ecuador to conquer and take the riches of Ecuador for themselves or for foreign kingdoms, whilst others tried to provide freedom for the Ecuadorian people. However, those who have suffered or been neglected the most in all circumstances are the indigenous tribes of the rainforest previously known as 'Indians.' The tribe that exemplifies the suffering the most are the Huaoranis.

The jungle and the rainforest has always been the home and sanctuary of this most famous and feared indigenous tribe for as long as their memories and their stories recall. Now it is their hiding place, as many of the tribe try to survive against all the odds. They were probably the last of the remote tribes to be contacted by travellers from the outside world. If only they had been left alone to continue life in their ancient ways. They have considerable knowledge about the jungle, its creatures, the insects and the plants, but much of this is being lost as they fight to survive.

The Huaoranis, as they are now called, were once better known as the Aucas, so named by another tribe, the Quichuas; a name meaning primarily the Savages but also meaning the Rebels and the Enemies. The Aucas were feared and respected by all other tribes as supreme fighters and hunters, who knew no fear and would attack without warning whenever they needed to, exacting a terrible price on those who opposed them. I prefer to think of them more as the Outsiders, as they have never wanted to conform to the rules of modern society, but have only wanted to be left alone and allowed to continue their jungle and rainforest lives without interference. This has not happened, and although some have unwillingly agreed to try and accept the rules and strictures of those with greater powers, many have fought back or vanished into the rainforest where they live undercover.

This is the story of this tribe who deserve more and from whom too much has been taken. The spelling of their tribal name varies, like many Indian names, and some will write it as Huaranis or as Huoaranis, or even Waoranis – the way it's pronounced. In this account of their lives I refer to the name of this fearsome tribe as the Huaoranis, meaning the Peoples, the name and translation they use and prefer.

For centuries the Huaoranis lived east of the seventy-seventh meridian, mainly within an area bounded by the Napo, Curaray, Arajuno and Nashino Rivers. As their territory was penetrated by 'strangers', however, and their land confiscated by prospectors and loggers, they have been forced to wander and have scattered into many different places. This has caused them to feel enormous resentment, even hatred at the way their ancestral ways and customs have been violated. The discovery of oil here, the 'black gold', has caused the rights of the indigenous peoples often to be ignored or at the very least discounted.

The Huaoranis are now being fragmented into different 'clans' as some of them have been 'persuaded' to change their religion and way of life, and to accept the influences of governmental organisations, missionaries and others who do not understand them, their history and their beliefs. Those who still and will always resist strongly and have hidden themselves away in even more remote and secret places are now known also as the Tagaeri and the Taromenani. They have become even more ferocious in defence of their traditions and customs and wish no contact with *cuwudi*, the strangers. Now they must live in fear of discovery and further harassment, and many seek total isolation in order to protect their privacy and their very existence. As a people they always were constantly on the move, exhausting one patch of land and then moving on to another whilst the first area was allowed to revitalise itself. Now their lives have changed dramatically; they rarely settle anywhere and can vanish overnight if they sense they have been found again.

In the past the Huaoranis thought of themselves as the lords of the jungle and revered the animals, especially the jaguar, the anaconda (the boa constrictor snake) and the caiman (the alligator). They incorporated these powerful and ferocious creatures into their own storytelling and in ancient times would carve their likenesses on their pottery and other objects. In archaeological diggings some ancient pottery and fragments have been discovered, although only very little due to the fact that once the regular monsoons arrived, the small sites would quickly be reclaimed into the mud and lost again.

In their stories they tell how Minimpera, the great mother jaguar, would guard their territory on the banks of the main river (the River Napo). She told them not to cross it as 'many, many people live over there and would try to harm them.' She also told them that much further on 'the sky and the earth meet in harmony'. The jaguar is their most respected animal and adversary and they have many stories of the contests with it. They admire the jaguar's grace and try to emulate it. In the past they have worshipped the sun (arising from Inca origin) and also the magic of water, believing the river to be all-powerful, with the ability to reward or punish either directly – by flooding or not – or through its strongest creatures such as the caiman.

Although small in stature the Huaorani men are ferocious to look at, especially when covered in war paint. They paint signs and stripes on their faces and bodies, often to symbolise the creatures they hold in equal respect, using mainly a red dye made from the berries of the Achiote tree. The men, women and children are naked except for a thin waist cord of vine or cotton called 'kumi', the males using theirs for holding their penises, whilst the females treat their cords as their only 'clothing'. They both cut the front of their hair short to hang over their foreheads, with the men's hair shaved at the neck and the women wearing their hair long at the back. The men and the women enlarge their ear lobes to quite incredible lengths by inserting balsa wood corks from a very early age and then gradually using bigger ones as they get older.

The men will carry a blowpipe or blowgun of 3 metres (10 feet) or more in length and it can fire a dart a distance of around 30 metres (100 feet) with incredible accuracy, hitting a moving target such as a small squirrel or even a tiny hummingbird. The blowpipe is made from the chonta palm, in two sections with the middle held together with hardened black beeswax. They also carry a quiver of barbed darts made from the veins of the large palm leaf, with the dart tips covered in curare, a poison taken from the Abuta vine, containing strychnine. The poison has a paralysing effect and will be effective within a very short time, usually less than a minute. The poison is only dangerous if taken through a vein into the blood, so it is quite safe to eat the meat of the animal killed in this way. In fact somewhat surprisingly you can actually drink the poison without ill effect. It has also proved to be useful as a muscle relaxant and can be used in operating on certain patients. The darts are notched using the sharp teeth of the piranha fish. The blowpipe has a very narrow shaft and it is the control by the hunter that really counts, judging the trajectory, the distance, the angle, in all creating the perfect balance between blower, the blowpipe and the intended victim. It is really a form of 'Zen in The Art of Shooting a Blowpipe' and is a skill learned in constant practice over many years.

The Huaoranis have learned to live as the animals of the jungle, and to think as they do. They have specialised techniques and skills, but it is in the mind where the action is created. The Huaoranis are part of the forest and this is why they should never be driven away or their ways sacrificed. They usually use a spear to kill a jaguar, a tapir, a boar, a caiman or another river creature and the shaft and barbed arrow section are made from a single piece of chonta palm; the spear adorned with Cotinga feathers. The Huaoranis fish mainly using another poison, made from the barbasco vine, which enters through the gills and paralyses the respiratory system of the fish so they drown and are easily caught in nets woven from chambira fibre. They look for good fishing areas where the currents are slow and throw the poison in upriver. There are shoals of piranhas in many rivers, but contrary to most perceptions of them they are not usually dangerous to approach and the tribespeople are not afraid of swimming in the same waters. If a piranha is not hemmed in or it has access to food it will not attack or bite humans. If it chose to, however, the piranha could tear human flesh to pieces with its incredibly sharp teeth. A greater danger yet is the stingray whose spine is so poisonous it can kill, or cause numbness that will last for years if not for ever. Surprisingly a Huaorani rarely uses dug-out canoes or rafts to navigate the rivers and prefers to swim or wade through, so needs to be aware of what's lurking down there. He is agile and extremely strong and will easily and quickly scale a large palm or a kapok tree carrying his blowpipe and quiver of arrows in order to search and hunt for prey.

The Huaoranis live in small communities, sometimes comprising only two families, in one or two room huts or houses that they build themselves, sometimes in a larger area on a plateau to give greater protection. They usually build their houses on stilts as a precaution against river flooding and attacks by wild animals (in particular snakes), as well as to prevent insects entering too easily and of course to protect against enemy attacks. Friends are invited to join them to assist in the building of their houses, and stay with them for the weeks that it may take, with food and drink provided for everyone throughout. The main supports and floors are made from the chonta palm tree, the sides from bamboo and for the roof they use vines, vine leaves and ferns which are interlaced to withstand the heavy and persistent rains. After the building has been completed there is a non-stop party for several days more. The Huaoranis believe in sharing, particularly at house building time, and this includes sharing wives. (They didn't realise they had so many friends!) One of the many tasks of the women meanwhile is to make the yarn for the hammocks, using sisal cactus fibre and chambira, cooked and dried in the sun, with usually the men completing the final stages. Occasionally they will dye a hammock red to make it more special and beautiful.

The Huaoranis often take two wives and have several children by each. It means that the relationships can get quite involved and confusing but no one seems to mind. The men and the women usually sleep in hammocks, but occasionally in a bed made from sisal, using skins and tree bark for warmth. The children sleep on the bare floors, as near to the fire as they can get. Everyone gets a turn in the hammock, though, and to see a sleeping Huaorani child of two or three swinging peacefully in a red hammock is a delightful sight.

The Huaoranis prefer to smoke their food and the method that they use for fire lighting is the ancient one of rubbing a pointed stick vigorously in a hole in a soft piece of wood until a spark is created. They then catch alight with the sparks some moss or other foliage and create fire. The cooking area is within the hut and near to it they will store their blowpipes and other weapons ready for fast use. A smouldering fire is kept going all the time for warmth and ease of cooking and also because of the difficulty in re-lighting it.

They hang stalks of yellow and green bananas and baskets of naranjillas in the house. There are two entrances, one opening out to the clearing whilst the other is more hidden, as it's an escape in case of emergency. Outside they maintain a compound or garden, in which they will grow various vegetables, the main ones being cassava, plantain and tapioca (manioc). The manioc vegetables' roots contain cyanide, which protects them from being eaten by insects. They also usually grow banana and other fruit trees at the edge of the compound. The two main palm fruits gathered by the women are from the chonta and maurita palms, and the reddish fruit of the latter is called nontoca. The women use large nets slung across their backs to carry these fruits and other foods. The soil is poor and therefore after two or three years they would abandon these homes, to move elsewhere and start the process over again.

Naturally, but sadly, one of the favourite foods of the Huaoranis is monkey, and although they are aware that, like themselves. the herds are also rapidly diminishing, they need to hunt for their families and cannot worry too much about the future of the monkeys, especially as their own future is so uncertain. However, they never kill wantonly and they respect all creatures as well as the rainforest. The

Huaoranis like to keep animals such as monkeys and parrots as pets, but in difficult times would not have any qualms about killing them for food. They will sometimes keep an eagle but would never kill it, as they revere it as the king of the air and admire its ability to fly so incredibly high and over such great distances. The Huaorani girls marry at very young ages, usually around 12. The girl and the boy are placed together in a hammock and the next day the girl must gather some cassava and prepare a meal. Once the food is eaten the couple are encouraged to copulate and are then considered fully married. Because of inbreeding, babies will often be born with six or more fingers or toes. The wives carry their babies in slings made of bark, worn around their necks and over their backs. If a man is sick or even dying he can request that his favourite child sleeps with him and is even buried with him. It's considered an honour and is not refused, but you can always tell the cleverest girls around; they are the ones who don't get on too well with their fathers!

On special occasions, at celebrations and festivals, the Huaoranis put on their 'jewellery', mainly animal quills, feathers and decorative leaves, and the musicians will play their rather monotonous bamboo pipes and wear rattles of seed fruits to create some further sounds and movements. There are many reasons for celebration including marriage, good harvest and victory in battle, and they can last for several days. There is a great belief in the magic of the forest and the tribal witchdoctor is called upon to perform whenever there is some great trouble or need. However, if he doesn't come through he may experience in retribution some anger which can spill over into actual violence. The Huaoranis are a 'stone age' tribe with a special history, and should be nurtured and encouraged instead of being forced to hide for fear of being destroyed. They have tried many times to make a stand against those they consider to be intruders on their land, but the greater force used against them, as well as the powerful commercial interests ranged against them, have left them in a perilous state. At times over the years they have been known to kill missionaries and workers who have interfered in their simple and naturalistic lives, but this has only allowed their enemies to claim that they should be punished and are definitely the 'savages' of the original Auca description. If you steal from the Huaoranis, hunt them or take from them, they believe they can kill in return. Only this strange word 'progress' puzzles and defeats them. They do not want much and do not understand why others want so much more; why people will destroy anything and everything for what they desire, whether it is gold or silver, animal skins or the black gold.

A few decades ago, although this emotive story is still remembered and re-told again and again as if it happened only weeks ago, they made a strong example of one person to show the extent of their feeling at their harsh treatment. They kept watch near a camp of the Tivacuno Oil Company and when the cook came to the river to clean a tortoise they quickly and quietly seized him. His body was found the next day with 26 highly decorated spears sticking into it. He would have died instantaneously from one but they wanted to show that they were all committed together and they were not prepared to tolerate forever the injustices they have been made to suffer. Those Huaoranis burned their houses and fled deep into the jungle to hide from the authorities. The Huaoranis have killed others, and they may feel forced to kill yet more people in their efforts to make understood the depth of their feelings.

CHAPTER 10

MORE TRIBES AND TRADITIONS

Her smile is as wide as the street. The varied items she has for sale are spread across several tables, and the contrasting and vibrant colours demand my attention. I hesitate only for a moment and then am of course lost, as she quickly drapes several scarves around my shoulders to show how wonderful they are and what an improvement they make. With her better English and my poorer Spanish I find her a fascinating character, and it is great to be able to observe her many skills. She shows me a range of paintings stretched over small wooden frames and explains why some cost twice as much as others. 'They're mine,' she says as she proudly points to herself and shows me the signature in the left hand corner and then with a flourish copies it onto a piece of blue sketch paper. They are excellent 'primitive' paintings, and mostly show scenes of wild animals, fishing boats, men in sombreros on horseback and women dressed in the same style as she is.

The painter is of uncertain age, wearing an embroidered blue blouse and large flowing skirt and has strong broad hands that are obviously used to being worked. Yet her delicacy with the paintbrush can only be marvelled at. Unfortunately I can't carry any of her paintings with me on the mountains, but I show my admiration for her talent and enterprise by buying several brilliantly coloured scarves. She is just one of the many skilled artists and

115

artisans I come across throughout my Ecuadorian travels and there are so many different traders, men and women, from different ethnic indigenous backgrounds that help to make up this multi-cultured society. Although there are rivalries between them it's always dealt with in very good humour.

Probably at least a quarter of the entire population of Ecuador belong to or are connected with one of the many different indigenous tribes that still remain. The main ones are the Quichuas, the Huaoranis, the Shuars (also known as the Jivaros), the Awas, the Chachis, the Tsachilas (also known as the Colorados), the Otavalenos, the Mantas and the Canaris. There were many more small tribes existing in previous periods but they have either been destroyed by the hostile and violent actions of others from outside the jungle, or by misuse of their environment by prospectors and loggers. Some have been forced to 'disappear' back into the jungle they love and only they seem to understand. There are still some very small 'stone-age' tribes who remain well hidden within the jungle, periodically frightened by the huge silver and evil 'birds' that roar through the sky overhead. The tribes know, or have learned to their cost, that they must never be found if they are to survive.

The indigenous tribespeople orally pass on their history, their culture and their traditions as well as their family stories, from generation to generation, father to son and mother to daughter; nothing is ever written down. Their religion is based on belief in Mother Nature (Mama Pacha) and worship of the sun, the moon and the stars, the mountains and rivers and the snake (anaconda) and other rainforest and jungle creatures. The land is everything and it must be protected above all. Anything that destroys the land also destroys the people. Many indigenous people have died due to disease, neglect and expulsion from their tribal and ancient lands, and tribe numbers have been decimated so that some can now only be counted in their hundreds, whereas before the Spaniards came they numbered many hundreds of thousands or even more. That was their time, and they enjoyed the jungle and rainforest as their own. Above all, they enjoyed their freedom. It is impossible now to turn the clock back and the only way forward can be to observe and learn from the past. The here and now should be treated as the present that it is, allowing us all the opportunities to influence what the future will become.

The largest tribe of indigenous people in the whole country is the Quichuas, who number approximately 1,500,000 and are primarily based in or around the Napo and Pastaza Provinces. In the Morona Santiao Province, the Quichuas and the Shuars tribespeople live side by side and together they total around 100,000. Many indigenous tribespeople do not always have the language or the ability to count in large numbers, which are often related back to the number two. One will be used therefore to mean one and also approximately one, with five often being expressed as two and two and one. Invariably they like to live in smaller communities, where the number of others with them may not exceed the number they can count using their fingers, and possibly also their toes.

The Shuars speak Quechua, the language introduced by the Incas, as do the indigenous peoples of the Sierra, although the Amazon and Sierra tribes lead entirely different ways of life. The Oriente (Amazonas) tribes live in the jungle in their stilted houses and they farm a tiny area, a chacra, on which they grow vegetables, mainly cassava, corn and rice. The soil is poor and every few years they must leave and move on, to build a new house and cultivate a new area. The jungle quickly claims back the old area and very soon it's as if they were never there. The burgeoning oil industry, however, constantly encroaches into their traditional way of life and threatens their lands, and they are harried by 'progress' and are always under threat.

Small numbers of indigenous people live in the coastal regions, primarily the Awas, the Tsachilas and the Chachis. The Tsachilas are famed for their shamans, the traditional medicine and wise men of the villages, always willing to dispense advice as well as medicine. Many Ecuadorians, including those living in towns and cities, use the shaman to provide jungle remedies and potions to deal with their problems of body and mind. The shaman can be asked to deal with all kinds of things ranging from a cure for malaria, to relief from anxiety, to providing a love potion. The tools of the shaman can include the whole range of plant and tree remedies, as well as guinea pigs, eggs, amulets, coloured dolls and their secret and guarded incantations and spells. This knowledge is passed down from generation to generation, usually from father to son, but sometimes from mother to daughter. All kinds of rituals accompany the passing over of this sacred information, as well as the secrets about cures, including the use of the jaguar, the anaconda, the caiman, the eagle and the incredible variety of spiders that abounds in the jungle and rainforest. The shaman's specialised knowledge of the herbs that can be used to deal with numerous ailments is quite incredible and there are thought to be over 900 different plants they might use.

However, like the indigenous tribespeople themselves, the knowledge of the shaman is dying out, as the rainforest where these plants grow continues to disappear.

A ritual which is still practised to test the courage of a young boy and initiate him into manhood is to fashion a 'glove' of leaves, fill it with red biting ants, put his hand inside and see how long he can survive the pain. Afterwards special herbs are used to reduce the swellings and ease the pain. Most tribespeople chew the coca leaf and it has many uses in dealing with pain and sickness as well as providing pleasure. Chewing the powder alone can make a person delirious, so unless that is the purpose aimed for, it is mixed with fire ash.

The indigenous tribespeople of the rainforest in Ecuador, as in many other South American countries, can truly be considered 'stone age' as they go back to a time when they communed with Nature to a degree which is not easily understood in this very modern world we inhabit. Their relationship with Nature has provided them with special skills and a lifestyle that allows them to rise above the conditions we all too readily accept as 'normal'. They had and still have the ability to 'feel' the forest, sensing the creatures within and communicating with them in a way which can be considered as possibly supernatural. They can even sense something before it happens and so can react to something simultaneously rather than re-acting afterwards. This ability has been described as a 'precognitive flash', a flash of insight into the future. It is part of the telepathic and extrasensory perception abilities that some people possess, although most of us do not. Perhaps we all had this ability once and it could still be rediscovered. This 'sixth sense' is such an incredible ability, it should be nurtured; we could all gain if they were encouraged to pass this knowledge on. Indigenous leaders from much of the Amazon Basin Region have started to collaborate in order to combine their greater strengths and promote an international appeal. They argue for more protection against those international companies who only seem to care about what they can extract from the rainforest, so little interested in who and what they contain, illustrating only too clearly that they lack the wider and longer-term viewpoint that the whole world vitally needs. Too many politicians will pay lip service to the rights of indigenous peoples without ensuring that effective action is taken to protect them. There are reports of tribal leaders, male and female, no longer being prepared to tolerate endless conferences and seminars on what is needed, but threatening to take stronger and more aggressive action to promote their cause. A saying that illustrates the abuse suffered over the centuries is expressed with considerable sadness: '*Al Lomo del Indio*', meaning 'On the Indian's back', referring to the days when those who considered themselves of high status even used the 'Indians' to fetch and carry them down from the mountains, as well as carrying their goods and other produce.

In the coastal areas, within the Esmeralda and Manabi Provinces and additionally in the Chota Valley in the Sierra to the north of Ibarra, there is also a large grouping of black Afro-Ecuadorians (known as Negro-afroecuatorianos). These people are descended from the African slaves who were brought over mostly in the eighteenth century. They have invariably retained their own way of life and love, song and dance, always using the rhythms of music to express their special cultures and customs. The bomba negra music is truly vigorous and exhilarating. They originally worked in the plantations and the mines owned by the wealthy Spanish landowners and were also used as servants in their sumptuous haciendas. These slaves were considered to be stronger than the 'Indians' and were given the hardest and toughest tasks. Slave trading was officially abolished in 1821, but it took until 1852 before slavery itself was totally illegal. Even then, the slaves still had few or no rights, and were left with outstanding debts to their 'masters', so they still had to continue as slaves in all but name. The current black population is estimated at around 1,000,000, less than 10 per cent of the total population. Sadly they generally still occupy a lower status generally, are known as 'negritos', and must live in a country where a lighter skin colour is still regarded as the preferred prize. Hopefully, that concept and attitude will eventually change in the way it has finally changed within the United States. What is definitely needed is an Ecuadorian Martin Luther King.

On the *parámos*, the indigenous people are called Chagras and are the 'cowboys' of the Sierra and the ranges, spending long days on horseback tending their herds of cattle and searching for strays. They are excellent horsemen used to riding through the difficult terrains without mishap. They are a tough, independent breed and are macho in spirit. The women are known as Chagrahuarmis and have a hard life but never complain, and certainly not to strangers; you get the impression they wouldn't dare. Indigenous women have difficult lives in this macho society, and there are many divorces or separations and many instances of domestic violence. This has also led to a large number of children living rough and having to find their own precarious ways of earning monies to support themselves.

In this region work starts early, sometimes at dawn. At that time the temperatures are often below freezing so warm clothing is essential, and as well as the colourful poncho they usually wear thick leather trousers called 'zamarros'. The further protection that you will not see them without is their local 'trilby'. The indigenous people here live at high altitude with less oxygen, and are exposed to strong sunlight and winds, so consequently have developed a wide thorax and heavily tanned cheeks. The children often walk long distances to school, but if lucky they might hitch a lift on a llama and the willing animals will carry three or even four young children at a time.

Perhaps the most famous of all the Ecuadorian tribes outside the country are the Otavalos or Otavalenos, who are renowned for their constant travelling, particularly throughout Europe. They can often be found in squares and streets, playing their musical instruments and selling their handmade cotton and wool garments and their huge range of handicrafts. At home in Otavalo, north of Quito, they hold on a weekly basis the largest indigenous market in Ecuador, and probably in the whole of South America. This market is based in the Plaza El Centenario and is still known as 'Mercado de Ponchos', although the poncho now only comprises a tiny part of what is on offer. The market has several different sections, the main ones being for livestock, fruits and vegetables of all varieties, some of which are not easily recognisable, as well as sections for textiles and pottery. If you can't find what you want there, then it probably doesn't exist! The main market is on Saturdays but there is also a daily one. The Otavalenos are renowned weavers, although it is the Salasacas tribe from the Banos area who are actually employed to do the weaving on behalf of the Otavalenos. The weavings are all extremely colourful and full of exotic and eccentric designs. There are rugs, jerseys, shawls, hammocks and of course many types of ponchos.

These colourful and exciting indigenous markets (*ferias*) are held regularly in towns along the Avenue of the Volcanoes, throughout the Sierra. Other interesting markets worth visiting are held at Guamote, Saquilisi, Zumbahua, Pujili, Cotacachi, Calderon, Tigua, Guano, Cacha. Every tribe wears different clothes and colours, which often relate back to the colonial times when the tribespeople 'owned' by a particular employer were made to wear different colour combinations to differentiate them from others. The Otavalenos women, for example, wear blue skirts and highly embroidered blouses while the men wear long ponytails, although usually tucked up inside their trilbys. The Saraguros wear black clothes, although this style is also thought to relate back to their ancient mourning of the death of the still-honoured Inca King Atahualpa.

On market day, the feisty indigenous traders are up at the crack of dawn to make their way to the town plaza to prepare for the day ahead. They can be almost bent double under the weight of the sacks that they carry, crammed with everything from vegetables to jewellery. Some traders will herd sheep, pull along pigs and other animals on leads, carry chickens, guinea pigs or various birds in crates, or find some other means of transporting whatever they have to sell or trade. It all adds to the tremendous bustle and noise which is part of market day. There's a sort of managed chaos with lots of sound, hardly any fury and a great time seems to be had by all, sellers and buyers alike. A woman may have a lamb slung around her back, either with or without a baby added, while some women will have chickens or cocks inside their heavily-embroidered blouses, adding to their already ample bosoms. With the air full of infectious laughter and shouting, and huge grins on the faces of the people all around, you can't help but feel a certain *joie de vivre*.

Music is an essential part of the life of Ecuador generally, but is especially important to the indigenous tribes as part of their wonderful festivals. There is the traditional folk music, but they also love to play the popular Spanish-European melodies and both kinds can be heard throughout the market. The main instruments used are the rondador (bamboo panpipes), quena (flute), maracas (hollow balls full of seeds), conchas (conch shells played like a horn), bombas (drums), charango (ukulele), marimba (xylophone) and the universal and versatile violin. In the markets musical instruments are played either to interest a would-be purchaser or to add to the gaiety, although often only one note is played loudly and constantly, perhaps to weaken the resolve of those considering whether to purchase or not. I am prepared to pay up on behalf of several purchasers at times, just for some peace and quiet. The pipes, the pipes, the pipes!

On New Year's Eve some years back, as part of another Ecuadorian journey, I was on a river boat on the River Napo, deep into the Amazonas. As it approached midnight we were all summoned to the deck to witness a special ceremony, celebrating the arrival of the New Year. The air about us was filled with the flickering lights of thousands of shimmering fireflies. On the opposite river bank there was a woman, strangely dressed in loose, ragged clothes, dancing slowly around a small bonfire, watched by a group of sailors and tribespeople. She (although later I learned it was actually a man disguised as a woman) was illuminated by a bright, focused spotlight.

As it reached midnight the beam of the spotlight suddenly went out and then quickly came back on again, to show the 'woman' being thrown into the bonfire, immediately catching alight. Obviously there had been a switch in the semi-darkness, and a dummy had been thrown on the fire, but it was done so smoothly and cleverly it wasn't possible to spot. Someone then held up something small, waving it vigorously overhead, wrapped in a bundle of white clothes, to represent a new born baby. The ritual was performed to illustrate the death of the old year and the birth of the new one. The ceremony was for the benefit of all peoples, Ecuadorians and foreigners alike and we all were happy to be a part of it. Being staged in the jungle, down this large tributary of the mighty Amazon, it was an example of combining ancient and modern traditions – like the markets. There was definitely a pagan element to the ceremony but it was accepted by all in the spirit of life and its changes, the inevitability of death and renewal.

It was clear night and the sky was filled with the light of many thousands of brilliant, shining stars, most of them dead but their light still reaching out to us. It was absolutely magical on so many levels.

CHAPTER 11

COTOPAXI BREAKS

I halt my travelling through Ecuador in order to attempt my next ascent. Climbing Cotopaxi, the country's second highest mountain, will make a very strong prelude to attempting Chimborazo. Cotopaxi is the highest active volcano in the world and probably the most beautiful mountain in Ecuador, as popular with climbers as Chimborazo. I am keen to climb, but reports of the present weather conditions on all the mountains are once again very bad and there seem to be lots of problems for all climbers at the present time. My climbing time will start to run out very soon, however, and I know I have to go for it despite the dangers. Marcos unfortunately again has other climbing commitments, and it is obvious why he is in such demand. As I am determined to give it a try, Luis, who is available, encourages me to attempt it with him. I try to find Axel to see if he would like to join us but he's still travelling and won't be back for days.

Cotopaxi is 55 kilometres south of Quito, within a National Park which includes three other high mountains, Ruminahui (4,712 metres), Sincholagua (4,898 metres) and Quilindana (4,877 metres). It's the second highest mountain in Ecuador at 5,897 metres (19,348 feet) and was climbed first in 1872 by Escobar and Reiss, and then by Whymper in 1880. Cotopaxi has the most violent history of all the volcanoes in Ecuador, as more people have been killed by its eruptions than by any other, and the surrounding villages and homes have been devastated many times. The records only date back to 1534, but it must have been extremely volatile for many thousands of years beforehand. There were three major eruptions in 1742, destroying the nearby town of Latacunga with considerable loss of life. This disaster was repeated in 1768, making that period of volcanic activity the worst ever recorded.

In 1877 the same catastrophe again took place and the volcanic ash even reached the steam ships travelling between Guayaquil and Panama in the Pacific Ocean, over 320 kilometres (200 miles) away. Smaller eruptions occurred throughout the eighteenth, nineteenth and twentieth centuries, but another big one has not happened for over a hundred years. This has led to some complacency among the locals, who seem quite content to live in close proximity to the mountain, assuming either that an eruption won't occur or that they will have sufficient warning to escape. History shows that it will occur, it's just a case of when.

The exact meaning of Cotopaxi is not clear, as with most other ancient mountain names, but the two most accepted translations are 'Broken Neck' or 'Neck of the Moon'. It's not certain whether the first is as a result of the volcano having had its upper section broken in an eruption or ironically it is referring to the number of climbers that suffer neck injuries on the mountain. The second translation could possibly refer to seeing the moon through the volcanic cone and connect to some ancient ceremony. The problem is that because of constant cloud cover usually it's not that easy to see the summit, let alone the moon, even when it is overhead! There's a third possible translation, 'Headless Poncho', which arises from seeing the mountain as wearing a shawl or poncho of snow around its shoulders without any head appearing above. Luis and I initially travel out to the Laguna de Limpios, where there is a large number of different birds constantly swooping over the water 'fishing', although I don't see any catching. We pass the cowboy town of Machachi but don't stop, as we need to press on. The weather has turned nasty again and I do briefly wonder if climbing with Luis is unlucky, but remember that we climbed to the Pichincha summits in good conditions. We drive on as fast as possible and finally reach our destination, the Tambopaxi Refuge. This is in super luxury style compared to most other refuge huts. Tambo is the name for a resting-place used by the Inca runners when carrying messages long distances across the country. This refuge is owned by four noisy but rather interesting individuals who host, cook and provide anything necessary to help travellers and climbers achieve their goals of either hiking the lower slopes, or attempting to climb Cotopaxi. Inside there's a huge group of climbers who have been waiting to attempt the mountain for several days but they or their guides have been deterred by the continuing bad weather and reports of dangerous conditions on the mountain. I try not to let it concern me and think that surely the weather must improve soon. Obviously I should never be allowed near a casino, with that kind of irrational optimism. If I could, I'd put everything on white.

Fortunately I have been allocated a large single bedroom which allows me ready access to the shower room, providing a welcome opportunity to wash myself and also clean some of my equipment. One of the Refuge owners also arranges to have my climbing clothes and boots cleaned, which is a real help as I've not been able to get off most of the clay since my time on the two Ilinizas. There is an apposite Zen saying that springs to mind, 'After the ecstasy, the laundry.' I think we all know what that implies, especially those who have young children. Sometimes it's a case of 'after the laundry, yet more laundry.'

The food provided in the dining room is excellent and, after scrubbing up and changing into some reasonably cleaner clothes, I am able to gorge myself on several kinds of meat, including steak and chicken, and many varieties of vegetables, followed by some terrific pies and desserts. The climbers waiting there are anxious for 'new blood' and I am bombarded with questions of where I've been and what the conditions were like on the other mountains. There's a constant flow of people checking in but none seem to check out, which indicates that climbing is off the menu at this time.

No one wants to go to bed early after dinner as it's so unlikely that anyone will be able to set off for Cotopaxi at any time during the night or early morning. Some are playing cards, others are showing photos of their adventures. Although I would prefer to read it's difficult to avoid responding to the questions put to me by those anxious for some assurance. I finally give in, joining in the banter to try and ease the deep concerns being expressed. We talk about the Galapagos animals, the problems of the indigenous tribes and the philosophy of climbing and exploration. I think it might help to take everyone's mind off the actual weather if I set out a weather-related puzzle. 'On the grass there are five pieces of apple, a carrot and a scarf. What's a logical reason for them being there?' After a long time of wild and far-fetched guesses I explain. 'Children built a snowman and they were left when the snow melted. Remember snow melts and it will here too.' Someone shouts out, 'We can't wait till Christmas!'

There's then a long discussion about whether the puzzle was fair and why five pieces of apple and not three or seven. All I can offer is, 'That's what the puzzle is, although it used to be with five pieces of coal, but I'm not sure if you all remember coal being used in snowmen and five heaters wouldn't work.' There's a plea for another one, to see if they can solve it and I finally agree to one more. 'A man lives on the tenth floor of a building. Every day he takes the lift to go down to work. When he returns he takes the lift to the

Hiding in the jungle

Huaorani girl bathing

Amazonas butterflies (the eyes have it)

Tribal warriors

Turtle frolics

River reflections

Amazonas walkway

Colorado tribesman and wife

Devil's Nose Railway

Llama and friend

Inquisitive monkey

Volcanic crater lake of Laguna Quilota (3,854 metres)

Chimborazo (6,310 metres) and Carihuairazo (5,020 metres)

Silver cloud haloes around the Chimborazo summit

Pinnacle Rock (Bartolomé Island)

On top of Guagua Pichincha (4,794 metres)

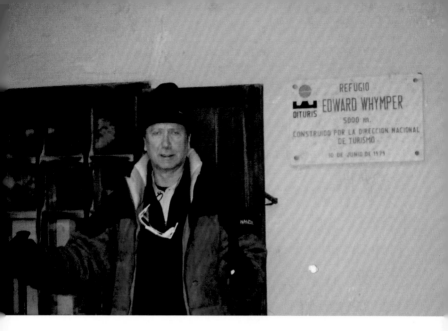

At the Edward Whymper Refuge waiting to climb Chimborazo

Arriving back from Chimborazo

Pelican feeding young

Blue-footed booby and chick

Land iguanas

Waved albatrosses 'dancing'

Galapagos snake

Brooding blue heron

Snuggling seals

Iguanas sunbathing

Sally-lightfoot crab

Boobies sky pointing

seventh floor where he gets out and walks up the staircase to the tenth floor. Why? What's a logical explanation?' The answers come thick and fast. 'He's scared of heights, he's in love with someone on the seventh floor, he wants exercise, he is a mountaineer and is in training.' No one comes up with the simple answer. 'The man is a dwarf and cannot reach any higher than the seventh button.' It's time to go to bed. I think I am almost too full to sleep, but later in a double bed with so much legroom for a change, I fall easily asleep. Strangely, I dream of being chased by jaguars.

The next morning I am up very early, only to find that the weather is worse and I can only just make out Cotopaxi which occasionally looms mistily in the distance but still looks formidable. Because of the weather conditions, several llamas have come down from higher slopes to nestle closer to the windows and the warmth of the Refuge, and they provide an interesting distraction to the practically invisible Cotopaxi. As it seems the weather will remain bad for several days, Luis and I discuss what the options are and whether to abandon the climb for now and travel to another mountain. I am against that as I am running out of time, so finally the decision is made to set off the following day, actually during the night, regardless of the conditions. We shouldn't wait for a break in the weather, as that may not occur in the foreseeable future and I must leave time for Chimborazo no matter what. All day long there are unsettling reports of deep snowdrifts occurring all over the mountain, with black ice conditions further up and very dangerous climbing conditions persisting. Alarmingly, there have also been a few small avalanches.

A German woman climber had left the previous night but returns mid morning after reaching 5,400 metres, with tales of deep snows and harsh conditions which made it impossible for her to continue. She is crying from frustration and her accent becomes more pronounced as she tries to explain what happened. Her guide shrugs; it's a gesture I've seen a few times. Some guides don't seem to understand the emotion involved and the pain felt by those who desperately want to succeed on the mountains, particularly after having made so much effort, travelling half way across the world, to get here and attempt their chosen mountains. It's just a job to those guides; they are hired to take people on the mountain and if they can't make it for whatever reason, then they have not lost anything personally and there's always another climber next time. I take Helga to one side to calm her down and she stops crying as I tell her about some of my mishaps on previous mountains, and that she must always be happy that she made the attempt but above all came down safely. The mountain will always wait for you.

It's a long day and I spend most of it staring out of the window at Cotopaxi, almost willing it to clear and become available to all of us. From times with one of my theatre organisations I remember a question illustrating the frustration of the acting profession. 'Why does an actor *not* stare out of the window during the morning? So he'll have something to do in the afternoon.' I continue to stare but nothing changes and it's definitely make-your-mind-up time.

Finally we agree we must go for it. Luis suggests that rather than trek from here before daybreak, to save time and improve our chances slightly it would be better to travel over early evening to a higher refuge on the flanks of Cotopaxi, the José Ribas Refuge at 4,800 metres, (15,744 feet). That's a good decision and I'm all for it. Luis decides to tell me the reason he hadn't suggested it before. In 1996 an avalanche fell on top of the Refuge and killed a large number of climbers and tourists. With reports of some avalanches higher up the mountain, even though they were small ones, he is nervous that something might happen again. I appreciate his telling me but now we've made the decision we should stick with it but be aware at all times of the danger. We enjoy a last early dinner, pack everything up, load it into the jeep and arrive at the Refuge just after seven in the evening. We prepare for a midnight start. I can't sleep at all and although I try to relax as much as possible, there's too much going on. It's too noisy and I feel very edgy. Probably the story of the avalanche is preventing me sleeping. I get up and wait until it's time to leave.

We are out on the lower slope shortly after midnight. Luis and I are roped together and I begin well, but almost immediately the steepness seems to be getting to me. I'm probably still not acclimatised enough, especially at this height, and soon I am starting to struggle as the snow drags my feet down and it's a tremendous effort to pull them back each time. The backpack feels extremely heavy and is weighing me down. My right knee starts hurting, not a good sign at such an early stage, although I hope it is more nerves than a real problem.

The conditions are terrible with loose snow and ice everywhere, and it's not easy to ground my steps. There's a scree section that is proving very slippery, and it becomes a constant struggle to ascend as I keep sliding backwards. I've always hated climbing over scree sections, although unfortunately most mountains have them and I know I must just fight my way through it. It's now very painful on both my knees and it's taking a lot out of me. I reach a long patch of ultra black ice, as hard as rock and as smooth as steel, and I can't get even a toe hold. I keep kicking my boots in hard to try and get the crampon tips to grip even slightly but to no avail. The tremors of resistance from the ice are reverberating all the way back up along my legs, through my knees and to my hips. I am desperate to prevent myself sliding backwards, and kick again and again. There is so much pain everywhere and my right foot as well as my right knee feels as if on fire.

It's essential to try and turn my mind away from the pain, with a Zen *shin* concentration and I reach inside for a mantra to guide me upwards. In the Japanese art of wrestling, *sumo*, there are three essential attributes, technique, strength and the mental spirit known as *shin*, the most important of all. Now I search for a strong mental approach to carry me through. For a moment or two I start to imagine feeling on my face the warm breeze of a summer afternoon but am quickly forced back into the harsh reality of the now. I try to use the pain as a force and am able to continue for a while before the pain reinforces its own strength.

I reach the glacier ridge of around 5,200 metres and worry about the continuing stress on my knees if I try to make it all the way to the top. I certainly don't want to scupper my chances on Chimborazo, which is my main goal, by struggling on now and using up too much energy and resolve. My mind has always been focused on Chimborazo, the tallest, with the other mountains only serving in my head as training for my main challenge. I continue to tussle with my thoughts and emotions as I climb higher. We come across a number of crevasses and must skirt them carefully. It's again the ones you don't see which are the deadly danger. I'm shuddering with the effort.

It's another 50 metres, then another and again another, until I have climbed to 5,400 metres. This is where Helga had to give up. My right foot feels in constant pain and I think I must have injured it in some way. I fear that it may not last the distance. I decide I will go on for a while, but don't think I have the inner drive and strength to struggle on for too much longer. A few others have already given up because of the atrocious conditions and with each one that passes me on their way down, it feels as if he or she is telling me enough is enough, give up now. Not yet I won't. I reach 5,600 metres and stop to take stock. I could possibly make it, it's actually only another 300 metres to the summit, but after that I will have to come down and there are still considerable concerns about the dangers of avalanches. They have a habit of hitting from behind, on the way down when you can't see or sense them, and that's when they will take you all the way down, burying you beneath their huge weight. Luis looks at me, I think sensing the tumult within, waiting for my decision. This is where some comment, some advice from him would be more than helpful, but it's not his way.

The worst thing would be to fight through these conditions and make Cotopaxi but then not have sufficient left mentally or physically to be able to attempt Chimborazo. Of course I might not make either. 'Ay, there's the rub.' Shakespeare has a word or expression to cover every situation. I wave Luis on and we go on for a while further but I soon have to stop again. I start going through the options, not knowing how long it's taking me. I have lost all sense of time and am in a white world with no shape or form.

I know my mind is struggling to think clearly. The aim was always to achieve, if possible, Chimborazo and I shouldn't do anything that could diminish the possibility of achieving that. If I don't make Chimborazo after trying my hardest, then that would be acceptable. Provided at least I have given it my best shot. My mind clears and I know what I must do. I explain to Luis I have decided to go down and he instantly accepts without comment; the mountain is far too dangerous a place ever to force a climbing decision on anyone. He tells me that anyhow the weather has now closed in so much that I wouldn't have been able to see the giant crater at the top, nor the Avenue of the Volcanoes, nor any other mountains. If I had continued and reached the summit it could be a Pyrrhic victory, if in doing so it ruined my Chimborazo chances. Luis waits for a few moments, leaving me alone to wrestle with my thoughts until he sees that I have definitely made up my mind to descend. I know from many previous climbing expeditions that the mountain will always be prepared to wait for you until you decide to return. I breathe in Cotopaxi's thin air.

Getting down is even worse than expected, and I realise it was totally the right decision to go down, and if anything I should have descended earlier. I am sliding all over the place and it becomes a torment trying to get back safely without an accident. It's necessary to stop frequently, to gain my balance and work out where best to place my steps to avoid tumbling over, knowing how easy it would be to fall a long way. I pass two climbers going down who are having greater difficulties but they don't need my help, just time and perseverance. They wave me on and catch up with us at the Refuge later.

Later in the privacy of my bunk I gingerly remove my boots and socks and examine my feet. They are very beaten up and look quite a mess. I gently coat them with Vaseline but they are going to take a while to recover. The right foot is much the worse and the nail of the big toe is a nasty-looking purple colour. The nail is in fact very loose and looks likely to come off soon. The question is whether to leave it alone and allow it to come off in its own time or pull it off myself. Whichever way, when it occurs it's going to be very painful. The toe itself is throbbing madly and it's obviously going to cause problems on my next climb; there's the possibility that it might not actually allow me to continue. Carefully I cut off the top of the nail to lessen the pressure, cover it with plenty of Savlon cream and bandage the entire foot. I will wait till the next day and look at it again before I decide anything further.

In fact, in the morning the whole nail has come away in the bandage, leaving very raw skin beneath where it was. It feels extremely tender and I pad it as carefully as possible, although I know it's unlikely to stand up to any hard ice kicking and rock scrambling.

As if in sympathy, the thumbnail on my left hand splinters, and part breaks away. I have to cut it down almost to the bone to try and prevent it splintering more. Both my toe and my thumb are now throbbing in some kind of painful unison and I take a yoga position in a corner of the room in an attempt to try to meditate the discomfort and pain away. Not with much success though. It leaves me in a quandary as to how I should proceed and whether I should or even could attempt another mountain. Vivienne Leigh, playing Scarlet O'Hara in *Gone With The Wind*, always dealt with her problems by proclaiming wistfully, 'I won't decide now, I'll think about it tomorrow.' That sounds the best way for me to proceed. I'll also think about it tomorrow.

I don't mention to Luis or any of the climbers about these problems as I don't want any sympathy. After all it's only a toe. Many polar explorers have lost toes and fingers and have still battled on to reach their ultimate goals. Although maybe they didn't need to kick their feet into very hard black ice. I still have time to decide, although I know in reality the mountain will decide.

CHAPTER 12

MORE MOUNTAINS TO CLIMB

Just being close to a mountain is a tremendous thrill. Undoubtedly Ecuador's most famous and toughest mountains are Chimborazo and Cotopaxi, but this country is a mountaineer's paradise and there are many wonderful high mountains, each with its own special features and aspects. All you need is the time, the determination and a little bit of luck. Better weather conditions than I am experiencing would, of course, be quite helpful. I will certainly return to climb here again and it would be a privilege. The following are some of the mountains that I'd love to experience, and are not listed in any particular order, either of height or difficulty, but merely as the fancy took me. That's part of the fun of climbing, 'finding' a mountain, and preparing to climb it or not.

COTACACHI was first climbed in 1880 by Edward Whymper and the Carrel cousins and is 4,944 metres (16,220 feet). It is on the northern shore of Lake Cuicocha and constant lake mist usually restricts visibility. Reaching the base of the mountain sometimes requires some ingenuity as the road approaches are often locked and vehicles can't always get through. Although it's possible to accomplish the whole expedition in one day, it's probably preferable to arrive early enough to walk in and pitch camp as far up the base as possible, ready for an early start the next day. At the foot of the mountain there is a military post which is manned, and you need to make certain that there are no special restrictions applying at that time. I am sure the soldiers based there will help you with most things, but I'm afraid you will have to do your own climbing.

Once you start, the best way is to skirt the military post to the left and head in a north-west direction, zigzagging all the way. A series of cairns will help to guide you on the right path. There are continuous scree sections, so if you prefer to avoid them as I do, you should climb higher to the right within the rocks although this can be painful climbing. There is always a great danger of falling rock, so apart from wearing a helmet you need to keep a watchful eye on the mountain and the conditions at all times. As you work your way upwards you will come across a large col to the south-west of the mountain which will take you through to a rock basin for an exhausting but not too difficult a climb to arrive at the summit ridge. There's more danger of falling rock there, so extreme care must be maintained at all times. It's a knife-edge ridge trek of about 15 minutes to the summit, but there are steep drops either side so don't rush it. There are other routes to the Summit but unless you intend to climb more than once it's better to stick to this Normal route. The name of the mountain is thought to mean 'he who grinds salt', deriving from the fact that salt deposits were found in the earth, which are still being extracted. This should be taken with a pinch of salt.

IMBABURA (CERRO IMBABURA) is an extinct volcano and its exact height is still being argued over. I have it as 4,630 metres (15,190 feet). It's approximately 60 kilometres north-east of Quito and also north-east of the famous Indian trading town of Otavalo. It's possible to tent overnight and climb the next day, or stay in nearby local lodgings. You can also stay in the village of La Esperanza and get someone to drive you in.

Once you start out do not deviate too much from the main path as the way is confusing, and whatever you do don't follow any path downwards, or you will be heading in the wrong direction and it will at least double your climbing time. You need to skirt a large ravine, Quebrada San Clemente, and you can do this on either side. Once you have climbed round the ravine you will pass a few houses and a cement water tank, and it should be easy to re-join the same track leading you upwards to the Summit. Along this path you will subsequently come across a set of rocks and you should climb down very briefly in order to circumnavigate them. Then you climb up again to find the ridge trail, which you should follow carefully around the rim of the crater. It's supposed to be extinct but you never know your luck! Admire but stand well back. The ridge curves round in a semi-circle to the left and will take you directly to the exposed pyramid Summit. The rock crumbles sometimes, so watch your step and particularly on the return. It's of course possible to ascend from the Otavalo side but it's trickier and the rocks are more unstable. This mountain's name is obscure and somewhat unreliably is said to derive from small fish in nearby streams and therefore to mean 'Breeding of small fish'. It could be one of those fishermen's tales. They have them in Ecuador as well.

CAYAMBE (NEVADO CAYAMBE) is Ecuador's third highest mountain at 5,790 metres (18,997 feet) and is the highest point on the surface of the earth through which the actual Equator Line passes (4,600 metres on the south side of the mountain). It is also the only place on Earth where its latitude degree and its average temperature degree are both zero. Although one can then jokingly refer to it therefore as 'the Big Zero', it is in fact considered to be the most aesthetically pleasing of all the Ecuadorian mountains. It is 65 kilometres north-east of Quito and looks over the volcano mountain of Reventador, 3,562 metres high, known as 'The Exploder' because of being one of the most active of volcanoes in the whole of South America.

Cayambe was also first climbed by Whymper and the Carrels, and its name means 'Great mountain of the boys'. A huge, glacial, extinct volcano, Cayambe has a reputation for being unpredictable regarding its weather patterns and conditions and there are often avalanches. There is in fact a refuge set at 4,600 metres, named after the three climbers killed in an avalanche in 1974, Cesar Ruales, Carlos Oleas and Joseph Berge. It is possible to drive fairly close to the refuge in order to stay there overnight and that's what most climbers arrange, but you can also tent nearby if you choose to.

You can still see clearly the remains of the pre-Hispanic agricultural terraces as you climb the lower slopes. There is an ancient glacial valley at the foot of Cayambe, and the *páramo* is usually damp and squelchy. The mountain climb start should be no later than midnight, as it's vital to climb on the frozen snow and get back down before it starts to soften in the late morning and midday heat.

Starting from the refuge there is a relatively short rock scramble and it's preferable to climb to the right side. Then you climb to the left around a large rock outcrop to reach the glacier base. This becomes a long but steady climb to the north-west, but there are large crevasses from the outset, so always be well aware of where you are walking and tread cautiously. There are exquisite stalactites and seracs to observe but stay well away from them, as they can be unpredictable and deadly. (Is that an ice dagger I see before me?). You need to head north-east towards a rock outcrop known as Picos Jarrin. Just before reaching that, veer east to another rock outcrop, which you can pass on either side. There is a massive rock face above you throughout but don't venture onto it, as it will delay your ascent enormously. Head now in an approximate north-east direction and you will eventually reach your goal of the primary flat ridge. Before, to the left of you is the end of the huge rock and ice cliff face. Here you are entering very dangerous crevasse territory, which you must climb through slowly and with great care. This route will eventually take you to an ice basin combining with a large crevasse or *bergschrund* at around 5,600 metres and this area is particularly dangerous. You will need to work carefully round the basin to the right, all the time staying very aware of avalanche possibilities. You may even need to descend partly into the crevasse. Once through you will finally reach the main glaciated summit ridge and from there an easy trek will see you soon at the Summit itself. The views, given the right weather conditions, are magnificent in all directions. Cayambe has an uplifting name: 'Healer of the Future'.

TUNGURAHUA is one of the five volcanic mountains to have erupted in recent times and is within the Parque Nacional Sangay. The last proper eruption was in 1999, the same year as Guagua Pichincha's, and before that it was some eighty years earlier in 1918, perhaps occurring as a celebration of the end of the First World War! Luckily it didn't notice when the Second World War finished. However there are small tremors from time to time, just to remind us that it can let off steam whenever it chooses. The last big one was in 1711 when it destroyed the nearest village of Pondoa. Any major eruption would also easily have an effect on the town of Banos, which is close by and has a thriving tourist industry thanks to the local hot thermal baths. Let's hope that the bath plug hole is only used for draining the hot water away and doesn't suddenly erupt with a massive geyser rocketing skyways, providing the unfortunate bather with a rather nasty surprise.

The mountain is at a height of 5,029 metres (16,500 feet) and was first climbed in 1873 by the two German climbers Alfonso Stubel and Wilhelm Reiss. Climbers are, in fact, often only allowed to go on the volcano with special permission, and are not usually encouraged to apply. Tungurahua is a beautiful mountain nonetheless, worth a visit just to view it, and is just over 10 kilometres south of Banos, as the lava flows.

To make the climb it's a trek in from a police check point and from there a gentle trail to follow to the right which then takes a very sharp turn further to the right towards the refuge. Before reaching it you come to the very small village of Pondoa where you can hire a guide if you want to. From Pondoa it's an easy but tiring trek to the left to the Sangay Park entrance. Once inside there is a further trail to the left to follow but this is steep and passes through all kinds of tropical vegetation including banks of differing bamboo. The refuge is set at 3,800 metres and also offers a view of the east side of Chimborazo. As always it's preferable to set off to the summit from the refuge very early in the morning, before the snow has time to soften and slow you down. Heavy rain can often cause mudslides from the volcano flanks. Gases are also emitted from the volcano which can be highly toxic and dangerous; definitely no laughing matter. The climb is not difficult technically but is extremely steep, it's not as easy as it appears to get up and down in one day and it's preferable to use the refuge as a staging post. The mountain's name means 'Burning Throat' and is thought to refer to the image of the volcanic fire bursting out of a headless giant mountain creature.

EL ALTAR is the mountain that took the longest of all to climb, as its summit was only reached in the comparatively recent year of 1963 by the Italian Marino Tremonti and his team. Even the great mountain climber Edward Whymper couldn't make it. It is now the fifth highest at 5,319 metres (17,451 feet) and its volcano is extinct but it's thought its cone was originally higher than Cotopaxi, until it blew its stack in a very violent eruption. There's a lesson for all of us in that. It has nine summits and the first time all nine were climbed in one expedition was only as recently as 1995, by two Ecuadorians, Osvaldo Freile and Gabriel Llano. It's considered the most religious of all the mountains, as the names given to all parts have some religious or clerical connotation. The overall name of Altar is self explanatory of course, but the actual summits are called El Obispo (the bishop) at 5,320 metres, El Canonigo (the canon) at 5,260 metres, La Monja Grande (the great nun) at 5,160 metres and the remaining lesser ones are El Fraile Grande (the great friar), La Monja Chica (the little nun), El Tabernaculo (the tabernacle) and three more friars, Fraile Central, Fraile Beato and Fraile Oriental. Tremonti and his team returned to climb El Canonigo and El Fraile Grande in 1965 and 1972 and the final summit of El Tabernaculo was climbed by a German team also in 1972. El Obispo and the others are not an easy one-day expedition. They should be taken seriously and it's necessary to prepare to stay a while.

It's a long trek in, whichever route you take and whatever summit or summits you decide to attempt. You can use mules to ease the leg work, but it's still too long to do anything but plan to get near enough, to give it your best shot the next day and the day after and the day after that. There are several camping areas you can use but the most well known is the Italian Camp; although you still have to trek and climb for the last three kilometres, no matter what means you use to get you close to the camp. When you are ready to set off from there you need to trek up to the rock ridge till you reach a gully, primarily composed of unstable rock and stone, and there you need to tread very carefully. A twisted ankle or a wrenched knee will put you at the lower end of the religious order. Climb carefully down the gully to the right to reach a plain covered with gravel and scree. Then it's a long steady climb northwards to the lower glacier, where you have to start ascending round to the right to reach the base of Obispo. You can push on but it makes a very long day. It's better to tent and be fresh and aware, as the rock areas are weak and unreliable and there are constant dangers of rock falls. There's a large couloir in the rocks to the left and, unless there has been a heavy snow fall recently, it's mostly a mix of rock and earth and ice and never to be trusted. After climbing the couloir you will be able to cross a higher glacier to the right which will bring you to another couloir which is very steep and tight. Climb up this and you will be on the summit ridge. It's now straight to the right to reach an extremely steep rock wall you have to climb to make the summit. Again as always be very careful of rotten and unstable rock which can give way at any time. Once you've made the summit, all you have to do is descend! Take it slowly. Although its name is now 'the Altar' it is always known locally as 'The Majestic One' because its indigenous name was Capacurco which translates as 'Majestic Mountain'. It's the only mountain of Ecuador to have had a name change.

CARIHUAIRAZO has two main glacier peaks, Maxim at 5,020 metres (16,470 feet) and Mocha at 5,000 metres (16,400 feet). There is a third, Loma Piedra Negra, but this is not considered the same challenge as the other two. Again this mountain was climbed first by Edward Whymper but with two Ecuadorian companions, Beltran and Campana. It is considered the sister mountain to Chimborazo and is about 10 kilometres away to the north-east. Neither of the summits is difficult to attain but you need to focus and put in the leg work. To reach Maxim you should start out from the Ambato-Guaranda road to travel across to the Laguna Negra (Black Lagoon). It's a long but pleasant trek to the north-west to reach an area below the glacier where you can camp at around 4,700 metres or push on. It's then a moraine climb up a fairly steep slope to arrive at the base of the glacier itself, and there's a clear route towards the right leading to the summit ridge. Always watch out for crevasses which have the nasty habit of suddenly appearing or not being seen at the most inconvenient of times – like when you are about to fall into one. Remember to rope up to someone. The last section is again a mix of rock and snow and ice, depending upon weather conditions. The rocks are unstable and you need to rely on prodding with a ski pole or your ice axe if you have one.

The climb up the lower Mocha is steeper and you follow a route leading from the ridge of the nearby Cerro Piedra Negra, which is relatively easily ascended.

The Mocha glacier is an interesting challenge as there's no obvious route to follow and you have to make or follow leadership decisions to accomplish this Summit. To climb both main summits is definitely worth considering but to do so you would need to allot at least three days to camp out. It has been given a name which contains the words for man, wind and snow. Although that seems to me a good name for a rock band (pun intended), you are entitled to put them into any order you think appropriate. Don't, though, come up with snowman has wind.

ANTISANA is also a volcano, the fourth highest at 5,758 metres (18,891 feet), and has four peaks, easily named and remembered as the North Peak, East Peak, South Peak and, the highest, the Main or Central Peak. Anti is the word from which Andes is derived. There are discussions, even arguments, as to whether Antisana is extinct or merely resting. The last known eruptions were in the eighteenth century but in the life of a volcano that is millions of years old, what's a couple of hundred years or so? The last eruptions resulted in two extensive lava outpourings, one of which created the lake at Papallacta after blocking the valley. This mountain along with Iliniza was one of the favourite mountains of the Incas and was used for burials and sacrificial offerings. There are a number of Inca fortresses to be discovered but they take some finding as they are built with local rock and over time have blended into and become one with the mountain.

Edward Whymper climbed the Central Peak in 1880 and claimed he could still detect the smell of sulphur from the crater. He may have been mistaken. however, as the socks of climbers are rarely changed during expeditions and tend to give off similar smells, and, unlike the volcano, Whymper himself seems to have been particularly active in 1880. As has happened with a number of the mountains with multiple peaks, the lower ones were not climbed initially and in this case the three lower ones were only achieved in the 1970s. The Central Peak is the highest in Ecuador with no refuge and therefore on an expedition provisions for a number of days are required. In all cases a camp should be established at South Crespo as the glacier is then only a short distance away. You can see the summit to the left and even in difficult weather conditions there's still some visibility to guide you. From there on it's not going to be easy at any time and you need to be on full alert constantly. The climb up the glacier will eventually take you to the central ridge but again crevasses are a danger and you should be roped with at least one other climber. Wand your route to follow back in the more dangerous places as it's likely that crevasses will appear. As you approach the lowest part of the ridge you will see a glacier to the left which leads to the summit. Climb the glacier to the east, then edge your way more to the north-west which will take you directly to the summit. You'll be particularly pleased to have set the guiding wands for the return. The routes to the other peaks are also difficult and this is not a mountain to be taken lightly. Its name is rightly inspiring, 'The Mountain towards the Rising Sun'.

SANGAY, although only ranking seventh in Ecuador's high mountains, is the most active volcano in South America, possibly the world, and that can make it at times the most dangerous. It is 5,230 metres (17.159 feet) and was only first climbed in 1929 by an American team comprising Robert Moore, Terris Moore, Paul Austin and Lewis Thorne. It is in a protected National Park, in a rather inaccessible region about 200 kilometres from Quito, so climbing it involves a lengthy expedition. It's almost essential to engage one or two local guides. Usually, however, they will not take you to the summit itself, but will leave you well below it, allowing you to make your own way there and of course back, where hopefully they will be waiting for you. You must be prepared to rely only on yourself, as people here can be as unpredictable as the elements. The fact that guides will not generally accompany you to the summit really goes to show how volatile and dangerous the volcano is, and how even the most experienced climbers will not want to take risks here unnecessarily. The best book to read before you attempt this mountain is Richard Snailham's *Sangay Survived*. His expedition will either put you off totally or inspire with the spirit he and his colleagues showed in the face of unbelievable conditions as the volcano erupted around them. Bonington's *The Next Horizon* is also a must.

To make your attempt you should first make your way to the camp site at La Playa, which will probably involve hiring pack animals, and you will need provisions for a week or more. You also usually need to ford rivers to reach La Playa and it's a tiring and cumbersome business, so you need from the outset to have your heart set on Sangay. If it's been raining very heavily, as it often does, the rivers can turn into torrents and can be obstacles to proceeding until they subside (it can take many days) but worse of all on the way back can also prevent your returning for as long. Always take sufficient provisions for an emergency or two and be happy if you have to give some food away. Overnight at La Playa, in your tent or wherever, you can and probably will hear the temper of Sangay, its volcanic explosions, which can be stimulating or off-putting depending on your own temperament. Remember you made the choice. The local guides should be able to tell you where the current activity is, so you can plan hopefully to avoid those sections. Rocks can and will fall at any time, so extreme caution is essential and a very strong helmet is required as well as fully padded clothing. It's important to take an early climbing start to avoid the later, more aggressive rock activity, as well as to be able to rely on the overnight hardened snow sections for a faster access and an even faster exit, should it become necessary. Initially, with or without your guide, you need to climb up from the *páramos* or grasslands to the ridges above. You will then need to clamber over thick slabs of solidified lava rock. Unfortunately there is usually fog or mist so it's advisable to carry a compass, particularly for the return. You can in fact end up climbing Sangay without seeing the whole mountain during the entire climb, only the lava rocks immediately in front of you. They can be very jagged and harsh, so solid gloves are also essential and don't wear your best climbing clothes (is there such a thing?), as you will likely end up with tears in several places.

It's not a technical climb, but you need to be agile to avoid any falling rocks or debris, and as it's quite steep it becomes a tiring process so you need your full mental commitment to reach the summit. Despite all the problems, once at the Sangay summit it's still a special place and is to be savoured, though not for too long. If you are lucky you might be able to peer into the crater, but invariably there will be rising steam and mist, which will prevent you having any worthwhile view, but use your imagination. Be very careful of the sulphurous gases coming from the crater as they can make you nauseous or worse, and it's a tough descent anyway, without feeling ill from inhaling sulphur fumes. Coming back down is particularly tricky as you need to keep an eye open (both eyes preferably) for anything coming after you and that's when it's easy to fall, if you don't watch your step. Hopefully your guides will be waiting for you and can then shout out advice and any necessary warnings as you descend from Volcan Sangay. There are many Spanish words used to shout 'look out' but the panic sounds in their voices will be sufficient enough to alert you to imitate the mountain goat.

CHAPTER 13

THERE'S A JUNGLE OUT THERE

I feel the need to contrast my mountain exploits with the other elements to be found in this vibrant country, so it's now time to explore the jungle. I am very lucky to find a marvellous and very knowledgeable jungle guide called Pablo, who is very willing to pass on his knowledge, and I'm a keen student. My time in the jungle and the rainforest prove to be absolutely fascinating and I learn so much even when standing absolutely still, just listening and observing. The Chinese philosopher Lao Tzu stated, 'Stillness is the greatest revelation.' Initially the creatures of the rainforest resent a human intruder, but if they see you mean no harm they will gradually be more trustful and you should see some amazing things. Whatever you do, do it slowly, without any sudden movements and always be prepared to stop and let any creature passing have the right of way. There are wonderful things to experience and each tree, each plant, each bush, is different and full of knowledge. I touch a tree, stroke a branch or a few leaves and discover a world of beauty and mystery. Pablo patiently shows me how to 'feel' the rainforest and to take the time in order to benefit from its secrets. I learn to spend hours within just a few square metres of rainforest, finding all kinds of things that I could so easily have missed.

The Amazonas Region seems to be a vast and intense wilderness of unstoppable growth and vitality, but although in some ways it is, the actual soil of the tropical rainforest is not fertile. The growth is caused by the fact that there is constant movement and change as trees decay and vegetation rots, with everything being absorbed back into the earth in order to help revitalise and recreate a new life cycle. The jungle and the tropical rainforest, in most ways actually the same and interchangeable, are intense areas, where there is constant death and re-birth and the struggle for existence continues without abating. Zen philosophers and Buddhists in particular will understand only too well what this constant struggle of life and death entails. It is possible to regard the whole of the Amazonas Region as being jungle but at the same time accepting that within it and yet part of it there are also vast tracts of tropical rainforest. Jungle and tropical rainforest co-exist, together and intertwined. You can always step from one to another, never certain or indeed needing to know which one you are in. The jungle is usually considered to be more dominant at the outer reaches of the forest, often closer to the edges of rivers and lakes, or as part of the swamp areas, therefore receiving more direct sunlight and having the freedom to expand more rapidly sideways, often creating almost impenetrable growth. The tropical rainforest, by contrast, is deep inside the jungle where it is difficult for the sun to penetrate. Everything has to therefore fight and force its way upwards, straining towards the sky, in the battle for sunlight.

The tropical rainforest has more varieties of trees and plant life than any other area in the world. The trees within the interior are also thinner and taller, often growing to some 30 metres (100 feet), although there are huge trees like the kapok and the ceiba, which can reach up to heights as much as 60 metres (200 feet). The tops of the trees are called crowns and invariably form an upper canopy with their leaves, so blocking the sunlight from reaching through to the smaller trees and particularly the plants and vegetation on the rainforest floor. The lower vegetation may receive as little as one per cent of the sunlight received by the highest canopies. There can also be one or more low canopies formed underneath by the crowns of the smaller trees meshing together. This means that the soil in the rainforest receives little rainwater, most of which is intercepted by the various stages of tree canopy, and cannot easily sustain the needs of the trees. The trees therefore must often spread and stretch their roots ever wider across the topsoil (which is rich in nutrients due to the layer of fallen leaves and rotting vegetation) rather than deep down into the ground, in an attempt to find more sustenance. At the ground level around those taller trees, the ferns and vines and other plants growing there have learned to expect little sunlight and will have adapted to that lack of energy.

Trees and plants do not live as long in the interior rainforest but, by rapidly decomposing, actually then provide more nutrients for the others to feed on and so their death enables the forest life to continue. Occasionally this balance will be disturbed by an unusual act of Nature such as lightning toppling one or more trees or causing a forest fire. As trees are interconnected with vines and creepers, one tree falling can topple several others in a domino effect. The sunlight will quickly pour through and will be hungrily absorbed by the grateful smaller trees and vegetation below, allowing them to flourish exuberantly as never before. Gradually the gaps are filled, the rainforest returns to its previous state and the cycle continues. The closed forest with its interlocked overhead canopies is referred to as primary forest, and where it has occasionally opened up to allow smaller trees and plants to flourish, it is called secondary forest. Even the winds cannot penetrate to any great degree, so it's more down to birds as well as insects to spread seeds throughout the rainforest floor and extend the growth patterns. Much of the animal wildlife of the rainforest is concentrated in the overhead canopies, and if you stop, be very quiet and wait, you can hear it and occasionally at times see it.

The rainforest is a wonderful, magical place and works daily miracles in replenishing and storing the resources it needs to continue. Leaves will catch the rain, absorbing what they need, and then it trickles downwards through other plants and mosses that also need moisture to reach eventually the rainforest floor where it will be soaked into the topsoil. The roots of the trees will then absorb what they need and the trees will pump the moisture up though their trunks back to the rainforest canopies above. There the moisture will evaporate to form clouds so the process can be repeated over and over again. The rainforest is the wettest part of Ecuador, indeed one of the wettest in the world, and many times I've been travelling in the rainforest and been so unbelievably drenched through, that I had obviously forgotten that's exactly why it has that name. The climate is more humid and rainy in the months from January to September and reckoned to be dryer in the other months, but don't bet on it. It's not called the rainforest for nothing.

As Pablo and I travel through the rainforest there are all kinds of secret sounds and strange movements that I almost understand, though there is always some tiny part of the intelligence missing. That's one of its many mysteries. Sometimes a large leaf suddenly falling can almost sound like an animal crashing through, and I quickly react with fear and apprehension, immediately feeling foolish as I realise there was no need. Another time there is a different kind of sound in the undergrowth and I look down without concern only to see the end of something slithering away, and guess that it must have been a snake. The question is whether it was a poisonous one or a harmless one, how close I came to being attacked and bitten, or whether it was a missed opportunity to see another of the amazing creatures whose territory this is. As Clint Eastwood often says in his *Dirty Harry* movies, 'Do you feel lucky?' There are signs of invisible life everywhere. Most leaves have either a piece taken from them or contain a spore or other deposit, perhaps to make a claim on it or to identify it to another insect. The jungle here can instil fear very easily, and it's the fear of the unknown. The pagan god Pan lived in the forest and has a lot to answer for, as it is from his name the word panic is derived, and if you panic in the jungle you will possibly die.

There is good and bad in the jungle and I need to learn the difference if I am to survive. Pablo teaches me what to touch, what to eat and drink, and what not to. If I were completely alone then it would be a case of trial and error, although an error could be fatal. Smell is also an important tool and Pablo tells me that something which doesn't smell right is probably dangerous and should be avoided; his knowledge and advice is immense. 'An animal can also be your guide, watch what it eats or drinks and particularly what it avoids. Lick something before taking the tiniest bite of it.' I again remember the Russian proverb I use on the mountains, *'Doveryai no proveryai'* – *'Trust but verify'*.

Pablo explains that we are trekking along the bank of what is known as a black-water river which has arisen within the rainforest only, not from the high mountains, and is therefore moving more slowly and does not carry any sediment. It transports seeds and berries, and the tannin from the leaves and plants creates the appearance of blackness. We stop to examine an ants' nest built underneath the nest of wasps hanging from a tree, in order to provide further protection from predators. The termites also have some of their nests nestled into a tree for the same reason, as well

as to avoid the direct sunlight drying out the nest. They
even create furrows in the side of the tree so they can reach
their nests without suffering from the blistering strength of
the tropical sun when it penetrates the canopy. Many trees
and plants act in a symbiotic manner to each other. Trees
allow different plant varieties (called epiphytes) to grow in
and from them. There are some 30,000 kinds of epiphytes,
which include ferns, mosses, cacti and bromeliads. Some
trees are so overloaded with 'visitors' of these various
kinds, also intertwined with vines and creepers tying them
to other trees, that it's not easy to tell which is what and
where one tree begins and another ends.

  Some plants combine together to cup their leaves to catch
the rainwater, and in turn these miniature water containers
play host to insects and frogs and birds who quite happily
share with each other. With flowering plants and fruits
growing from the trunks of the trees, the rainforest animals
are able to access them more easily. The animals will in
turn help to disperse the seeds further afield in many
ways, including being swallowed and passed through their
digestive systems onto the rainforest floor. In this way there
is a wide potential dispersal area. Of course many fruits
or seeds fall to the floor and break open, or are assisted to
break open by some helpful creature. Insects set up home
inside leaves, and in return protect them from predators
that could harm the plant. Pablo shows me a Viola tree,
which has a deep red sap and looks like chicken blood.
It's very rich in nutrients and therefore attracts many
insects. Patiently he explains about many features of other
rainforest trees. The fruit of the monkey pot tree produces
its fruit in a large round pod containing thin seeds laced
with poisonous selenium. The chonta palm, which is a vital
part of indigenous tribal life, is covered with thousands of
needle-sharp thorns that can tear the skin to pieces if it's
not handled carefully and correctly. Even the sap of the

very useful rubber tree congeals on exposure to the air, to prevent any insect from benefiting after biting through its bark. The insects get to know this and don't bother, as there are other more edible items to forage for. There are many leaves that are self-protectively inedible, and after a quick bite to test are then quickly left alone.

There are two types of liana vine that take control of a tree, the strangler and the trunk-climbing liana. The strangler starts at the top and climbs downwards, all the while encircling and tightening until the tree is literally strangled to death. The trunk-climber does the same but from the floor upwards. In both cases, the tree finally topples and decomposes into the jungle floor, and the lianas claim their jungle space. It looks as if the tree knows what's happening to it but can do nothing about it. It's a slow, sad death but can only be viewed within the context of the cycle of life and death occurring within the jungle and the rainforest. The giants of the rainforest, the kapok and the ceibal, tower over their thinner neighbours, and can usually reach open sky and also claim their right to greater soil territory and to the nutrients it contains. They sometimes greedily or cleverly, depending on how you look at it, claim most of the nutrients from their patch, so the other trees die and they end up in splendid isolation. In the rainforest it's always necessary to understand how creatures and other life forms evolve together, in order to boost their own chances of survival.

The whole area of the Amazon Basin is very malarial. The indigenous people are not immune to the deadly mosquito, and make up part of the frighteningly high statistic of one to three million people that die every year from malaria in Africa, Asia and South America. A staggering half a billion people are said to be infected annually. Half a billion pounds sterling is the unbelievably generous sum donated by Bill Gates, the Internet king, through his charity The

Gates Foundation, to continue the urgent research needed to try and find some cure or antidote or preferably some preventive treatment. To emphasise this huge and very serious problem, the British and Norwegian governments have also promised to provide sums equivalent in value. A recent result of this ongoing research is that the scientists have discovered that the malaria parasite has the ability to trigger a genetic masking device, to prevent the immune system recognising it and therefore switching itself on in order to fight it off. If this masking can be prevented then it's another step forward to encouraging the body's own defence systems to respond automatically and possibly destroy the parasite. But malarial dangers continue to be enormous and the benefits of halting the spread of malaria would be equally massive.

Finally there seems to be a scientific explanation which will help in the continuing fight to find a permanent solution to this terrible scourge of the traveller, whether professional or amateur. It seems some people give off a scent that attracts the mosquito, whereas others give off a masking odour which actually throws the mosquito 'off the scent'. Scientists are trying to isolate the natural masking odours (there are several kinds) and will experiment in order to produce a formula to protect against the unloved mosquito. Possibly they could even work in the other way, producing an attracting formula would persuade the mosquito to bite into something that would prove deadly to itself, such as a pair of mountaineer's socks.

It's so hot and humid that I long to stop and swim in a river or lake but Pablo doesn't have to warn me not to. I know from previous expeditions how dangerous the waters can be. There are extremely tiny fish organisms known as the candiru catfish that lurk in them, and they are always looking for warm 'nests' in which to lay their eggs. It can be bad enough for a woman, but they can easily swim inside the urethra entrance to a man's penis and then are impossible to dislodge. They have minute inverted spines enabling them to enter, but once inside then cannot be dragged backwards. There are frightening stories that the only cure is castration but in fact there are other lengthy, more painful procedures. You wouldn't want to imagine them, however.

The rainforest is a place for me to reflect and to try and be alone within myself, even if for a few moments. Pablo seems to understand this, and leaves me alone quite often for some quiet moments of thought and reflection. It is scary at times as if he didn't return I wouldn't easily find my way out, but that is part of trusting him. The rainforest is always teeming with life and activity, yet there can be moments of absolute silence, so that nothing intrudes into your inner mind and you feel you could be the only thing existing there. There may be something watching you of course, but then again it may not see you, as, not being of its world, you do not exist. There's a wealth of knowledge to be found in the rainforest, waiting to be revealed to those who keep their minds open. The poet and artist William Blake declared, 'Some scarce see Nature at all. But to the eyes of the man of imagination, Nature is imagination itself'. I see a very beautiful emerald-coloured beetle.

There is a timeless question and koan that I always think worth re-visiting, and this is the perfect place. 'If there is no one to hear a tree fall in the forest does the tree falling really make any sound?' Does silence remain unless someone else witnesses the action? Yet the forest is always full of life and there must always be something to hear or to see the tree fall. Krishnamurti, the renowned philosopher from India, always implored us to 'Look at a tree, really look at a tree.' We rarely do, which is such a shame, as trees are full of history and life and deserve our closest attention. There is so much in every tree to observe and discover, its texture, its width, its height, the kind of leaves and nuts or fruits it has, the insects and birds that use it as a home, its proximity or not to other elements of nature, rivers, lakes, mountains. The list becomes endless and each tree is a book, perhaps an encyclopaedia, without it ever having to be cut down to become one.

Night and day are very different in the jungle and many creatures can only move around in one and not in the other. There are so many nocturnal creatures who will only 'come to life' after dark, after spending the daylight hours sleeping and gathering energy. In the jungle you will usually be warned when night is approaching by the crickets and the frogs sounding off as dusk occurs, and then will be energetically awakened by the dawn chorus of the birds and perhaps the morning screeches of the howler monkeys.

It's great to learn to love the jungle and the rainforest. They are full of the past and must be part of the future. Yet an area the size of Austria is being destroyed each year. This is a result of indiscriminate logging, burning or slashing in order to provide more farming, or prospecting for oil and metals. It sounds impossible when you see how much rainforest there still is, but, if this rate of destruction continues, there will be very little left within thirty years.

We do not have the right to neglect the rainforests. Trees touch and influence all our lives and as Krishnamurti stated we have to stop and think about what a tree really means. One large beech tree can provide enough oxygen for the daily intake of ten people. Every person in a town or city on average consumes the equivalent of twelve trees each year. One hectare of forest allowed to grow to maturity and protected will absorb the carbon emissions of 100 motor vehicles every year. These are facts and must not be ignored. George Orwell, in his book *1984* stated that, 'The planting of a tree… will far outlive the visible effect of any of your other actions, good or evil.'

The hardwoods, such as mahogany, teak and ebony, take hundreds of years to grow and mature so no amount of tree-replanting will compensate in the short term for their destruction. Only sensible and planned tree felling methods should be employed, so that the fragile topsoil held in place by the roots of trees and other vegetation is not allowed to vanish, as it cannot be replenished. These are all problems and concerns of such immensity that they cannot be ignored, and we all owe our commitment to influence governments and multi-national companies to think and act in responsible ways and never to think short term. The jungle and tropical rainforest took millions of years to develop and yet now could be wiped out in decades. They have rightly been called 'the lungs of the world' and without them all life is at risk. The signs and the effects are all around, and we ignore them at our peril. Protecting our future should always be part of any action taken by anyone at any time. Indeed it is an action to be taken at all times.

CHAPTER 14

THE MOUNTAIN
IN THE JUNGLE

'Fancy climbing another mountain, now?' Pablo is grinning from ear to ear.

I am sweating with the heat of the jungle and trying to swat a persistent mossie away from its intended target area of uncovered flesh, so he persists. 'Yes or no, are you up for it, are you feeling strong enough?' I presume his remarks are just part of his Ecuadorian banter, perhaps trying to upstage one of my usual European style jokes which are usually about as successful as my focused intention for the mosquito.

'Absolutely, I'm raring to go,' I laughingly reply. 'Just point me in the right direction and I'll have my boots on in a jiffy.' I'm not sure if he knows what a jiffy is but his grin if possible grows even wider.

'OK then, great. You're on. There are actually two mountains in the jungle. Either of them is not too far from here, and the choice can be yours.' He laughs out loud but it seems it's really no joke. Over the next few minutes Pablo explains more about these two mountains, and it does sound a really exciting challenge which I am determined to be up for.

Although the other mountains of Ecuador are either soaring out of the Cordillera Occidental, west of Quito or towering from the Cordillera Oriente, east of Quito, with a few actually within the 'Avenue of the Volcanoes', there are two potentially active volcanoes much further to the east that are actually in the jungle region. One is Reventador at 3,562 metres, more recently and aggressively active, and the other is Sumaco at 3,723 metres, usually considered less active, although both have the potential to 'explode' at any time, so we must certainly be aware of that possibility and prepare accordingly. Neither is over 4,500 metres, which I had initially put as my benchmark of mountains to attempt or consider, but they are a fair height and it's too good an opportunity to pass up. Pablo tells me we are roughly equidistant from each. A full day's trek and bus journey is needed to see us through the jungle and bring us to their lower slopes. I decide to opt for the higher one, so Sumaco it is.

Sumaco is located and protected within one of the National Parks. It's known as a wild area and is relatively unvisited, having yet to prove of much interest to loggers and prospectors, and long may it remain so. The volcano was first climbed in 1865 by the Ecuadorian Jimenez de la Espada, and the British explorer George Dyott achieved the summit in 1924. Due to its remoteness and possibly the 'call' of the higher mountains, it has not been climbed often and as I like to experience 'virgin' trails, that also makes Sumaco very appealing. In Quichua Sumaco means 'pretty beast' and the contradiction is what appeals, as the mountain can enchant or terrify. I will have to wait to find out which aspect is waiting for me.

I check my feet out – they have recovered well and the redness has mostly disappeared. I have been coating them night and day with Vaseline and Savlon and together they seem to have done the trick. I hope I have enough left to see me through to Chimborazo. Sumaco shouldn't be a problem, however, and there's definitely no ice to worry about. We quickly collect the necessary gear together, divide up our food and water, fill our backpacks to the brim and then turn in straight away, as we will need to set off very early the next morning. The alarming thing is that Pablo has provided me with a large machete and his is even larger. What size mosquitoes are we likely to encounter?!

I awake to hear Pablo moving around in the darkness, getting the final food provisions packed, and I quickly join him. We strike out along an overgrown pathway that skirts a tributary of the River Napo and trek in semi-darkness for about two hours. There are constant rustlings and sometimes Pablo whispers, 'Sssh, caiman, don't make a sound.' I try to obey but my heart starts pounding so loudly that any creature within 50 metres must surely hear it. How does he know it's a caiman, perhaps it's an anaconda. That thought is no more comforting though, and I therefore decide that any noises are the result of beaver action or perhaps the scampering of forest rabbits. Still I keep my machete at the ready and practise a few sweeping swipes at an imaginary adversary. Pablo doesn't comment on my odd actions but as trailfinder uses his machete for the appropriate purpose of cutting aside the dense interlocking vegetation and vines that so often try to impede our proceeding. As it becomes lighter the sounds increase, and there is now a lot of activity overhead. I see the shadowy shapes of troupes of monkeys as they swing through the canopies. There are increasing bird songs and they all seem to be alerting one another that there are intruders making their way through their territory.

I had expected a full day's heavy marching through the jungle, but we finally break out of it to reach a cleared road. Pablo announces with another of his mystical smiles that we can actually save ourselves several hours, hard slogging by getting a bus to the village of Humani, which is on our route. Taking a bus to cut down our trekking time is definitely ok by me but we still have to continue for another hour before the lumbering vehicle overtakes us and, responding to our frantic waving, pulls over to take us on board. There are some dozen passengers already on the bus, all with huge bundles, many of which bulge alarmingly in several directions all at once and emit very strange sounds. Pablo tells me they contain chickens or pigs or other livestock, although a few might have snakes that have been caught to take to the local witch doctor. The machetes they all seem to carry are even more perturbing. They are twice the size of mine.

When we reach Humani, Pablo asks the driver to wait, which he is quite willing to do as timetables don't really exist here and the driver is very willing to stop for coffee and much more, depending on whom he knows in the village. Pablo knows two guides here and he wants one to take us up Sumaco but disappointingly neither is here. We will need to look for one nearer to the mountain but there's always the possibility that we won't find one to hire, which could cause us problems. Pablo hasn't climbed Sumaco for over two years as it's so remote, so doesn't know it well and could easily lose the way. It seems several trekkers and climbers have been lost before and it can take several days to find a way through and back. Pablo tells me that there were two climbers who never made it back to any of the nearby villages, but that hopefully they continued on through the jungle on the other side and reached a road to get a lift from a passing vehicle.

The driver is ready to move on and after taking on board even more strange moving sacks and bundles and a few women wearing scarves or hats and voluminous skirts of many colours, the bus trundles off. The road has now become a trail and at times it seems to be covered by vegetation which has spread across the track in an effort to link the jungle on both sides. Soon we reach Guagua (baby) Sumaco and Pablo again tries to find us a guide. No luck again and he is beginning to look worried. I pull out my compass and continually set down various positions as the bus winds its way noisily upwards, in case there's a real need to try and find a route back. I even buy more water in the store just in case! It's not his intended way but with a little haggling and some earnest discussions the driver agrees to take us further up the trail to Pacto Sumaco which will save us several hours hard trekking. We are in luck once we get there as Pablo finds a guide who agrees to take us up the mountain. He speaks only some local dialect and it is difficult to understand him, but he knows the region well and that's what really counts. I think his name is Bosca or something similar, and he has few teeth and a thin wiry body but is strong and quick and we have to move fast to keep up with him. He arranges the Park entrance fees and we are allowed in. It's up to us from now on, or rather, it's up to Bosca.

Bosca's aim is to get us up to our first camp, take us to the summit the next day, and then return very fast as he has some reason why he needs to get back to his village within two days. We can't get from him exactly what it is – it seems to be something to do with a wedding although we can't work out whether it is his or his son's or his brother's. Everyone is going and we are invited as well. We are in no position to argue as he seems to be the only guide available and without him I have the feeling we may be here for days. He's ready in moments and quickly bounds ahead.

The trail Bosca takes us is along a lengthy area of cut logs and it's very hard going. There are no signs and it's so easy to get lost and without a guide I think Pablo and I couldn't make it through. It's hot and humid and soon water is pouring off me. However I take my dress code from the others and don't change into shorts as the long grasses can hide a multitude of insects, all of which could feast for hours on my whiter skin. We cross several small brooks and then reach the hill going by the name of El Mirador, its name indicating the spectacular views over the jungle, and from there we drop back down several times before re-climbing other high sections. Again we are dipping in and out of jungle, it's hard machete work mostly and we take it in turns, although Bosca and Pablo do the bulk of the cutting. The bamboo areas are particularly difficult to penetrate as they are thick and unwieldy and don't move easily as we push through. We are climbing slowly upwards as well and my back pack feels like some rainforest creature has hitched a ride, as it is getting heavier by the minute and my back is bending under the strain. There are some very high strangler fig trees and many trees have coverings of blooms. We come across a small but spectacular waterfall which I would love to enter, but Bosca gestures there's no time and insists we must keep going. 'Jaguar look, jaguar.' They seem to be his only words of English or certainly those he uses every time he thinks I'm slowing. The words are accompanied with a fierce look, presumably meant to instil fear and he points into the jungle, as if the animal is about to hurl itself out at me.

With Bosca leading, the three of us continue trekking like this for about seven hours, although time has little meaning and the only thing keeping me going is the prospect of being lost in the jungle if I stopped. There's only these two, one of whom I can't converse with, who knows where we are. The next sight though is very welcoming, particularly as I know it's our camping area for the night. In front of us is a lake or lagoon called, like the village we left so much earlier, Guagua Sumaco. It makes me realise how easy it would be to go round in circles if one were to keep asking for directions to Guagua Sumaco. We are at a height of around 2,525 metres. I am also advised not to go swimming, as there's a huge serpent that lives under the water and feeds on unsuspecting travellers. I manage a laugh but then see by Bosca's face that it's no joke, and even Pablo seems to believe it. Although tempted I decide not to take chances, as perhaps the fable came about because there's an underwater eddy or current waiting to suck someone down, so I don't wade in too far, though I have to remove my boots and bathe my aching feet. The water's muddy and swirls pleasantly around my feet, feeling very soothing. I have developed some small but painful blisters and afterwards I coat them with Vaseline and stick some plasters over.

I am starting to feel almost human again, and there are great views in all directions with flocks of birds swooping low over the lake before nesting down for the night. It's time for us to do the same. We have one tent to share but there's a broken hut that seems easier so with the quickly dropping temperature we huddle inside as best we can. I cover myself with mosquito repellent and use a net, although this refuses to cover all the places it should and I know that I am probably providing dinner, and can only hope they prefer their food home grown. In my dream of the mountain I am already on the summit. There is a rumbling as it erupts all around me, and the serpent from the lake is emitting fumes of fire, which set light to the long grass. I am struggling to breathe, and the continuing rumbling suddenly wakes me. It turns out to be Bosca's or Pablo's snoring, or possibly both. The next dream is quieter.

In the morning, although it still seems night, I am woken for a very early start. We leave everything behind except for small daypacks to carry water and food, and I just take my waterproof top. It's a tiring climb up and down several ridges before dropping down to a saddle at over 2,800 metres, stretching between one peak and the mountain proper. Eventually we leave the jungle areas and reach the *páramo*, and then it's a relatively easy climb to the summit ridge itself. It's taken about three hours from the first saddle, and now at about 3,250 metres we cut down to the right to another saddle. From there we are able to climb the summit cone to achieve the summit of 3,732 metres, from where we can see, way below, the River Napo snaking its way through the rainforest. There are two uninteresting telecommunication huts on the summit that look totally out of place, and I have no inclination to visit. I need to stop instead and think about this special jungle mountain climb, and despite my tiredness I experience real joy. The weather's extremely clear and I can see over the jungle canopy in all directions to a number of mountains in the distance, to the west and to the south. Pablo points out the other jungle mountain, Reventador. There are some wisps of light cloud above it which look like smoke, and for a moment I wonder if it's erupting. Perhaps there's someone on Reventador looking at Sumaco and thinking the same. I imagine I can see Chimborazo, the tallest, in the far distance. The more I stare across the more I seem to see it, until it seems to start beckoning me, although this could just be the sunlight reflecting on the snow peaks of the several majestic mountains. I have to believe that soon I'll be there and perhaps I might make the summit. After the last few days I feel anything is possible. Bosca is very impatient to return, the wedding or the bride won't wait and soon, too soon, we are plunging back into the jungle, struggling hard to keep up with his incredible pace, so as not to be left behind.

CHAPTER 15

FLORA AT THE EQUATOR

I see and smell such wonderful flowers and plants in Ecuador that sometimes my senses are overwhelmed. Many are 'exotics', generated through the intense tropical heat of this equatorial country. There are exquisite blossoms and vibrant greens of every shade, and an artist could spend a lifetime here and only paint a small fraction of what is on offer.

Ecuador, although relatively tiny in size (it covers just two per cent of the Earth's surface), is home to ten per cent of the world's plant species, mostly growing in the north-east of the Amazon region, where over 10,000 species exist. The entire total of different flowering plants in the country is estimated at more than 20,000. 'The sensation of delight which the mind experiences' are Charles Darwin's own words and they help to express and convey the extravagant and staggering beauty which he and so many others have experienced in coming to this 'Garden of Eden'.

Evolving over millions of years the vegetation in these regions has adapted to the power of the climate, whether receiving the intense rays of the sun from being at the Equator or experiencing the night and early morning harsh frosts and icy conditions of the high mountainous regions. Plants and flowers in Ecuador, as in most South American countries, were given their Latin names by the conquering Spanish, as part of the mandatory introduction and instillation of the Catholic faith in the sixteenth century. As a rule these Latin names have been retained, along with the addition of a few nicknames, rather than the flora acquiring more ordinary and colloquial names as in most European countries. Of course the indigenous Ecuadorians have had to contend with the more immediate and harsh reality of coping with the difficulties of survival within a volatile environment. They and the incoming settlers learning to live in 'the New World' did not have the time to become a nation of gardeners, so mostly the Latin botanist names have remained.

There is one clear exception to this rule however and that is *flos pasionis*, the *pasionaria*, the *pasiflora* or passionflower, considered the most glorious flower in the country and indeed in many other South American countries. The name was given to it by the Jesuit priests in the sixteenth century, who believed that this was the flower of God and that it contained special messages to be understood only by the faithful. Every part of the flower was taken to symbolise something relating to the crucifixion, the five outer sepals and the five petals being taken to be the number of the apostles present, even the leaves representing the Roman soldiers and their spears. It was actually officially noted by scholars and priests that the religious meaning had been 'hidden from the heathen people of those countries until the time pre-ordained by His Highest Majesty'.

Whatever your belief or religion is, there is no denying the passionflower is a real beauty and produces a range of intoxicating fragrances. The flower is mainly star-shaped and the colour combinations are immense; all shades of blues, reds, pinks, mauves and purples, including the pure white, and even a rare yellow variety. The leaves are usually dark green and leathery but can be lighter and roughly textured. The main vine stalk is thick and strong, enabling it to carry a wealth of flower and leaf, the ten flower petals feel waxy to the touch and there are alluring 'eyelashes' sprouting all around the central corona. There are many kinds to be found throughout the country and the names include Purple Rain, Amethyst and Incense. Initially examples were carefully transported to Spain but couldn't flourish in the cooler climate, and it wasn't until the invention of the glasshouse and the conservatory that a passion for this flower could be more easily developed and its cultivation then quickly spread throughout Europe. It has a special use to aid the explorer and mountaineer as it can be used as a timepiece because it opens fully at midday. It's not a lot of use at other times but the smell is always special.

As usual the main colour of the ordinary plants here is green, although there are a number of different shades of other colours with red in particular to add some variety in the landscape. The reddish lipocodio, a slim elegant tight stick of a plant, often grows in groups within the otherwise green sea of plants. In the higher regions due to the harshness of the weather and the extremely low temperatures experienced overnight, the leaves of plants as a rule generally have curved, waxy skins to absorb or reflect the sun's radiation. They are also smaller and thicker to protect against the bitter cold conditions, and are covered with a fine down that acts as further insulation. Many of the plants growing on the plains of the *páramos* particularly are rather small and grow in tight and concentrated formations spreading over huge areas. There are the green almohadillas, which are multi-leaved and grow in colonies in vast bunched-up profusion.

Moreover, there are the unusually-shaped, giant frailejones (part of the espeletia family) and, with their bulky leafy shapes waving in the grey mists, they have been mistaken for groups of monks praying, which is why their common name translates as grey friars. They can reach almost human height and are usually found near water where the area around can be very swampy and treacherous. The flowers tend to be rather small and grow low at ground level to protect as much as they can against the strong winds and the intense cold they bring. They will nestle amongst the grasses for further protection. The cenecio plant, which has curly, velvety green leaves and bulbous tops, together with some of the hardier grasses can grow in heights up to 5,000 metres.

At the highest levels lichens will cling to rocks that the snows of the glacier, for whatever reason, have ignored and they have gradually fought their way upwards as the ice has retreated. Further south there are also the puyas which grow even taller than the frailejones and have short spiky leaves, growing up from a narrowed trunk, usually within the grasses covering the *páramos*. The tall chuquiraguas, used as lookout perches by a variety of birds, can be found at the approaches to many mountains as if being the outlying sentinels to warn of strangers approaching. Bromeliads abound everywhere of course and in some dryer areas are used to extract drinking water. There is a long, spiky grass plant called zigzes which grows amongst the pajonal and is the most common of all. A legacy of the last glacier age means that within the *páramos* there are many small lakes and ponds with all types of water plants happily cohabitating. These water plants help to attract birds and insects with which to interact and surrounding the streams and ponds often are pantsas forests. Though it is primarily the jungle and the rainforest that are filled with the really useful medicinal plants, the properties of which have still not yet been fully explored or utilised, the Andes region itself has alone more than 8,200 plant and vegetable species.

Orchids are in abundance everywhere and over 2,700 species – 11 per cent of all the world's species and 30 per cent of the species classified in Latin America – are found here, with new ones are regularly being found. The Galapagos itself has 600 indigenous species and 250 more have been introduced. Fifteen new species were even recently found in the uninhabited Llanganates National Park and there must be many more for the adventurous to discover.

There are continuing and determined attempts to transplant and grow orchid species in many parts of the world. The internationally famous Kew Gardens in Surrey, England, have grown many kinds in their 'hot houses', although their experienced gardeners and horticulturists know they cannot hope to compete with the natural conditions of the tropical and equatorial treasure trove that is Ecuador. Orchids in the wild are generally rare in the British Isles but a new kind has recently been discovered on Holy Island. DNA testing has proved that the tiny green orchid, once thought to be part of the same family as the dune helleborine group of orchids already known on the island, is genetically different. It is being classified as a species in its own right. If that can be the outcome in a country like Britain, then there is a very strong likelihood that the orchids in Ecuador, if examined and DNA tested in the same way, may be found and to prove the existence of many more species.

The wisdom and knowledge contained within the plant world is largely untapped and there are so many species that need careful examination and research with immense potential benefits. One example refers to the curare poison used by the indigenous tribes to coat their arrow or dart tips which can render any creature targeted unconscious for several minutes, so it can be collected and bagged for future cooking and eating. The indigenous tribes know exactly how much curare to put on in order to kill or just to render unconscious. This poison after being clinically analysed led directly to the creation of d-tubocurarine, a very potent muscle relaxant. Administered during surgery it has helped considerably in reducing the level of anaesthesia required. This is extremely important, as many patients cannot either tolerate the use of anaesthesia generally or they have a low threshold of tolerance.

The indigenous tribespeople have many uses for the bamboo and it grows in profusion throughout the jungle. They use it for hunting, fishing and building, even in creating a stretcher if one of them is hurt and needs to be carried through the jungle. It's a very versatile bush and it has an extremely quick growth rate of over 12 inches a day. The shamans of the rainforest have also learned to use the secrets of the yage plant and combining it with other plants they have been able to produce hallucinogenic and psychoactive substances and drinks. They then allow at certain and special times some tribespeople to drink them in order to experience mind imagery which can be beneficial in dealing with mental problems and anxieties (of course they can also produce these effects). These substances can have positive, negative or even nil effects, depending on which other compounds they are mixed with. The shamans and many indigenous tribes are able to recognise easily which plants have these appropriate properties, even if there are thousands of plants and leaves to choose from. They also know in what proportions to mix them with other plants in order to achieve the many different effects possible. This knowledge, complex in so many ways, has been passed down from generation to generation. Another interesting plant is called yoco, which contains caffeine stimulants and can allow someone to stay awake for very lengthy periods. Yoco is often used by hunters who will trail an animal for days in order to catch it. They believe it allows them to be as one with the forest.

Health in the rainforest comes through balancing the spiritual with natural forces, achieving harmony and equilibrium. There is so much to be gained in this way. The destruction of great swathes of the forests can indeed be only a very short term benefit to a few, leading to so much greater and continuing loss in the future to the many. Unfortunately those at such terrible risk cannot make their voices heard and we must speak and shout out for them, acting now whilst there is still time.

CHAPTER 16

CREATURES GREAT AND SMALL

I am fascinated by the animals, birds and insects to be found in Ecuador, and Pablo agrees to travel on with me to see what we can discover together. We plan to stay in different eco lodges for a few days so we trek out very early each morning as well as late at night, to observe some of this country's creatures in their natural environment. We agree to spend more time in the jungle as well as in the mountain regions, and Pablo has a wealth of knowledge, which he is very happy to share with me. I learn so much from him and use my research in the Libri Mundi bookshop in Quito to add more information.

The most fearsome of all the flying birds by far is the eagle, which can spot prey over three kilometres away. The eagle is an out and out killer, the top of all the raptors and a superb flying machine. Its beak and its talons can only be described as razor sharp and if it decides on an attack the odds are very much in its favour. It can even see through water and the fish, which is a creature with poor eyesight, is unlikely to spot the eagle hovering above. The fish would have no chance of surviving the attack, as an eagle's grip is stronger than a dog's bite and it won't let go until it has carried out its deadly intention. Its legs are as thick as a man's wrists and its claws about the size of a man's hands. Knowing the strength and power of the eagle, it is not surprising that the tribesman will strive to capture one by luring it with a small prey and then trapping it in a net. He will keep it in his home and would only consider eating it if the family circumstances are very dire indeed. There are three kinds here, the crested eagle and the hawk-eagle, with the harpy eagle, black and grey in colouring, being the world's largest at over one metre in height.

The Andean condor is also a colossus of the bird kingdom although as its Latin name implies (*Vulture gryphus*) it is carrion eating and does not seek out its own prey. It has a wingspan of approximately three metres, larger than the eagle's and indeed larger than that of any other flying bird in the world. Moreover, its weight of about 12 kilograms makes it one of the world's heaviest birds. The female is very slightly smaller than the male and the only other difference is that the male has a skin plume on its head. As long as the male can spot the difference, that's all that matters I suppose. From afar it is a magnificent flying creature but close up it's very ugly, with a wrinkled, bare, pink head, a white neck ruff, set atop a black body. Presumably it is not ugly to another condor though. The condor roosts and nests high on the mountain and rock faces in extremely inaccessible places. It uses the rising air currents called thermals to fly, the feathers opening or closing to control direction and the very broad tail is used as a rudder to guide it in flight. It has exceptional eyesight and can spot a carcass from a long way off, and when it dives down to it several other condors will usually follow, as they all generally like to keep a condor eye on each other to see where any kill has been spotted. As the condor lives for up to 50 years it has a slow breeding rate and will usually mate for life. A pair will breed only a single white egg at a time, laid either on the bare rock face or in a crevice, and will share incubating and feeding duties. Sadly it has been hunted extensively so there are only now about 150 condors in the wild. Its close cousin is, of course, the vulture, and there are many everywhere in Ecuador, on the *páramo* and in the forests.

One of the most admirable and abundant birds also on the *páramo*s and in the jungle, although also known to fly high in mountainous areas, is the tiny hummingbird. Its name originates from the sound made by some of the species. It's actually the smallest bird in the world but no one seems to have told it that as it's bold, self-assured and totally unafraid as it goes about its very important daily business. Hummingbirds have even been known to attack hawks and owls. It can actually survive intense cold by lowering its metabolism by up to 95 per cent, as if in a state of hibernation, although just for one night at a time. This process is known as torpor. Its wings can flap at the extraordinary speed, invisible to the human eye, of more than 100 times a second and the heart beats at up to 1,000 times a minute as it hovers seemingly motionless. It mostly feeds on nectar although it will also consume very small insects. It can also fly backwards and that's quite bewildering to observe. Its bursts of energy are so draining, as it can reach speeds of more than 100 kilometres per hour, that it must eat every half hour in order to store body fat for its lengthy travels. It can eat half its own body weight and drink eight times its weight in water every day. The females are quite flirtatious and will use their feminine wiles to get first to the special flower they are after. Mating can be quite an elaborate procedure with often very acrobatic displays in order to impress. The hummingbird is multi-coloured, although mostly iridescent and a delight at all times to watch in action. There are many varieties and some of the names indicate its versatility and dominant colourings: sword-billed, velvet-breasted, fire-crown, ruby topaz, booted racquet-tail, sparkling-tailed. The sword-billed is one of the larger as its bill is longer than the whole body and likewise the streamer-tailed has a tail much longer than its body. The longer bills in particular often end up with nectar all round the tips, so some of the nectar is carried to and so pollinates the next flower.

There are plenty of noisy snipes and lapwings around and you should try not to tent near their habitats otherwise they may wake you up earlier than intended, particularly as they can fly during the night-time. The owl is another night-time caller and its persistent sound, charming at first, can become a source of considerable irritation as it continues to look for a mate.

The parrots in Ecuador are many, varied and loud, and often screech out so unexpectedly that it makes me wonder why they are endeavouring to use their mainly green camouflage to remain hidden. They are in fact very sociable and like company but have parrot eyes for only one and will mate for life. I suppose when you've got used to the screeching of one, you don't want to listen to another. Their jaws are exceptionally strong and they can easily crack a hard nut whilst turning their heads to one side, as if quizzically observing to see if you are watching their special skills. They can also use their upper jaw as another claw to climb trees. The macaws, although part of the family, are more multi-coloured and range from yellow and blue to bright reds or scarlet. All parrots are at risk from poachers and the loss of much of their habitat.

Although not of the parrot family, its colourful plumage and its beaked nose make the toucan seem very much part of the tropical rainforest bird 'exotics'. They are great fun to observe and they love to be watched, being tremendous show-offs in the nicest sense of the word. They have developed their enormous beaks or bills in order to reach inaccessible fruits and berries and can only eat by cleverly flipping bits upwards to catch and swallow. There are many wonderful varieties in the jungle and these include the blue-eyed, the white-throated toucan boasting a black bill with a central yellow stripe, and the mountain toucan that naturally lives high up so it can look down on its forest cousin.

In Ecuador there are also more than a million species of insects; it's impossible to know how many species are as yet undiscovered. It's in fact estimated that there are more unidentified insect species than the total of the world's identified animal species. Surprisingly it's not the ant but the beetle that has more of its kind in the world than any other creature. There are more than 4,500 wonderful butterfly species, some of them absolutely gorgeous and riveting in colour and design, of which 2,500 species are nocturnal. The large, electric-blue morphos butterfly is outstanding and to see a huge grouping is a truly wonderful sight. There are so many colours and sizes and those with markings like an eye on each wing can be startling when you come across them affixed to a tree or a leaf 'staring' straight back at you. Further research carried out into the habits of butterflies has also revealed they are more sophisticated than previously thought, and know exactly where they are going in life. Tiny transponders have been fixed to their backs which show they will carry out reconnaissance missions to search for food and can spot sources up to 200 metres away. The attaching of the radar 'backpacks' was one of the most intricate technological feats ever attempted on any form of wildlife. The butterflies had to be very gently held whilst the transponder weighing one 12-thousandth of a gram was fitted to their backs.

The ant, possibly the most dedicated and hard working of all creatures, can carry twigs and leaves up to several times its own weight and size to help build the ant nest. They usually work 18 days non-stop and then procreate for 18 days before continuing the cycle. One can only conjecture what an ant, coming to the end of its ultra-long work period, might call out to a colleague who is now returning and just starting its own 18 day stint. There is a particular ant to be avoided at all cost, called sometimes the soldier ant, or the suture or the surgeon ant or even the rain ant. It is large, can be the size of half a thumb, has very strong pincers and it will not let go once they have gripped onto something. The indigenous tribespeople sometimes use it to suture or bind their wounds when they are out in the jungle and have no other remedy. They hold the ant over the cut or wound and carefully lower the ant over it until it feels contact when it will instantaneously grip the skin around the wound and so holds it tightly together. There are some very potent berry and plant juices in the rainforest which an ant will drink from, and it's said that an ant when drunk only falls over to its right side. It's not easy to test this theory out. There are reckoned to be more species of ants in one Ecuadorian rainforest tree stump than in the whole of Britain. The acacia ant has an extraordinary symbiotic relationship with the acacia tree where it makes its home. In return for staying there it will attack any other creature whether it's another ant, a beetle, a caterpillar or even something larger that tries to make its way onto the tree.

There are so many mysteries within the rainforest and its creatures and they are in danger of being lost unless sufficient time and care are given to unlocking the invaluable information stored there. It has been discovered that a protein in the saliva of certain flies speeds up the clotting process so enabling a wound to heal faster. Also the saliva of the vampire bat has been analysed and is now likely to be used for treating stroke victims. Certain grubs can be used to clear up skin problems; some grubs are very nutritious, and are used by the Indian women to create healthier breast milk. The eating of insects by humans is called entomophagy and has always been practised. Insects are low in carbohydrates, high in protein and have very worthwhile nutritional value. They just look so wriggly! There are obviously so many more possibilities just waiting to be discovered or understood. The jungle is undoubtedly a green storehouse for those who know or want to know.

The three great jungle and rainforest creatures revered by the indigenous tribespeople will always be the jaguar, the anaconda and the caiman (also spelt cayman). The foremost of all is the jaguar and it is the most respected as being the largest and most powerful cat animal in the tropical regions of the whole American continent. Its place at the summit of the animal kingdom is firmly established, and other creatures of all kinds will always give way to it and try to avoid it. Gorgeous in colour, style and grace, its absolute ferocity makes it an implacable enemy. It can measure up to two metres in length, without including the tail which can add another 75 cm, but its legs are short and thick, giving it its incredible power although its head and body are very large. The jaguar has a magnificent tawny yellow coat with dark spots, some of which are jet black. It's not a runner unless it absolutely has to but relies on its speed of attack and power to overcome its victims. It inhabits cool, shady areas, usually close to rivers and lakes and is an excellent swimmer. Like any cat it can climb trees and any other places, and will use that height to launch itself on any unsuspecting prey. It only eats meat although it likes fish as well, and will usually go for deer or capybara but will also attack caiman and monkey, if the opportunity presents itself. It is not meant to attack humans unless forced to defend itself so if you meet one in the jungle, don't back down, make a lot of noise and shake your fists and it should saunter off. If it doesn't you won't be able to argue about the advice you were given. The female jaguar can have up to four cubs after a gestation period of around

100 days and will nurture them for two years. Jaguars can live up to 22 years but are now an endangered species through having been hunted so vigorously and with their habitat constantly under threat. It has protection within some national parks but in the wild will mostly be found in the Esmeraldas region.

The anaconda is considered the most mysterious and deadly of all snakes, and its ability to fall suddenly upon its victims (including humans) without warning makes it the most feared. It is a close cousin of the boa constrictor and is the largest snake in the world, growing to nine metres and weighing over 200 kilograms. The anaconda will often hide in the swamps to catch its prey but is also known to drop suddenly down from an overhead branch where it's been lying in wait. Its colouring is green with black patches so it blends into the forest background well and is not easily seen until it's too late. It is nocturnal and in the dry season it mainly sleeps but if you wake it unwittingly it will come very quickly alive and mount its attack. The anaconda's bite is not poisonous but it is so powerful that it can easily crush animals and people to death. Its method of foreplay is to knock its victim somewhat senseless with a hammer blow and then wrap its coils tightly around and wait. As the victim struggles and exhales it tightens its grip each time so eventually there is no room to breathe. The worst bit is still to come and it's better not to be conscious when it occurs. The anaconda is able to unhinge its jaw and thus swallow any size of creature head first, including a caiman. It will then lie on the ground waiting till its digestive juices are able to get to work. This can take several hours and the good news is that it won't want to eat again for many days.

The Latin name for anaconda is *Eunectes murinus* and the English is boa constrictor. Both sound just as frightening as the attack action of the anaconda itself undoubtedly is. How to avoid them is the question. Well, they do have a strong, unpleasant, fishy smell, although in the rainforest there are so many smells it's not easy to distinguish one from another. The best way is to react quickly and to travel with other companions, not on the basis that they may be attacked instead of you, but that there is safety in numbers and, assuming the others don't run like hell, it is possible one of you will be able to hack at the coils so the anaconda will release whoever it's hugging to death. Otherwise you can only try singing, while you can, the international hit song of the singer Englebert Humperdinck, 'Please Release Me, Let Me Go'. Anacondas however don't have a great sense of musicality or indeed of humour. What they do have, however, is a great sense of reproduction and anacondas are sexy beasts. They are very willing to indulge in week-long orgies, that is one female with up to ten males inseminating her like mad, until complete exhaustion sets in. The females are viviparous and therefore produce up to 100 baby instantaneous wriggling snakes born alive at one time. That can also be quite an alarming sight.

The caiman is considered part of the lizard family. It is similar to an alligator and is sometimes treated as one, and is small in comparison to crocodiles. It has a short tail, a smooth head with a high skull and a large, pronounced overbite, and has short, backward curved teeth. It will walk with its head raised somewhat inquisitively as if looking for someone. Perhaps it is but hopefully someone else. Primarily it goes looking for snakes, birds and capybaras but has been known not to be too choosy. The caiman lives in a burrow and travels from there to the rivers, streams and lakes in which it will swim or more usually float just under the surface. It patrols its territory along the waterways and usually forages at night. The female builds the nest out of the available vegetation and its incubation period is between 90 and 115 days. The female will shepherd the young after the first day of birth into the water where they can very easily fall prey to many predators, and therefore often die young, although the ones that make it to adulthood can live very long. Caiman, however, like many other rainforest creatures, are an endangered species. Their habitats are being constantly reduced and they are hunted for their skins and meat by many who don't think of the consequences of their actions.

Of course there are all kinds of other animals inhabiting the higher forest regions on the mountain slopes, and many of them are quite strange and wonderful. One of the strangest is the fascinating mountain or woolly tapir (*danta*). The tapir is the largest mammal in South America and one of the oldest, older even than the dolphin. However the mountain tapir is the smallest of the tapirs. The tapir is now on the endangered list as its numbers have declined rapidly due to much of its natural habitat being destroyed by clearing and burning by farmers, loggers and prospectors. It is also hunted more than ever as its hooves and snout are believed by the Highland peoples at least to contain medicinal properties, especially in treating epilepsy and heart problems (non emotional that is, although the witchdoctors might still use some bits for love potions). The tapir generally is nocturnal but the mountain variety is more versatile and can be active during both the day and the night. It prefers moist areas, as it likes to bathe whenever it can, and in the rainforest there are usually plenty of opportunities. Sightings are rare, as it likes to keep in deep cover. With its thick, heavy body, large ears, altogether strange look and an extremely long snout always sniffing amongst the shoots and ferns, it easily gives rise to all kinds of tapir tales, imaginary or otherwise.

It is rumoured that to find out where you are at any time in the rainforest all you need to do is go to the nearest palm (chonta) tree, just tap here and a tapir will appear and with its snout will point the way out. That may sound like an old folklore story but in these regions anything can happen. You can more easily spot its tracks and the way it's heading, as it has four toes on the front feet and three on the rear feet.

Another animal that lies to keep a low profile is the sloth. To see one, you will need patience, good eyesight and plenty of sandwiches. Walk far into the forest very quietly, as it usually found asleep, and search amongst the thickest trees until you see a tattered bundle of matted fur precariously fixed to the top of a long, high branch. That could be your sloth and if you are prepared to wait it out, you might see it unbundle itself and move very slowly to another comfortable branch. If not in luck at first, eat a sandwich and start all over again. You must remember it's the slowest animal in the world and only travels around four metres or less each hour and that's only when it's decided to move, which isn't often. It invariably sleeps around 18 hours each day and always upside down. When looking for your sloth it's also worth remembering it often has blue-green algae growing and mixed into its hair, which forms its natural disguise.

There are actually two types of sloth, although it's not easy at first to tell them apart, unless presumably you are another sloth. There is the two-toed sloth and there is the three-toed sloth. You may indeed wonder if a two-toed ever falls in love with a three-toed and would their offspring then end up with 2 ½ toes?

Luckily there aren't similar physical conditions existing with the amphibious toad, as calling it a two-toed toad would be pretty confusing. It's also worth noting there are more frogs and toads in one hectare of the lowland forest here than in all of North America. When trekking over the *páramos*, particularly after a heavy rainfall, remember to be careful wherever you step, as that can bring out an abundance of the black and orange variety of toads, slowly hip-hopping their way through the grasses.

The sloth only gives birth to a baby sloth once a year and only one at a time; it just don't believe in rushing anything. Sloths are herbivores and particularly love to eat shoots from the cecropia tree, although in line with their normal pattern of behaviour about everything, it takes them about one month to digest their intake. The sloth is surprisingly a very clean and tidy creature and climbs down from its tree (very slowly) to dig a hole in the ground in order to excrete, which is probably why it only excretes once a week. As it does that the moths that live on the sloth in the algae fly off to lay their eggs in this ideal breeding place, before rejoining the sloth for another one-week sleep session. The sloth has many predators including the jaguar and the eagle but as always man is the worst. Apart from the poachers and hunters, much of a sloth's natural habitat is being destroyed, as trees are logged and the forests slashed and burnt, and oil prospecting continues regardless of the cost to this incredible wilderness. The sloth has therefore become, like so many other extraordinary rainforest creatures, endangered and under constant threat. The sloth has its long curved claws for protection and its skin contains toxic chemicals to help ward off attack, but primarily its best defence is its ability to blend into the rainforest and the trees and not be seen.

All the monkey varieties live in the trees and will only leave their sanctuary to cross an open space or if they spot some readily available food. You certainly don't need to ask why the howler monkey is so named, after spending time listening to them going on hour after hour. It can be heard up to five kilometres away, that's some howl! There are also the tiny marmosets and tamarins that have the faces of miniature lions on tiny monkey bodies and are less afraid of contact, as they have learned over time they are not generally hunted as being hardly one mouthful. They are no howlers of course and can only chirp or whistle, making almost inaudible tiny sounds.

On the *páramos* as well as elsewhere there are also three species of deer, puma, and the smallest bear in the world, the endangered spectacled bear, so named because of the lightly-coloured eye patches it has over its black facial hair. Its body is also mostly black, although sometimes brown and is dappled white. It's the only bear in Ecuador and weighs around 80 kilograms. Its paws have very powerful claws, used for climbing trees where they build platforms of branches to rest up and think where to bear next.

The llama (pronounced yama) is a typical South American animal and is recognised the world over for its woolly and shaggy appeal. In fact they have started to be exported all over the world and even in Britain there are also llama farms.

The rainforest creatures are still so mysterious in many ways and research into their habits and behaviour patterns should be undertaken before their numbers decline any further, provided of course that the research does not cause harm of hasten this decline. Many indigenous Indian tribes believe in the powers of the jungle and rainforest animals and there are many examples of the 'sixth sense' which creatures in many parts of the world are thought to possess. It is often conjectured that animals can predict imminent danger and can then react to save their lives, with their actions helping to forewarn humans. Following the great loss of life caused by the 2004 tsunami in Asia there were several reports of animals acting strangely there before it occurred, or even fleeing to higher ground. There were also several reports of flocks of birds flying inland on the morning of the disaster. Whether the animals anticipated the tsunami, heard the killer waves before they could be seen, were reacting to underground vibrations or changes in the magnetic forces cannot be known, but it's certainly a field well worth investigating further. At the time of the large earthquake in Turkey in August 1999, near the Sea of Marmara, there were advance reports of dogs howling for many hours before the earthquake struck. Also in the Alps there have been continuing reports of animals running away from valleys before an avalanche strikes. Over 2,000 years ago (373 BC) there was a report of rats and other creatures deserting the Greek city of Helice, just hours before an earthquake struck the city.

In the lagoons attaching to the Napo and Aguarico Rivers there are very powerful manatees that no other creature would dare attack. The Amazonas area in this region supports over 600 species of fish and more than 250 species of reptiles and amphibians. There are considerable numbers of different species of fish in the rivers and lakes, and the indigenous Indians are expert fisherman, whether spearing, netting or the slower, less aggressive way of casting rod to water and just waiting. Indigenous Indians can be extremely patient. The species to avoid are the stingrays and the electric eels, both of which can give you a shocking time.

The piranha fish do not totally deserve their very harsh reputations, inspired in no small part by the James Bond film, *Dr. No*, which involves Sean Connery being threatened with being cast into a tank full of hungry piranhas. Piranhas in fact only attack and bite when they are very hungry or cornered, otherwise it is even safe to swim amongst them. Just take some sensible precautions (like feeding them first).

Also in these waters there are cuttlefish. The male is very jealous and protective of its female and does not allow any other male cuttlefish to approach her. In order to circumvent this, another male cuttlefish will adjust its skin colour to a female tone and pretend to be about to lay eggs. This enables it to sidle up to the female and actually fertilise her without arousing any suspicion and the female, for whatever the reason is, doesn't give the game away. Another interesting fish is the leaf fish, which has the cunning ploy of pretending to be a dead leaf as it floats in the river, no doubt hoping there isn't a leaf-eating bird about.

Although the bird species seem at first glance to be inexhaustible, there are some extremely alarming statistics to contemplate. It is predicted that out of the 9,787 known bird species (with 129 already now extinct), approximately 10 per cent will vanish by 2100 and a further 15 per cent will be on the brink of extinction. If we allow the environment to deteriorate only slightly faster, those frightening statistics could leap to 14 per cent vanishing and 25 per cent pushed to the brink of extinction. The bird that has recently become extinct in the Amazonas vicinity is the yellow-eared parrot. That's one too many.

In November 2004 3,000 more animals and plants were added to the Red List of endangered organisms by the World Conservation Union, which now has 15,589 organisms at risk of extinction. Its findings make terrifying reading; one in eight bird species are under threat, one in four mammals, one in three amphibians and close to half the species of tortoises and turtles. The current escalation in loss of bird species, for which we must take responsibility in our industrialised societies, is all the more apparent when it is understood that since 1500 up to this last 30 years, there were only 1.3 per cent bird species lost. There are many knock-on effects from the loss of huge numbers of birds, which are not always apparent. Such effects include vast increases in rodents and feral dogs that are then responsible for spreading diseases like Lyme disease, and causing rising incidences of rabies. Exciting and important news is the recent announcement that the genetic codes of the world's ten million species are now to be stored in a DNA barcode library, the work planned to be completed by 2010. This will also enable new species to be catalogued very easily and clarified into which organism they actually belong. This will be of great assistance in trying to stem the loss of any species.

We inherit the earth and all that lives on it, for our children and our grandchildren, and we are all guilty of colossal neglect if we allow any creatures to vanish. It's so essential for all of us to assume more responsibility for our actions, before it is too late.

CHAPTER 17

GALAPAGOS STORIES

Now it's my time to leave the Ecuadorian mainland and journey across the Pacific Ocean to reach the fabled Galapagos. I feel very excited to travel to the islands Charles Darwin reached and from where he developed his theory of natural selection. To paraphrase and adopt some words of the song by the singer and film star, Harry Belafonte, 'these are the islands in the sun, where life has begun.' The Galapagos Islands, straddling the Equator line, are definitely in the sun, and the many endemic creatures to be found here in many ways represent the beginnings of life and as such pay homage both to creation and evolution. The islands were formed approximately five million years ago as the peaks of volcanoes during a series of eruptions, this being one of the most active volcanic regions in the world. They were first 'discovered' accidentally in 1535 by the Bishop of Panama when his ship was blown off course.

Each island has some amazing species and unique features, and my island hopping is a thrill. Going ashore often involves me in a wet landing, but 'getting your feet wet' in the name of exploration and discovery is a small and acceptable price to pay in order to 'get close up and personal' with the incredible array of Nature's fauna and flora found on these wonderful islands. The pirate and navigator, William Ambrose Cowley, in 1684 prepared the first charts, choosing English names for each island with

191

most islands now being known by two or more names, both in Spanish and in English.

Baltra (South Seymour). My flight in is from Mariscal Sucre Airport in Quito, with a stopover in Guayyaquil to arrive at Baltra, my first port of call. It is a very tiny island and is still the major entry point into the Archipelago for most travellers. Originally it had the only airport, built by blasting into the rock, as part of the base created by the United States during World War Two, after the assault on Pearl Harbour. It was agreed that the Americans would be allowed to station here in order to protect the Panama Canal from any surprise attack and was handed back after the war ended with Baltra gaining a very useable airport under the control of the Ecuadorian Air Force. There is now also an airport on Isabela, and San Cristobal has an airstrip. There are ferry services to the port of Puerto Ayora and access crossing the Itabaca Channel leading over to Santa Cruz. Although an island in its own right, the even smaller island of Mosquera lies in the channel between Baltra and North Seymour and is primarily sand coral packed with sea lions. After a quick visit to listen to their energetic barking I transfer to a small sail yacht, the *Samba* and prepare to dance my way through as many islands as I can, starting with Santa Cruz.

Santa Cruz (Indefatigable). Its capital is Puerto Ayora, the largest town and the port for most vessels arriving on a trading basis as well as hosting the large work force dealing with visiting scientists, international travellers as well as the needs of those living on other islands. Santa Cruz is considered the Archipelago's centre, has a large dormant volcano reaching to 864 metres and is the second largest island. Volcanic activity last took place about a million and a half years ago and as witnesses to that there are two huge holes formed after the collapse of a magma chamber, known as Media Luna and Los Gemelos. Santa Cruz has a somewhat chequered past, as the original Norwegian inhabitants founding Puerto Ayora were encouraged to settle there in the 1920s by false promises of easy wealth and prospects of starting gold and diamond mines. They all lost their investments and savings and eventually their hope.

My first visit selected naturally has to be to the Charles Darwin Research Station. It was founded here in 1959 and is where the continuing research into the habits and breeding of the giant tortoises is carried out. Scientists travel from all over the world to visit and work at the Station, as well as to participate in the research programmes. I am first of all shown the pens that are used for rearing the giant tortoises and can only admire a number of the 'baby' or miniature giants still waiting to grow up. That can take very many years, and all those tortoises there now will probably outlive me and all those presently caring for them. This dedicated nurturing should always be thought of in the same way as our planting new trees; it's for the future, theirs and ours, and particularly for those generations not yet even thought of. It must be our way of creating part of the natural and geographical history of the future.

The conservation head of the Darwin Station is Graham Watkins, and he has the enormous responsibility of trying to protect the species of the islands. It's a delicate balance between funding research, promoting tourism and working with the islanders. I am introduced to Lonesome George, the last surviving giant tortoise of Pinta Island, brought over in 1971 to Santa Cruz. He wanders around near the Station, probably pining for the old days and remembering his former loves. George must have a lot to remember. They keep trying to pair him up with new dates but George is very choosy and maybe he just won't mate again or has forgotten how to.

Mating between tortoises is, as you might imagine, a complicated business and doesn't seem to be enjoyed by either party, but they are driven by a primeval urge that usually has to be satisfied. These creatures are not communicative normally but at mating time the male will signal something, we can only conjecture what, by grunting on a fairly continuous basis, as if he is in constant pain. The real pain is about to follow. The coupling can take an hour or longer and I was allowed to watch one such encounter (in the name of scientific research of course). I can only describe it as astounding, but it made me feel sorry for both the male and the female equally. In brief, the male tortoise has to mount the female from behind and in trying to achieve his purpose he strains every sinew, so that it looks as if he's about to collapse with a heart attack at any moment. After the event takes place, the female carries the male sperm for several months before fertilisation occurs.

This is also tough boot country, as I have to walk for long distances to experience much of the fauna in its natural surroundings. Whilst trekking across the island I enter some giant cacti fields. It is also a particular delight to find the native passionflower (*pasiflora*) growing so profusely, and it seems to be providing a welcome landing and feeding base for the carpenter bee as well as several other insects homing all along the stems. Travelling for about six kilometres north out of Puerto Ayora I eventually reach the cattle village of Bellavista (Beautiful View) where there are avocado and papaya growing amongst the elephant grasses (but no elephants!). A further nine kilometres trek on from Bellavista, I arrive at the Santa Rosa orchards and pass (forgive me for picking one apple) through them to the Chato Tortoise Reserve, at the south-west of Santa Cruz, where there are many living in the wild. It's a world of difference to the penned ones although I do wonder whether a tortoise of whatever size can ever be considered really wild or whether frisky would be a more appropriate adjective.

Isabela (Albemarle). This is by far the largest island and is especially important to visit as it straddles the Equator Line at its northern end, enabling me to again stand with one foot in the Northern Hemisphere and one in the Southern Hemisphere. Reaching the water's edge I perform this same trick in the Pacific Ocean and am joined by a shoal of tiny fish that also cross Hemispheres around my feet.

Isabela is a very large lady, covering nearly 4,600 square kilometres, 60 per cent of the total area of the Galapagos and having six large volcanoes spread across it, five still active. I am told that sometimes two or more erupt at the same time, with each spewing igneous material such as burning basalt into the air, running as molten lavas down the hillsides; an awesome sight. These periodic flames bursting from the centre of the craters can either flow inwards, or manoeuvre their way down to the sea to create volcanic 'tuffs'. These provide further sanctuaries for more marine life, each time helping to change the shape and contour not only of the volcano but the island itself. I wait for an eruption to occur. Unfortunately it doesn't happen on my watch, although I feel sure that as soon as my back is turned there will be a fireworks display.

Approximately in the centre of the island are the cliffs of Tagus Cove, several of which are signed and etched with names of ships going back hundreds of years and are very helpful to the study and history of pirating in this region. It's fascinating to see this record at first hand, and I note a few names and dates have been added from the 1930s when the yachts of many millionaires (back when a million really meant something) dropped anchor for a day or two whilst on their ocean going jaunts. Some might consider them as the pirates of modern times, but I couldn't possibly comment. South of Tagus is Urvina Bay, where in 1954 a huge slab of reef was upended and pushed out of the water leaving exposed the skeletons and remains of the sea creatures taken with it. It's a clear illustration of the potential power of any sudden movement by the tectonic forces. It seems to be an ideal landing spot, but I completely misjudge the steepness of the beach and am immediately up to my waist in the ocean before realising. I wade ashore holding my pack above my head, as if surrendering, but the iguanas are not interested in taking prisoners and quickly ignore me, raising their heads towards the sun in a prehistoric pose that doesn't allow for any intrusion.

As a reminder of the darker side of life, Isabela is also the island with the infamous 'Wall of Tears', so named after the then President of Ecuador agreed to the creation of the infamous penal colony which was to house some 300 prisoners. The wall was the 'brainwave' of the director of the penal colony, Velasco Ibarra, who arranged for it to be built and then unbuilt by the prisoners of the penal colony established there. They were forced to construct a wall without cement and after laboriously building it were then made to unpick the stones, level it and then start the process all over again. Many prisoners died as a result of the inhumane treatment meted out to them and it was finally closed for good in 1959.

Fernandina (Narborough). I was particularly keen to visit this island as it has had no introduced creatures and is therefore considered the largest pristine island in the world. It also has the greatest number of flightless cormorants – the rarest seabird in the world. This was my first encounter with this wonder of the bird world, and it lived up to all my expectations. The cormorants, having 'traded' their ability to fly for an incredible diving ability, have very large bodies and feet and find it difficult to walk. Certainly the term 'waddle' could have been invented for them, and their 'rock hopping' was fascinating to watch. They are really only comfortable keeping close to the shoreline, and build their nests just above the high water mark so that they can get back into the water at the earliest opportunity. It's not easy for males or females to gallivant so they more or less share nest duties equally. Although their wings have shortened, as far as I can see they seem to prefer to keep them stretched, so giving the impression they are about to launch into flight.

Fernandina is the third largest island with the youngest geological volcano, only up to 300,000 years old and it is listed as very active. Many years ago inside the Volcán La Cumbre, there was a deep mineral lake where birds of different kinds came to feed on its insects, including black-necked stilts and white-cheeked pintails. Eventually there was one eruption too many and the lake vanished. Despite the disappearance of the lake, their instinctive knowledge somehow remaining, the female land iguanas still make their long journeys there from different parts of the island to lay their eggs in the warm volcanic ash. It's almost unbelievable but they will travel for up to 15 days to arrive at the base of the volcano and then 'mountain climb' for 1,500 metres to reach the caldera walls. Then they must climb down a further 900 metres of sheer lava rock to locate the best places in the ash to lay their eggs. After ensuring their nests will survive they then leave them and make the long exhausting journey back to where they started out from.

After three months the baby iguanas are born and they then must climb the caldera walls, go 'over the top' and make their way to the region their instincts tell them is to be their home. On the way they have to try and avoid being killed by falling rocks and stones and being snatched by the hawks. They never question why their mothers chose to birth them so far away in such a dangerous place, or why they have been left on their own, all they know is 'that an iguana's got to do what an iguana's got to do'. Their will is just enormous and we can all learn from our prickly friends the meaning of true grit and determination.

The iguana is a prehistoric looking creature and actually has three eyes, the two on either side of its head and the third eye (parietal) protected within a slight depression on top, used to gauge the brightness and strength of the sun. If it's not strong enough the iguana goes into a slight depression. An iguana feels the changes in temperature more than most creatures and after a freezing night will need to attract the heat by basking in the sun for several hours. If the heat is insufficient it draws all the warmth it can from the hot lava rocks. Once it has reached the correct body temperature, as it's difficult to find any shade it adopts its 'gangster' pose by raising itself on its feet, head held high, facing directly into the sun and allowing its body to receive any slight breeze. By adopting this position, the iguana also creates a shadow underneath itself to cool it down and the position can be held for hours at a stretch. The face of an iguana is a sight to behold. It's craggy beyond belief, like someone with a hundred-a-day smoking habit, covered with scales that no amount of moisturiser will alleviate, and the crown of its head is covered by blunted spines which are used to head-butt rivals trying to interfere with their intended mating. Darwin somewhat aptly named the black 'brooding' marine iguanas the 'imps of darkness'.

Bartolomé. This tiny island only has one name and is special because it contains the Pinnacle Rock, the most photographed point of the Archipelago. I trek across the harsh landscape, where you can look for the Galapagos snake, but secretly hope that you don't see it. Once at the base I have to make the Pinnacle climb which is certainly worth it as the view from the summit, at 114 metres, is absolutely spectacular. Opposite is the lunar landscape which is dotted with lava and tuff cones and channels, seemingly lifeless but impressive nevertheless. I can also see several Galapagos penguins gambolling carelessly in the shallows below the Pinnacle in the midst of brightly coloured fish of all shapes and sizes. They work as a team in catching fish and encircle a school constantly darting and retreating, so forcing them into an ever decreasing grouping until they become so tightly bunched they become an easy target to pick off by constant attack. The Galapagos penguin, the second smallest of the 17 worldwide species, is the only one actually to cross the Equator. I take a swim on the shore but it would take me a lifetime of practice to do a backflip like a penguin.

There is a trek worth taking through the mangroves and across the dunes to another beach, although swimming there is not permitted. More fascinating marine life is readily available in abundance, including turtles and reef sharks, rays and ghost crabs. I can carefully observe the green marine turtles work their unhurried way along the shallows, stopping now and then to nibble on the luscious undergrowth of weeds and vegetation, swaying rhythmically with the gentle thrust of the currents. The female usually comes out of the ocean at night to lay her eggs. She takes a long exhausting crawl through the sand to be away from the incoming tides and digs a very large hole in which she buries her cache of eggs. She then covers them with several layers of sand, scraping the sand in all directions to hide her tracks and hopefully protect the eggs from the many predators anxious for a juicy snack. She can leave behind up to one hundred eggs and is desperate for them to survive, to make her painful work worthwhile. By sunrise her job is done and she then starts the long weary journey back to the sea. She can do this several times in a season but when she is finished will not return and Nature must take over.

Española (Hood). It's the most southerly and the oldest island, and its remoteness has led to many endemic species surviving. Española is another must for me as it's also the prime home to the waved albatross, the only tropical-breeding albatross (the only other habitat now existing being on the Isla de la Plata off the Ecuadorian mainland). The albatross can have a wingspan of up to 2.5 metres and can spend up to seven years out at sea, and on its return will search for and find its mate for the rest of its life. Some sailors say they behave the same way but most of their wives would declare that to be an old sailor's tale. The courtship rituals of the albatross are certainly a sight to behold and they are not shy to perform in public. They slowly dance around each other and appear almost to kiss as their bills encircle each other. They continue by pointing their bills skywards in unison, clapping, preening, making odd clunking moans and other noises as well as many other quirky movements, the meanings of which are really known only to themselves. I can't resist a laughable imitation of the courtship dance when no one else is looking and think my skypointing at least is up to scratch but I don't receive even a glance let alone a wave from any albatross, none of whom are fooled for a moment.

The waved albatross can live for up to 40 years. They enter into a life-long relationship and will faithfully return from the ocean together every April, to create and raise just one chick during the year, leaving again in December to go travelling. Interestingly they do not travel together but separately, perhaps feeling it adds some spice of romance to their lives when they are reunited. They may all appear to look more or less the same to us but when the pair finally returns to the cliffs, almost within days if not hours of each other, they will immediately recognise each other and leap joyfully into a new dance of renewed courtship. This happens no matter how old they have now become and they will repeat their original courtship ritual, although not quite with the same fervour. Still, it's the thought that counts.

Floreana, (Santa Maria or Charles). In past less regulated times (it actually ended in 1790), the famed wooden postal barrel was sited here, to be used as a post drop for all those passing through the Archipelago. In recognition the bay was subsequently re-named after this curious but very beneficial service as the Post Office Bay. The very early nineteenth century saw the arrival of 'the first settler', in the Islands, staying on Charles Island as it was then known, Patrick Watkins. He had been put ashore after a heated dispute with the captain of the sailing ship in which he was travelling. Watkins became more and more eccentric and an even stranger sight as he roamed the islands. He refused to wash, never shaved and was always likely to abuse or behave violently to anyone he came across. To get away he finally commandeered a crew and stole a ship which he sailed to Guayaquil. He arrived there, however, with the crew no longer on board, and was promptly arrested and then sent to prison in Peru. The Peruvian prisons of that period were certainly no holiday camps and Watkins wasn't heard of again. I wonder if the new head of conservation at the Darwin Research Centre, Graham Watkins, is a descendant but decide it is better not to enquire. My curiosity and humour have already got me into enough trouble.

The islands were claimed in 1832 for the new Republic of Ecuador by General Jose Villamil who based himself in Floreana and designated the Spanish names for all the islands. The authorities on the mainland had thought it very convenient to use the islands as a place in which to park unwanted criminals and any others they wished to banish. Very soon Villamil tired of the life of the orchilla business (or lack of it) and also of having the low life of Ecuador thrust upon him to be his main companions, so in 1837 he retired from this colonial and barren existence. Not before, unfortunately, handing over to the infamous and brutal Colonel Jose Williams who had to keep a pack of wild, ferocious dogs to protect him. The nickname of the islands soon became known instead as, 'Kingdom of the Dogs' and it had obviously 'gone to the dogs'. Williams in 1841 eventually had to flee for his life but inconveniently left the dogs behind. It's not recorded what happened to the hated dogs but in those times no meat went to waste. Nothing much really happened for nearly 30 years until Jose de Valdizan tried to take charge but he didn't fare any better and he didn't leave in time and was assassinated in 1878.

It then went relatively quiet again for many years until the sordid 'Galapagos Affair' occurred. Two Germans, Freidrich Ritter and Dore Strauch, arrived on Floreana in 1929. They were apparently lovers, although their behaviour to each other teetered on the edge of the bizarre and the downright wicked, with severe beatings, removing each other's teeth, burnings with the lava, being just part of their very strange practices and 'love habits'. The torments inflicted to each other were certainly at high earthquake levels on the Ritter Scale. They were then joined in 1932 by another odd German family, Heinz, Margaret and their son Harry Wittmer, shortly followed by the arrival on the island of Baroness Wagner de Bosquet and her two lovers, Rudolf Lorenz and Robert Phillipson. There were even wilder goings-on within the extreme relationships existing between them all, which ultimately culminated with the Baroness and Phillipson mysteriously disappearing together. They were presumed murdered, though nothing was proved and no bodies were ever found.

San Cristóbal (Chatham). This is the most easterly island and has the only freshwater lake, El Junco, in the Archipelago. The lake is in the crater of a volcano and is called the Leon Dormido. There are herds of sea lions which are great fun and I am happy to sit relaxing on a rock while they entertain me. Each bull is powerful, territorial and will quickly fight its corner if a new challenger seems too inquisitive, or actually attempts to take over. The sea cows are content to suckle their babies, making available their tiny retractable nipples, whilst at the same time seeing that their other excitable youngsters, surfing in the shallows, don't come to any harm. Wave surfing is as much an attraction to the young sea lion as it is to the surfers of Bondi Beach in Australia. They swim out looking for the 'perfect wave' and will ride it all the way to shore and then swim out and do it all over again. They are a delight to watch and their enjoyment is infectious.

The birth of a sea lion baby occurs quickly, and immediately the mother will use her teeth to bite off the amniotic sack in which it has been born and start to nudge it alive. It responds within minutes, automatically searching for the food which the mother is happy to provide. The babies have no protective blubber when they are born, so cannot spend too much time in the sea. Surprisingly, if seals are separated from their young, they do not recognise them very easily (the same problem occurs with the polar bear mother and her cubs in the Arctic, they really do all look so much alike). The first few weeks are therefore spent 'vocalising' so that the mother and her pup will be able to call to each other when apart, hear the distinctive voices or sounds and hopefully find each other again. The young sea lions are extremely playful and curious and will chase anything that moves. This includes the iguanas, who are prepared to tolerate their interest as part of their growing up, being well aware that they are not rivals for food or love. The sea lions are very noisy creatures when awake and the air is filled with grunts, growls, barks and bleats from all sides, as they presumably pass coded messages across, indicating some decision or request. They are all very sociable and spend a great deal of time snuggling, sniffing and 'helloing' as they move laboriously around their beach territory. They all like to sleep a lot, and a little exercise seems to tire them out quickly, so everywhere on the sand there are groups of sea lions, sea cows and pups lying in comatose mode, looking as if nothing except an earthquake would ever wake them.

San Salvador (Santiago or James). It's the fourth largest island but has an unfortunate zoological history. Captain David Porter of the US Navy in 1812, at the time of his conflict with the English whalers, set free on the island four goats which continued to multiply so that in the late twentieth century their population had reached around 100,000. Porter wouldn't have realised the harm four goats would cause but it's a Zen observation to be remembered; always think through the consequences of your actions, no matter how small they may seem at the time. The goats were extremely destructive and killed off much of the island's fauna. A necessary decision was finally made to eradicate them, but at the same time the huge pig population that had also been allowed to expand without control also had to be dealt with. Because of the large area through which the animals had been allowed to roam freely it took nearly 30 years and was only completed in 2001.

There are very many places to visit but time is short so I have to limit my travel initially to Puerto Egas (Port Egas),

Espunilla Beach and Bahia Sullivan (Sullivan Bay). Hector Egas was an old salt or even an odd sort and the port named after him still contains some of the salt buildings. He left in a hurry to the mainland to obtain some further funding but never returned. His staff waited for him for some years, possibly salting everything away for his return, but finally realised he wasn't coming back and all they had was a huge amount of salt, with no orders. If they ever got hold of him I'm sure they would have delighted in rubbing salt into an old wound.

Seymour (North Seymour). It is north of Baltra, from which it is only separated by a narrow channel. At certain times this channel can be walked carefully without getting one's feet wet, or not enough to worry about, although the lava can be very slippery. It is a flat pack of an island, only about two square kilometres. The fascination for me is to see at first hand the colonies of both of the magnificent and great frigate birds as well as blue-footed boobies and swallow-tailed gulls. The male frigate bird walks around with a saggy bright red pouch sac most of the time, but in an inspiring moment can puff it out to an enormous size, in order to impress the female or intimidate his rivals. I am equally impressed. It beats a red sports car any day. The males are in constant rivalry and many may surround a solitary female, each putting on his best puffing act. Once the mating is complete, the nest chosen, it's all over bar the shouting. The pouch stays deflated, the vibrant colour disappears and the job of the male is only to search for twigs for the nest. The two frigate kinds are generally similar (well they would be, wouldn't they) but because of the inbuilt rivalry each may also want to be 'the best'. The great species have a green sheen on their feathers and the female a white chest, whereas the magnificent have a purple sheen and the female a red eye-ring. A colour-blind frigate could get into some real serious trouble by making approaches to the wrong species. It could even turn into a real contest. The wingspan of the magnificent (up to 2.5 metres) is slightly larger than the great but who's really counting. Perhaps size does matter, even with birds!

Genovesa (Tower). It is the only one of the five northern islands open to visitors without special permissions and because of the huge numbers to be found there, it is also known as Bird Island. I am keen to visit, as here are numerous colonies of masked boobies, the largest in the world of red-footed boobies, great frigate birds, swallow-tailed gulls, red-billed tropic birds and yellow-crowned herons. The air is rent with the whooping, screaming and cries as each tries to call to its own kind, with the males simultaneously warning off intruders and exhorting the females to stay available and within an area where they can be protected. When the shoals of schooling fish are spotted offshore, the boobies immediately take off in pursuit and dive down repeatedly until they are fully satisfied. The fish of course never learn and next day they will probably return and the feeding ritual begins all over again.

The male booby, in order to attract the female, has to go first through an elaborate nest building courtship ritual with any twigs he can muster. The female will watch him silently and if unimpressed she will walk away. It can be a humiliating process particularly if he gets turned down by several females. It's the same the whole world over and it's why some men are often referred to as 'great boobies'. Next there is an elaborate skypointing with his beak, earthpointing with his feet, to show off his brilliant 'footwear' colours and then some more posturing until he waits for the female to decide. If he is accepted as a mate he can expect to be rewarded with up to three eggs which will become little boobies all of his own. A booby chooses a new mate every year but he is not very faithful. He might even choose the same female a year or two later, though neither will remember, as it's a rather spur of the moment decision on both their parts and it's like hopping on a bus and off again, although here you don't have to buy a ticket. The female booby has the instinctive motherly task of during the day shading the eggs from the burning heat of the sun, then spending the cold night with her feet wrapped around the eggs to keep them warm.

The front view of a booby's face can be alarming in its intensity. Its long pointed beak makes it appear to be almost cross-eyed, but it is all part of its precision diving technique. It can zoom into the water from 30 metres or more at high speed without damaging itself, pick up a selected fish, and re-emerge all in a matter of a few seconds. To dive it tucks its wings behind it to give better aerodynamics and then bombs down without any concern, particularly as it has a head air-sac to cushion the impact as it hits the water.

Plaza. This island is tiny and volcanic and is situated north of Santa Cruz. I learn this is one of the best places to see and study iguanas and I jump ashore, splashing through the surf and find myself almost immediately in the midst of iguana country. The land and marine iguanas are believed to have gone their separate ways after arriving in the islands and keep themselves to themselves now that they are separated by biological history. The land iguanas have very bright colours, yellow and orange of every shade, which makes them stand out from the surrounding dark lava slabs on which they spend most of their time. The males will assert their rights over a certain place or area and then will fight furiously any other male that seeks to invade. The cleverer male will make his home inside a spacious cavern, possibly created from a lava rock bubble, as this proves a great draw to the ladies. There's never much else to get excited about.

A number of the females will then congregate outside in anticipation and wait for the call. It isn't long in coming and one by one they will enter and obediently take the 'receptive' position. They obviously haven't heard about equal rights, after all it's a long way from the mainland, several hundred years in fact.

The pregnant iguana then starts a long, exhausting, tenuous journey to what must seem in iguana terms the centre of the world. It takes at least a month, sometimes two, with her slowly and painfully crossing the hardened lava slabs, suffering in the intense heat. Then a tortuous crawl down through the crumbling caldera of the volcano walls until they arrive at the warm ash beds on the actual floor of the caldera. They will gradually burrow inside and then half-submerged, wait for the birth.

The marine iguanas have concentrated head glands which can excrete the excess salt into their nostrils so they can snort it out. This is a gradual process, and it's possible to hear all over the islands slumbering iguanas snorting vigorously. Some scientists used to think it was a mating call but as nothing ever happened afterwards, decided it must be a waiting mating call, until it was eventually discovered to be a wake-up call instead. Iguanas are also very adept at adapting to circumstances.

During the devastating El Niño of 1982/1983, when all their food seaweed stocks were decimated, the iguanas took to eating the beach Batis salt plant leaves and developed such a liking for them, they continue to eat it even when there are plentiful seaweed supplies. Iguanas mate during the warmer months of February and March. The males stake out their individual territories and the impregnated females (don't ask how they do it, it doesn't look comfortable) choose a sandy area along the beach where the tides don't reach to bury their eggs. The sun incubates the eggs, and provided the eggs are not stolen by beady-eyed predators, bakes them out two to three months later. The baby igs, without a backward glance immediately head off to the shoreline (hawks and herons permitting) to get their first bites of seaweed. The marine iguana has a symbiotic relationship with the sally lightfoot crab, as it will sit and stare impassively forward whilst the crab clambers all over it, picking off bits of shredding skin to eat. It's unlikely they share any common language, although perhaps there is a way of interpreting a twitch or a shrug, when the iguana might want to indicate, 'A little lower, now to the left, harder, perfect, that's just right.' An iguana would never, however, allow anything to crab its style.

Santa Fé (Barrington). This is a very small island, not quite in the centre of the Archipelago and is about 25 kilometres south of Punta Ayores. It's definitely a wet landing to reach its beach, but at least this time it only comes up to my knees. I am told to look out particularly for the Galapagos hawks and land iguanas (an unusual pale colouring marking them out from the other land species), endemic to this island. There are three endemic species of the rice rat, but I prefer not to look for them. Trekking across the island I come across plenty of endemic giant cacti woods with giant prickly pears intermingled amongst them. The giant Opuntia cacti can grow to over ten metres and they provide interesting colour combinations as a reaction to the surrounding, somewhat drab vegetation and scrubland. They have the usual green prickly tops but their trunk coverings have contrasting flaky, dark rusty hues, the bark so hardened it's almost impossible for the iguanas to chew through. As the cacti store very sought after water, they are, however, a constant draw to insects, reptiles, rodents and birds, all of which have long discovered how to avoid being snared on their prickly spines and they all certainly know the way to Santa Fé. There are also some dwarf cacti, which I'm careful not to overlook.

Mating and Waiting in the Galapagos. Mating time is the same the whole Archipelago over, with the exception of the iguana who likes to make an early start. It is something like the Rio De Janeiro Carnival mixed with the Mad Hatter's Tea Party, with the addition of several artistes from the Cirque de Soleil performing extraordinary acrobatics. There are thousands of bird and animal voices screeching, honking, whistling, all in effect shouting noisily in their bird imitations of the singer Tina Turner, 'Look at me, I'm simply the best.' Some are sky-pointing, some toe-pointing, some pumping their chest pouches, for all they are worth, preening themselves in all their finery in untrue Hollywood Oscar Party Night. This time, however, many are desperate to win the Booby Prize. Everyone gets someone and the mating takes place quickly and urgently before the mood lessens, as time waits for no male.

Seabirds in these islands are never solitary parents; there's always a mate for each parent to rely on, whether just for the season or for a bird lifetime. Sometimes one partner may be away for weeks, as it may have to forage far and wide to look for food to bring back to the nest, leaving the other to stay on guard duty. However long it takes, the remaining parent will wait patiently, without food or water, unable to leave the nest for a moment, in case a predator, whether another bird or another creature, takes the brief opportunity to strike. When eventually the travelling partner returns, there are only short moments of exchanges of food and possibly news, before the roles are reversed and the foraging and journeying starts all over again. It's a complete dedication and commitment within the bird world, which can only be admired.

However, there are always tragedies. A bird may not return for many reasons, perhaps it's been killed in a storm or in an accident, or even by a larger predator. The home-alone parent cannot know what has happened and will stay until the chick eventually starves, as may the parent, if it no longer has the strength to find food for itself. Sometimes the growing chick will need greater feeding and both parents will go off to find food. Left alone the chick is then very vulnerable to predators. If it survives till it is time to leave the nest and make its own way, it's not certain by any means that it will be able to find enough food to feed itself. It's a wild world out there.

You have left me nothing to stand on, said the bird as it began to fly.

CHAPTER 18

THE WORLD'S TALLEST MOUNTAIN

C himborazo is now in my mind, crowding everything else out. I am prepared for my last mountain, and it's now time to see whether I can accomplish the final goal of my expedition. This is the highest mountain of the region, a strange, remote place where I am hoping to find some answers. I need to make the attempt, even if the summit ultimately eludes me. My torn toe has mostly recovered and is feeling easier and I hope I will be able to live with whatever pain that it causes on the ascent. My knees are another matter, but I've climbed before with the pain and I must try to accept it this time as well. If I don't try I'll never know. Only on this mountain am I likely to find a part of any inner knowledge, even if it proves momentary. However as the Zen master, Shunryu Suzuki, states, 'You can't make a date with enlightenment.' Only by allowing myself to be exposed, mentally and physically, climbing 'into harm's way', will I create the conditions whereby possibly and only possibly there is even a chance of experiencing some kind of enlightenment. A Zen saying echoes this thought, 'Gaining enlightenment is an accident. Spiritual practice simply makes us accident prone.' What better place to experience an accident than on this high ice mountain!

Chimborazo has long been regarded as one of the world's special mountains, a place where it is always possible to dream. Sometimes those dreams will come true. It was once considered the highest mountain in the world, even up to the 1820s, and has inspired many explorers, writers and poets. The poem 'Romance' written by the playwright and poet, W. J. Turner (1884–1947), refers to the two best known of Ecuador's mountains and has been taught and learned in schools for generations. This poem conjures up the magic that is waiting for those who are willing to travel to their icy slopes and it has encouraged many to begin their own adventures.

When I was but thirteen or so
I went into a golden land;
Chimborazo, Cotopaxi
Took me by the hand.

The houses, people, traffic seemed
Thin fading dreams by day;
Chimborazo, Cotapaxi,
They had stolen my soul away!

Chimborazo is a five-summited mountain, the southernmost mountain in the Cordillera Occidental range of mountains and is 150 kilometres south-west of Quito. It is visible from Colombia to the north of Ecuador, and also from close to the border with Peru to the south, as well as from far out in the Pacific Ocean. Since those heady days of being thought, erroneously, to be the highest in the world, it has had to settle for being acclaimed as the tallest. As I mentioned earlier, this is due to the natural bulge at the Earth's Equator (more than 8,000 metres). If you had the inclination, a techno-smart measuring instrument and the means of accomplishing the task, a line taken from the very centre of the earth to the summit of Chimborazo, would reach higher than a similar one taken to the summit of Everest.

It's totally academic of course, as we all now accept Everest at 8,848 metres (29,028 feet) above sea level is the highest mountain in the world, but the Ecuadorians are still rightly proud of this unique and powerful mountain that stands at 6,310 metres (20,703 feet) and is still a difficult climb by any mountaineering standards.

Even Simon Bolivar, successful at achieving so much else, was unsuccessful in his Chimborazo attempt. The famed traveller and scientist Alexander Von Humboldt nearly made it in 1802 but also had to give up, although he set a record at that time of being the first to reach nearly 6,000 metres (19,500 feet). Subsequently I was to understand only too clearly how frustrated he felt. Eventually it was first climbed in 1880 by the superb English mountaineer, Edward Whymper and in his honour the main Refuge at 4,880 metres (16,400 feet), bears his name. Whymper was accompanied on this incredible climb, as indeed on so many of his mountain attempts, by the Italians, Jean-Antoine and Louis Carrel, in whose joint honour the lower Refuge, 4,020 metres, is also aptly named.

It's important to remember that it's always the mountain that is the master, the climber is only ever allowed to climb on probation, the mountain can always withdraw permission. It can decide to send you away at any time it chooses, never more so than when a mountain is also a volcano. Any mountaineer venturing onto its huge glacier walls must always accept Chimborazo is the master.

Its five peaks have been built up over extensive rock and lava formations rising up from the Andean *páramos*. Four of the summits are Veintimilla Summit (6,270 metres), North Summit (6,200 metres), Central or Polytechnic Summit (6,000 metres), and Easter or Nicolás Martinéz Summit (5,500 metres). However, the one to climb if you want to say you have really climbed Chimborazo is the Whymper or Ecuador Summit of 6,310 metres. This is permanently covered in ice and snow and can only be climbed with crampons, axe and harness and plenty of guts. Also more than a fair share of luck, as you will definitely need the right conditions, positive and supportive climbing companions and above all the right and committed frame of mind. In Zen terminology that is usually termed the *shin* approach, using the special spirit of the inner mind.

There are always several routes up any mountain and weather conditions will often dictate which one at any particular time it is preferable to follow. Also every mountaineering guide will have his own preferred route, usually the one on which he has had most experience. As I have no previous experiences of the mountain I have no personal preference at all, so am quite content to follow whichever route is suggested by the guides. On my first attempt I am led by a guide with whom I am unable to relate at a level which might encourage me to try and overcome the difficult and dangerous climbing conditions. We do not share any karma and I feel he is negating my determination to continue. Therefore after struggling up the initial slopes for several hours I choose to stop and return down the mountain and to climb again.

On my second attempt not only have I become more acclimatised to the high altitudes of the region, but my torn toe seems to have recovered considerably. I am also now definitely in the right mindset to give myself an acceptable chance of summit success. This time also there are now four of us, two guides and Axel, the German climber I met in Quito at the Libri Mundi bookshop. The guides are good friends, Jorge and Enrique, who have often climbed Chimborazo and seem to understand my need to feel and to experience the mountain as much as to climb it.

Enrique has a Volkswagen car which we agree to hire and we drive for several hours out of Quito, passing Riobamba in order to reach the Carrel Refuge (4,800 metres). It's about 7 p.m. There are already several cars parked haphazardly in every direction.

We share out our gear and food equally and quickly set off together to trek up to the Whymper Refuge. I am feeling energetic and I decide to lead for the first few minutes but then think it advisable to take it more slowly. Everyone comes up level with me and we stay more or less like that until we reach the Refuge. Even though we are only climbing as a small group, I am feeling more confident, as I now know the initial route. It has also taken us much less than an hour to climb to the Refuge, and I arrive feeling pretty good and in no way tired. It's sleeting slightly and very cold, and the first thing is to drink several cups of tea and then try to eat some of the food we've brought with us. I'm not hungry but know it's essential to eat as much as I can, as the mountain will drain energy away fast at high altitude. I don't sleep but am able to rest fairly comfortably, although it is pretty cold. I keep my boots on, waiting for it to reach midnight, which is when we have agreed to start up the mountain. My right foot feels a little painful but I have packed it well, hope it will last out, and intend to use my left for the really hard stuff.

The Whymper Refuge is spacious and there are plenty of bunk beds with the usual well-used and rather dank mattresses, although no climber ever expects anything other than the very basic amenities. I pare down my clothes and equipment to the minimum, as the less weight I carry the more chance I'll have of climbing higher. The helmet is a necessity however, although it's definitely a lot of weight and I still decide to take both ski poles, as I know they will help to surmount some of the trickier rock and ice sections I will encounter. There are several routes but the two main ones are the shorter Whymper route, that Edward Whymper himself took over a hundred years earlier, and the Castillo

Route. This is a steeper climb but more direct leading to the very long climb to Veintimilla Peak. Whymper's own route, veering right then straight up, before cutting back to the centre, has become more dangerous over the years, due particularly to global warming causing the snow cover to diminish. There have also been increasing rock falls and a number of deaths have occurred from traversing across the ice skirting the seracs, which too often tend to crash down without warning. The Castillo would also definitely give us a better chance in these harsh weather conditions.

We set off fairly shortly after midnight, and it is a very misty and bitterly cold night, although with intermittent moonlight breaking through the drifting cloud formations. Since we arrived at Whymper the weather has worsened; the snow and sleet now drives fiercely into my eyes and I must immediately put on my goggles. There are several other climbers planning to try their luck on the Castillo Route at the same time, several already ahead of us and a few start out hard on our heels. The head torches all the climbers have are like dancing lights sparkling in the darkness, but also illustrate the driving sleet, which seems to intensify with every step we take away from the Refuge.

We are climbing to the left of the Thielman Glacier and through breaks in the mists and clouds which drop down to envelop us, I can see the ghostly whiteness waiting and looming like some apparition just waiting to claim more victims. The initial scree and rock faces are hard going, and there is plenty of slipping and sliding as the rocks are wet and very uneven. I use the active form of Zen meditation, *kinhin,* to balance myself and take me forward. The snow is sleeting down so hard it's impossible to see much and to judge which rocks are stable through the thin layers of ice and snow which are covering all sections. I have learned the rocks are becoming more uncovered each year, causing many more accidents than before, and it becomes a slow and painful process climbing up and across them. There is no obvious route to follow so I try to step whenever possible in the footsteps of Enrique, the leading guide and Axel just behind him, although they aren't at this stage leaving any footprints to follow. Even though they are just ahead of me it isn't always easy to see where they have been. Several times my boots become locked into rock crevices, and it takes a considerable effort to prise them free which is more draining each time.

There are many sections of further loose, slippery scree to climb up, and it often is a case of two steps up and one step down. Occasionally, and this is immensely frustrating of course when it happens, I take one step up and slide two steps down. At such moments I almost feel like giving up, but then the sight of my fellow climbers silently making their own way upwards always makes me determined to carry on a while longer. I am breathing really hard, gulping in the thin air, forcing myself forwards and am finding the higher rocks even more treacherous. I am worried I may take a tumble, which can easily cause considerable damage and prevent me continuing. If I have to give up I want it to be because I just can't go on any longer, not because of some stupid accident which could have been avoided.

I start to practice *samadhi*, the Zen practice of intense concentration, to force myself to climb on. Despite it becoming increasingly difficult to manage a proper balance on the jagged and protruding rocks, we don't rope up for some time and I am surprised at this but feel I can't suggest it. However eventually it is quite clear to all of us the rocks are becoming too dangerous, are looking extremely unsafe from every point of view, and it will be much better if we are all roped together. I am roped third after Axel, so feel it necessary to climb at a faster pace than I really want, in order not to slow the others down. Enrique and Axel continue to climb at quite a fast pace, I also sense Jorge behind me is also impatient to move ahead, and therefore I feel the pressure to keep going at their quicker pace. Anyhow I reason to myself, perhaps it isn't such a bad thing, as otherwise there is the real concern we may not have the opportunity to reach the Summit slopes before the sun rises. If that were to happen it would quickly become extremely hot and we will suffer the effects from the sun's intense rays, particularly with the bulge of the Earth in this region bringing us even closer to direct exposure.

In fact the weather throughout the ascent and the subsequent descent becomes steadily worse. It snows and sleets incessantly, and we do not see the sun for the whole time. We climb to the left away from the summit approach, and at last I start to achieve a good rhythm and make steady progress. It seems as if it has been going on forever, but finally we at last leave the sliding scree and ultra slippery rock sections. It's real ice time and there's an ice wall to climb so we remove our lifeline ropes and go for it. There's the use of a step ladder, which though unstable still helps a bit, and with a huge scramble and struggle I reach the ice ramp of El Corredor (sorry, no marks to those who guess this means the corridor). It's set between heavy layers of rocks stretching way below and the higher outcrop of several large rocks known, because of the shape of the highest one, jointly as El Castillo (the castle).

We stop on the snow at the entrance to the ramp to put on our crampons, and I am certainly glad of the breather. We then trek, still roped together, across to the right along El Corredor and edge steadily forward fighting against the extreme winds for about an hour. There are a few minor rock falls and we can hear the small rocks ricocheting down the mountain for a considerable time. It is quite a worry as there are always dangers of larger rock falls, and if any one of us is hit and falls the remaining three could easily end up being dragged downwards as well. After trekking past the rock outcrops and now veering to the left, we make a long, laborious climb up the ice to reach the Castillo Way.

The ice here is rock hard and it is very painful to kick my crampons in, particularly with my right foot. I feel it twinge all the way up to my knee. My plan to rely mostly on my left foot has proved impossible, and both feet have to share equally the considerable pain of kicking in and pushing hard on the ice. There is suddenly a crevasse right in front of us and we skirt it carefully, all too aware it can extend for quite a distance below the ice, unseen, but ready to suck us into it if we don't exercise extreme caution. In Zen false thoughts or actions are known as delusions and I must remain totally aware to avoid taking any false steps. We move very slowly forward, all the time prodding the ice with our axes, hoping we will only encounter more hard ice and the axe won't break through into a void. At El Castillo itself, apart from encountering a few small crevasses, it becomes relatively straight forward, with us now heading in a direct north-west direction.

After several painful hours of slow, hard climbing we reach about half way along the massive glacier heading towards the Veintimilla Peak (6,270 metres). This is unfortunately known as the false summit as it's not the one you must achieve to complete the climb successfully, and we all know we need to keep something in reserve to make the real summit. There are several unstable seracs to avoid as well as snow towers to be carefully passed, which are all very difficult to overcome and my ice axe is sometimes essential to wedge me through and occasionally up and over. Another, larger crevasse presents itself for inspection, as if anxious to welcome us into its depths, but we resist its siren call and edge around it, to continue cautiously upwards.

My legs are very tired and I can feel very dull aches in both my knees. This is somewhat ominous but I don't want to mention it to the others, just as they would keep any pains they have to themselves. My right toe has finally decided enough is enough and is throbbing madly, but I try to use the pain to force myself on. Both the two guides are still looking quite relaxed and Axel also doesn't complain about anything so I certainly am not going to. I try to get into more of a rhythm, chanting my Zen counting mantra and sometimes I manage it but mostly I don't. I am starting to run out of steam and am not certain whether to announce I've had enough or need a longer rest to try and get some of my strength back. I must concentrate harder. *Susoku* in Zen is counting the breathing to ten, repeating again and again, to focus the mind. I start to feel focused again, but will it last?

There is no real choice of course but to continue, as the alternative would be for me to go down, and that would probably mean one or more, or possibly everyone would then have to return with me. No one speaks now and it seems as if even the guides are finding it as tough. In a perverse way that thought spurs me on. There are constant belays to set up and I feel I am being dragged upwards and try desperately to go with the flow. A few jazz numbers keep echoing through my brain and they help to propel me upwards. Towards the end of this section, the weather clears temporarily, as if encouraging us all on, somehow we all seem to find renewed strength or courage and suddenly it isn't proving as difficult as before. We take a final rest but it is so cold and we are so exposed that we can only stop for a few minutes and it is preferable to continue.

We now gain some momentum and keep going regardless, and with a further spurt we are at the Veintimilla Summit. Now we all know there is no turning back and we must see it through. The final climb up the Whymper Steps to the actual Summit however is horrendous and feels so painful in all ways; my chest pounding, my legs hurting, particularly my right knee and foot, my head a dull ache. I don't really know how I will manage to keep going. On my own I don't think there would have been any chance, with one other climber I doubt I could have managed, but with the four of us there is a real force created, and it becomes possible and somehow we make it. Thank you Jorge, thank you Enrique, thank you Axel.

The summit crater, with mists swirling across it, is huge. I am standing on the point in the world that is furthest from the Centre of the World than any other. I have actually achieved my three goals; travelling from Britain and starting out from the longitude of 0-0-0, arriving to Ecuador and reaching the latitude of 0-0-0 and now climbing to the top of Chimborazo, the 'tallest' mountain in the world. It is definitely a special moment in time but not one in these bitter conditions to savour for too long.

It is icy cold, the intense chill is fighting its way through me and the winds are so fierce it isn't even easy to stand upright. I lean on my ice axe to allow myself a final few moments to experience the mountain. I feel its deepness, its remoteness, it is another place, in another country and it has its own being, and for some moments I am privileged to be part of it. René Daumal expressed his philosophical take on any great experience in a way so appropriate to my feelings at this intense time. 'You cannot stay on the summit forever. You have to come down again. One climbs and one sees; but one has seen. There is an art of conducting oneself by the memory of what one saw higher up. When one no longer sees, one can at least still know.'

Jorge and Enrique gently insist it's time to leave this mountain top, otherwise it might not let us leave. The way down is horrendous, almost more so than the ascent, and first the ice and then the rocks are tearing at my knees and I continually feel as if they are on fire. The Zen teacher Yamada Roshi stated, 'Pain in the knees is the taste of zazen,' but he was really referring to the pain from sitting with bent knees and practising zazen to empty and free the mind, not arising from reactions to the ice and rock of the mountain. Of course there is no other choice, we have to climb down or perish, but it is a slow, painful and long descent. I fall a few times and it isn't easy to get up, but as we are roped together that always helps me to regain my balance. Axel actually falls more than me and I guess he is also feeling as much pain but neither of us comment either then or afterwards, perhaps each waiting for the other to speak first, but in the end neither of us say anything.

Despite everything, the atrocious weather, the pain of knees and toe, the toughest conditions, I have achieved a successful ascent to the Chimborazo Summit. But is it one I would want to repeat? Who knows, perhaps with a third attempt it would actually become easier. Once you know the way, you know when to pause, when to move ahead and more importantly what to expect. I will just have to wait and see what the future holds and if the mountain beckons me again. I know it will always be difficult to ignore its call.

The name Chimborazo has many meanings and one is 'the Snow that must be crossed', another 'Snowy Pass', and it has certainly been a mixture of great pain and extreme pleasure for me to cross the snow of this mountain. I know that it is only because the mountain allowed me to do so and it always retains the right to refuse. There are several other nicknames and translations including 'Woman in Ice', 'Icy Home of the Gods', 'Sacred Winds of the Moon', I decide to give it my own one, 'the Mountain Nearest to Heaven'.

CHAPTER 19

HIDDEN IN
THE FOREST

He is asleep, he is awake. In between is a special moment, a secret moment. He always has many secrets and he is forced to live a secret life. The enemy are always looking for him and his family and they only want to destroy. He can't understand why that is but he has seen their work over too many years to have any doubts about their intentions. He listens carefully, trying to hear any unusual noises which might indicate danger. The forest is stirring, there are rustlings of movement and several birds are starting to call out. He loves these early morning sounds as everything about him comes slowly to life. There is never a reason to rush and there is a natural rhythm of pace which every creature will follow. His woman and their children are still asleep but will also waken soon. He can hear their soft breathing and he feels content, his job is to protect them. There is a slight glow from the fire and they will need to bring more wood to add to it during the day.

He slips quietly out of the hammock, but before his feet touch the floor she is also up and ready. He smiles at that, she is a light sleeper and never wants to let him leave without offering him food. He isn't hungry now but takes some strips of meat that she offers him that have been cooked over the last few days. They don't speak, in order not to wake the children, but he touches his knife and she knows he is going hunting and may not be back for one or two days. Of course if he is really lucky he might come back sooner, only the jungle could know that. She touches a finger to the long, jagged scar running down his right leg and then to his forehead. She is telling him to be careful and he nods his understanding. He had been lucky once and he couldn't expect to be as lucky again.

The anaconda had saved him and it wouldn't save him again. That is the rule. He accepts his debt and has no more right to ask for its help again. It had suddenly swung out of its hiding place, angry and ferocious, and had wrapped its coils about his attackers. It had thrashed about so wildly that they had all tumbled into a bush of poison nettles, so everyone had started screaming. Only he had kept silent, his wounds dripping so much blood he was able to slide his feet out of his bindings and start to run. The pain was a gift he could use to spur his race to freedom. He hated leaving his father's knife behind, but he knew his spirit would understand. The monkey was also gone and he would not be able to return here. When you are given a second chance you must learn from it.

They hadn't pursued him, perhaps they feared another creature attack, but they still might try to find him and he didn't stop until he had left their territory and had recognised some parts of the forest that could offer him sanctuary. He couldn't know what had happened to the anaconda but he hoped it had escaped, as it would not suffer from the nettles and could disappear as quickly as it had come. It was now sacred to him and he would never try to harm one again. It had taken nearly a day to return to his home as he had taken a very long route back, in case any of them were still trying to pursue him and exact revenge. When his woman saw his wounds she didn't react, that was not their way, but set about washing and cleaning them. She sent the boy quickly to fetch some plant roots and boiled them before pulping them into a paste. He lay still whilst they spread it over both legs and they waited patiently until he was ready to tell what had happened. The loss of his knife was upsetting but he had others and it had no life of its own, only carrying a memory.

It took seven days before he started to recover but the right leg had the worse wound and it healed into a long snake-like shape that he took as a sign. Every day for a month they made an offering to the anaconda and at the end he was as before, only the scars on his leg and in his mind to remind him of how close it had been.

He takes his blowgun and darts with him and starts down the trail leading to the river. He chews on one piece of meat as he walks but saves the rest as he might need to use them as bait. The forest is now really alive and he hears the plaintive cry of a lone monkey in the distance. He hadn't attempted to capture one since that time, as he felt it had happened as its curse and he believed in listening to the jungle

Several butterflies start their ritual dancing ahead of him, seemingly beckoning him forward and he follows their path further into the forest. They are gathering more as they move until he counts a dozen, all with the same vibrant blue and extra large wings. Then they all suddenly vanish and he is alone.

He is near the river and moves quietly through the undergrowth till he reaches the bank. The waters are sluggish and it is still early for the caimans and the other water creatures to be active although he can sense he is being watched. There is a shimmering of something reflecting near the opposite bank and there seems to be something moving over there but he can't make out what it is. Perhaps it is an anaconda or another snake. He continues downriver, stepping carefully within the foliage, trying to remain unseen, but still keeping a look out on the opposite side, as there might be another tribe out looking to hunt and he wouldn't want them to become aware of him.

It is a gorgeous day and he travels a long way, feeling so right with the world. There are plenty of berries to pick and he cuts into a large bulbous leaf to drink from the water it contains. It is his land, his forest, he belongs here and it is a place to live and be at peace. Then he hears the strange humming, as if a million bees were angrily buzzing around some intruder. He reaches nearer and the noise becomes louder, more insistent, more threatening. Blending into the ferns and vines surrounding the trees he edges cautiously forward. His first instinct had been to go back and leave but he needs to see. Now he can hear voices, noisily shouting above the humming. Then his heart freezes, they are here as well. A large, circular area of forest has been cleared already and a machine full of savage intent is being used by one huge man to saw at another tree, which starts to topple even as he watches. This is the cause of the humming. There are several piles of cut tree trunks rolled to one side and four other men with metal hats are shouting about something, in a language he can't understand. Each one has a gun stuck in his belt. They are enemies of the forest and are therefore his enemies. Immediately he inserts a dart, raises his blowgun and gets ready to aim. Now. Do it now, kill. Then he lowers it again, uncertain as to how and whether to proceed. He could kill one, probably two but then they would know he had seen them and would come after him. They are very strong, they control the machines, they are more powerful than the jaguar and the anaconda and he could never know what they could do. They might be able to find him and take his family away. It had happened before, to others of other tribes. Two blue butterflies dance daintily towards them, only to be waved aggressively away. They obviously have no forest soul. They are here only to take, to destroy and to leave nothing of value behind. The sun has stopped shining, replaced by a line of spreading darkness stretching eagerly towards him. Now he must move his family again, to find a deeper hiding place. What will happen when there are no more places left in which to hide?

APPENDIX 1

LUCKY THIRTEEN

A s the creatures that pushed Charles Darwin to the edge, making him suddenly realise what he had discovered and enabling his theory of natural selection to become a reality, the Galapagos finches definitely deserve a bird note all of their own. They are rightly called Darwin's Finches, in homage to an original thinker who dared to question and who, as an early theologian himself, was only too aware of the dramatic and traumatic effects his findings would cause. That's possibly why he hesitated for so many years and why he was so reluctant to publish his findings. Who knows, if Alfred Russell Wallace's own writings hadn't pushed him into action, whether he would have even told the world his startling theories. How many times, over so many years, Darwin must have stared at the stuffed sets of finches and wondered if he dared. An eagle yes, a cormorant perhaps, a booby possibly but the humble finch! This was his inspiration to change and challenge the world!

There are finches on most islands and there are several varieties on the same island, with often a minute change in their physiognomy being the difference between one species and another. There are 13 species within the Archipelago and the subtle adaptations evolved were eventually the final proof Darwin needed to convince himself before he could try to convince others. Possibly the finch, which started his brain reeling with the possibility of what it could mean, is the sharp-beaked ground finch (*Geospiza difficilis*) found only on the northern Darwin (Culpepper) and Wolf (Wenman) Islands. This is the 'dracula' or 'vampire' of the finches, as it sips the blood of nesting boobies and frigate birds by perching on their backs and with its 'sharp beak' puncturing through their wing or tail feathers. They surprisingly don't seem to mind, and perhaps even view it as a form of bird acupuncture or even bloodletting, which would encourage healthy bird living. They certainly don't seem to suffer any harm and don't resist the intrusion. However not content with taking blood, the sharp beaks also steal their eggs when they aren't looking; that seems a little too sharp!

The toolers of the finches are the woodpecker finch (*Cactospiza pallida*) and the mangrove finch (*Cactospiza heliobates*). They use twigs and cactus spines they have fashioned into their own sharpened tools in order to tap into trees and cacti to extract wood boring insects like grubs and termites. They have an amazing ability rare amongst birds, to use something to provide them with the means of carrying out a required task. There is then the vegetarian finch (*Platyspiza crassirostris*) which has the largest body of them all and it has a very sharp cutting beak to accomplish its mission. The cactus finch (*Geospiza scandens*) and the large cactus finch, bigger than the other, (*Geospiza conirostris*) actually living on different islands, have very long sharp beaks to enable it to pierce the cactus flower and later in the season the cactus fruit, without causing injury to itself. The large-beaked ground finch (*Geospiza magnirostris*) cracks the hard seeds and nuts that other finches would find impossible, and by contrast the small-beaked ground finch (*Geospiza fulginosa*) concentrates on the easier grass seeds. There are also the medium-beaked ground species (*Geospiza fortis*) that goes for the seeds and nuts that aren't too big and aren't too small and they consider 'just right'.

Sounds rather like some kind of 'three bear Goldilocks' complex.

Guess what the grass-eating warbler finch (*Certhidea olivacea*) likes. Well not totally, it also has the special trick of eating the ticks off the backs of iguanas and giant tortoises, enjoying the blood content as an added source of protein. It doesn't tick the igs and torts off though, as the warbler reaches the parts that others can't and they become quite complicit in the ritual by standing stiff-legged to raise their bodies for inspection and this special dry-cleaning service. There are three sizes of tree finches (in descending order, *Camarhynchus psittacula*, *Camarhynchus pauper* and *Camarhynchus parvulus*) living primarily in the higher areas where trees and tall shrubs grow more easily, whereas the different species of the darker ground finches live in the arid scrubland regions. Thirteen can be an unlucky number for some, but in Darwin's case it proved to be the opposite and indeed in this special circumstance for most of us. In this case at least, this number thirteen has definitely helped to unlock some of the major mysteries of life.

Mr and Mrs Finch should also take a bow and surely deserve to be ranked amongst the upper echelons of the bird world, for the integral part they have played in Darwin's theory of natural selection. Rightfully they have jumped up the bird queue and rather than being 'commoners' they are now truly 'blue bloods'.

APPENDIX 2

EL NIÑO

I n recent years there have been constant references
to the awesome power of El Niño and the tragedies
it continues to cause, and the Galapagos Islands and
the mainland of Ecuador have also suffered considerably
from its terrible forces. It occurs because of a drastic
change in weather patterns, which in turn have a dramatic
effect on tides and winds and will invariably create havoc
and devastation on those areas, both inland and offshore,
that are affected. Inland, villages, roads, trees, animals
and people can be badly harmed and even destroyed and
offshore ships, small boats, coral reefs, sea creatures and
people can also suffer similarly.

El Niño translates as 'the Christ Child' or 'the Young
Boy', and the name originates because that's what the
fishermen of Peru called the arrival of the warmer waters
that would arrive in from the ocean around Christmas
time. At that time it was primarily welcomed, which is why
the effect was given such a benign and religious name at
the outset, but now it has come to signify an onslaught of
unpredictable weather conditions which can bring death
and misery to thousands, if not millions, of people. There
are records of these changes and 'storms' occurring as far
back as the sixteenth century but only recently has this
weather phenomenon been identified and documented.

The name of El Niño all over the world has now taken
on a much darker and frightening aspect. Previously an El
Niño occurred rarely, perhaps every few years, but now

it occurs more frequently and seemingly with increasing ferocity. There is also a domino effect from an El Niño occurring in one area, as it causes equivalent effects in other areas, which compound the general destructions taking place. The basis of the force unleashed is related to the balance in atmospheric pressures between the Eastern Equatorial Pacific and the Indo-Australian regions, with one set of pressures rising as the other set falls and vice versa. Previously it seemed to be reasonably well balanced so there were few occasions when the weather conditions were 'abnormal'. It is known as the Southern Oscillation and was an acceptable part of the weather patterns of the world. Now it seems that this gentler seesaw effect that used to occur is more like a pendulum gathering increasing speed with massive changes inevitably taking place. When the trade winds fall the layers of warm waters of the West Pacific are pushed back across the ocean thereby warming the East Pacific and cooling the West Pacific. This generally allows air temperatures to even out across the whole Pacific and the trade winds lessen. If however this is occurring at this 'abnormal' rate of change, the effects are more profound and extreme and as the warmer waters continue to spread across the Eastern Pacific the Western Pacific waters become even colder and the rainfall intensifies and lashes the South American coastlines.

The reverse is then also happening elsewhere as little rainfall is occurring in other places. This warmer water effect pushes the cold Humboldt Current deeper which then starts to kill off huge numbers of fish and this reduces the food supplies for birds and mammals, many of which will die as a consequence. There is then a traumatic chain reaction throughout the regions affected and this will cause considerable damage to the marine infrastructure as well as resulting in loss of life for all creatures. If the Southern Oscillation happens in a more violent way than usual there is a knock on effect to all of the world's weather systems, often with far ranging results. It is argued with some validity that the increasing effect of El Niño and therefore also a more pronounced Southern Oscillation, is a direct result of the global warming generally agreed to be taking place. The greenhouse effect is actually shown nowhere to be more potent than in the colossal destruction occurring within the rainforest. Nature's 'greenery' is being replaced by huge open spaces created for cattle grazing, oil drillings and farming, whether for animals, fruit, vegetables or shrimps! The failure of 'civilised' society to limit and reduce the emissions of greenhouse gases is nothing short of a calamity and we, whether our skins are white, yellow, brown or black, may well be known as 'the savages' by future generations if they are allowed to be the future generations.

The Galapagos Archipelago is obviously very exposed within the Pacific Ocean and the islands have suffered from a vicious El Niño on a number of occasions. The worst in living memory was undoubtedly the one taking place in 1982/1983, when over 3,400 millimetres of rainfall occurred and many islands were flooded.

This compares with a usual annual rainfall of less than 400 millimetres. The sea water rose by approximately ten degrees as a consequence, which in turn reduced the nutrients available to the fish. They consequently moved further offshore, thereby limiting the fish stock available to the birds. The flightless cormorants were particularly badly hit as a result, their numbers decreasing to half, and the penguins totally dependent on catching fish in shallow waters decreased by three-quarters. The marine iguanas also decreased by half as vast numbers starved because the oxygen-depleted and nutrient-deficient waters couldn't provide the algae which they relied on. The sea lions also suffered tremendously, with the sea cows abandoning their pups as they were forced to search further afield in order to try and find food. Many bulls also died as they lost their strength and then tried unsuccessfully to achieve dominance as before over a herd on the beach. It wasn't totally bad news however, as the vegetation and plants grew in greater abundance and this encouraged the appetites of the insect kingdom which seemed to expand enormously, although it proved too difficult to organise a census. The tortoises and those birds, such as mockingbirds and the Darwin finches, normally eating green leaves also did rather well, as there were extra rations for all. However this growth of plants and vegetation also resulted in the nests of the waved albatross becoming covered up, so no new chicks could be hatched and its population seriously declined the next season. The marine iguana also suffered considerably when their sea weed diet was vastly reduced as it was decimated by the algae created.

The El Niño of 1997/1998 was also very serious but this time was equally devastating, if not more so, to the mainland. In the Galapagos the rainfall again hit the 3,400 millimetres levels with the marine iguana numbers again suffering badly and reducing to half, similarly the number of sea lions dropped drastically away. Penguin numbers were again devastated and again reduced by three-quarters. There was however a very disturbing effect of this particular El Niño, as many new insects, especially ants, were carried in on the powerful winds to the islands. Fire ants attacked the nests of some of the giant tortoises, breaking into their eggs and preventing the babies from hatching. If the number of new introduced insect species continues in this way it can seriously affect the existing order of creatures throughout the Archipelago and upset the balance which has taken centuries to achieve. It's not right to argue an El Niño is just a force of nature and whatever will be, will be, if its force is totally exacerbated by the actions of human beings.

On the mainland there were tremendous floods and landslides, killing over 200 people, many of them children and many thousands of families were made homeless. Bridges and roads were washed away to cause absolute chaos over many months and the damaged infrastructure still has to be repaired in many cases. Disease of course was widespread through the infected waters entering reservoirs and water systems as well as lakes and rivers, thereby affecting fish stock. In fact many parts of the world were similarly affected, which only goes to emphasise how dependent we all are on one another and the actions of others, sometimes only a relative few, can affect so many more. We should have warnings stamped across things, not only on cigarette packets, something to the effect that, 'Your Actions Can Destroy Future Lives.'

APPENDIX 3

PROTECTING THE FUTURE

E cuador has an enlightened policy (mostly) to protect its wonderful treasure house of fauna and flora and has designated more than 17 per cent of its small country as protected National Parks, Reserves and Special Areas, covering over 46,000 square kilometres (nearly 18,000 square miles). Included within many Parks and Reserves are most of the high mountains, so they can be also kept under appropriate protection. They also provide tremendous trekking opportunities in wild and not so wild countryside; it's always great fun and certainly eye-opening to see a number of extraordinary creatures roaming freely in the forests and across the grasslands. That's probably from the animal's perspective as well. There are 10 main National Parks and 14 Nature Reserves and several other important areas, covering overall an immense area of nearly 5 million hectares of land and over 14 million hectares of water and the most important include the following:

Cotopaxi National Park is 60 kilometre (44 miles) to the south of Quito and covers over 34,000 hectares (84,000 acres). It's split between the Cotopaxi, Pichincha and Napo Provinces. This is the mainland's most exquisite Park and is full of wonderful flora and fauna, including pumas, wolves, condors, wild horses, llamas and deer (usually trying to avoid becoming puma dinner). There are also dwarf deer and marsupial mice. Within it of course is the world renowned Cotopaxi Mountain, 5,897 metres (19,347 feet), the highest active snow-capped volcano in the world. It's accepted to be the most beautiful of all Ecuador's mountains. The Park also contains the Limpiopungo Lagoon where it's possible to see many kinds of birds including waterfowl, as well as the jet black toad with its orange underbelly. The lagoon is very near Carachaloma Mountain (4,068 metres) and not too far from the Rumiñahui Volcano, whose main Central Peak is 4,712 metres (15,492 feet), combining with the slightly lesser North and South Peaks. The mountain of Morurco (4,850 metres) is also here, just south of Cotopaxi and several others including Chiguilasin Chico, a rather enjoyable and non taxing climb. There are some important and interesting Inca ruins at Pucara. Also at the foot of Cotapaxi Mountain is the Inca palace built by Tupac-Yupanquil in the fifteenth century, which was turned into a monastery two centuries later by the Augustine Catholic Order.

Sangay National Park is 280 kilometres (174 miles) from Quito and covers nearly 500,000 hectares (1,235,000 acres) and is in three provinces, Tungurahua, Chimborazo and Morona Santiago. It is accessed from the Pan-American Highway at Riobamba. The northern area is a World Heritage Site. It has extensive flora and fauna and is named after its highest mountain, the Sangay Mountain 5,230 metres (17,154 feet), an existing active and often non-climbable volcano. Also included in the Park are two other powerful volcanic mountains, Altar 5,320 metres (17,446 feet) and Tungurahua 5,029 metres (16,452 feet). Animals include the endangered mountain tapir, the spectacled bear and the ocelot. There is also the giant otter, the jaguar, the gazelle, the condor and the largest hummingbird in the world. The rivers are stocked with fish and there are many types of amphibians. The Quichua-Canelos indigenous Indians live in the north and the Shuar indigenous Indians in the south.

Yasuni National Park is also one of the largest parks with over 545,000 hectares (1,350,000 acres) and is 305 kilometres (190 miles) from Quito, sited in the Napo Province. Its biosphere reserve has the largest bio-diversity in Ecuador with some endemic plants which have continued growing there since the Pleistocene Period (around 20,000 BC). Over 700 species of vegetation, 500 bird species and 200 different animal species have been identified. The indigenous Indian tribe, the Huaoranis are known to live within the Napo River embankments, but you will not find them too easily and be careful they don't find you first. They have a number of well-founded grievances and sometimes want to share their grief. The Tiputini, Cononaco, Nashino and Yasuni River basins are also part of their secluded habitats and they are always ready to move on to avoid intrusions. Some of the wonderful creatures to be experienced (at a distance) include jaguars, harpy eagles, king buzzards and crocodiles. Also piranhas, catfish and very colourful and ornamental fish can be found in great quantities.

Cajas National Recreation Park is 520 kilometres (323 miles) away from Quito but only 37 kilometres (23 miles) from Cuenca and its area covers over 29,000 hectares (71,000 acres) It has over 230 lakes of glacial origin, connected to each other by streams or small rivers. Two rivers around Cuenca commence here, the Tomebamba and the Yanuncay. Here there are spectacled bears, pumas, the Andean tapir, the white-tailed deer and the *páramos* deer and countless rabbits. The bird species include the grey-breasted Andean toucan, the spectacled duck, the snipe, the condor and the caracara. The Incan site in the area of Molleturo is believed to be a resting place (known as a tambo) used by the Inca messengers running from Cuzco in Peru to Quito (or Quitu as it then was known).

Llangantes National Park is one of the most inaccessible and hostile landscapes in the whole of Ecuador and has numerous lagoons, waterfalls, large valleys and wild moorlands, with dense and tall vegetation stretching everywhere. It's great machete country but don't swing it too wildly and keep control at all times, as it can prove to be a very dangerous weapon if used incorrectly. As jazz music maestro Louis Armstrong always said, 'It don't mean a thing if you don't have the swing.' A compass is also essential as are long rubber boots, as your trekking boots will quickly accumulate too much mud and you'll soon feel as if you're dragging heavy weights around with you. It's actually easy to get really bogged down, literally, as there are many bogs, which will suck you in and welcome you with open legs. You will come across the dwarf quinus trees and there are all kinds of mosses and lichens, mushrooms and fungi to be found everywhere. An abundance of moorland rabbits should provide great opportunities for sightings, weather permitting and there are also the jungle (sacha) rabbits and weasels. Although not very common you may come across the spectacled bear, the puma, the moorland fox, the tapir, the condor and the moorland and white-tailed deer. The highest mountain in this area is Cerro Hermoso 4,571 metres (15,618 feet), which for the reasons explained is very infrequently climbed. To actually spell it out, it's because you will sink frequently into black, squelching, stinking mud, trekking on your way to reach Hermoso. If you're lucky the weather will occasionally clear and Hermoso will live up to its name, which surprisingly translates as 'Beautiful Mountain.' There is a relatively unknown mountain range called Sacha Llanganates, it's not been officially measured and little is actually known about it and the surrounding area. If you want to explore uncharted territory, then this is definitely the place and there are all kinds of flora to discover and possibly name after yourself, your loved ones or even your favourite schoolmaster.

Rumoured to be hidden in this region and long sought by explorers and adventurers is the buried gold of the last Inca warrior emperor, Atahualpa. Clues to where his gold is hidden are contained within this book and any reader finding his treasure must share it with the author and the publishers (they made me put that last part in).

Sumaco-Napo-Galleras National Park has an area in excess of 205,000 hectares (506,000 acres). It contains the Napo-Galeras mountain range, cut across by numerous rivers and deep valleys. with its highest peak being the Sumaco Volcano at 3,900 metres (12,792 feet), which itself is surrounded by lowland forest and set well apart from the rest of the Andes mountains. It is a wilderness and has largely been left to its own devices, fortunately ignored by loggers and prospectors and this means it has remained a hidden region, potentially full of secrets and long may it be so. Endemic species are sometimes found there by the occasional visiting scientists and there is obviously much still to be discovered. A number of the mountains, not being of great height, seem never to have been climbed and this means again many creatures will probably be living around them in isolation and seclusion. This offers the exciting concept that the pristine forest and jungle areas here have provided wonderful opportunities for creatures of all kinds, as well as indeed exotic flora, to flourish untouched and unmolested for centuries. The regular tree types in the forest are rubber, cedar and canelo and the wide-ranging creature species include spectacled bears, armadillos, marsupials, eagles, bats, reptiles and many kinds of amphibians. Near to the Park there are several indigenous Indian tribal communities also living in isolation and nearby are various archaeological sites of the Cosanga Culture.

Podocarpus National Park has over 146,000 hectares (350,000 acres) and is over 700 kilometres (435 miles) from Quito, sited in Loja and Zamora Chinchipe Provinces. It includes over 100 lakes also containing many cascades and crystalline currents. The extensive fauna includes spectacled bears, tapirs, sloths, pumas, toucans, parrots, tanagers, hummingbirds, woodpeckers and many kinds of reptiles. There is also what is known as the Andean wolf, although it is actually a fox. Whenever a chicken is taken, the real culprit will blame it on the Andean fox, which in turn will blame it on always being misunderstood, because of the misnomer and will hope to just get off with a caution. That's what's known as being foxed. The Park is also brimming with sumptuous orchids of every colour and size, overwhelming everything with their heady fragrances. Podocarpus is the official name of a kind of very large conifer tree, native to Ecuador and can grow up to 40 metres and may have a trunk circumference of three metres. It was in danger of being destroyed by over zealous loggers but fortunately the remaining specimens in the park are well protected. The mining operations once very active in this area have now also been drastically scaled back.

San Jorge Botanical Reserve is only 4 kilometres (2.5 miles (away from Quito along the old road which goes to Nono (yes it does). It comprises 150 hectares (375 acres) of virgin Highland tropical rainforest containing over 250 native plants, some 80 species of birds and numerous mammals, marsupials and rodents. It also contains 15 natural waterfalls. There are some worthwhile ancient Incan trails leading to Nono (I've already done that joke), to Mindo and to Calacali where the second official Monument to the Centre of the World stands.

Limoncocha Ecological Reserve is located 370 kilometres (229 miles) from Quito in Napo Province and covers over 4,600 hectares (12,000 acres). An indigenous Quichua tribe lives in the Reserve which contains vast tracts of jungle vegetation, primary and secondary forests and majestic rivers. The reserve includes the Laguna Limoncocha. It is home to approximately 350 bird species, many mammals and reptiles and it's famed for being the home of the black caiman.

Pululahua Geo-Botanic Reserve is in the Pichincha Province and is just 40 kilometres (25 miles) from Quito and its area covers 3,400 hectares (8,400 acres). On the mountain, using the Mirador de Ventanilla (small window lookout) there is a spectacular view of the Pichincha Crater. In the Reserve the many varieties of birds include hummingbirds, tanagers, toucans, owls, flycatchers and gulls. The animal species include ocelot, gazelles, *páramos* wolves, armadillos and spiny rats. A large variety of trees can be found including walnut, palm, alder and laurel. There are also many varieties of orchid and of course the *páramos* grasses and various ferns.

Cuyabeno Fauna Production Reserve is in the Sucumbios Province, 314 kilometres (198 miles) from Quito. It is another of the largest reserves covering over 655,000 hectares (1,600,000 acres). It includes parts of the Cuyabeno and Aguarico Rivers and is between the basins of the San Miguel and Aguarico. There are numerous lagoons, swamps and flooded areas where the Siona indigenous Indians prefer to live and there are supervised opportunities to visit them. Extensive bird varieties including macaws, trumpeters, herons, fisher eagles and king buzzards. Exceptionally noteworthy is the pink dolphin. The larger creatures include jaguar, ocelot, boar, monkey, otter and manatee. In the rivers and around them are caiman and snakes and various fish species and the insects are particularly plentiful and varied. The flora and fruits include ivory nut, chambira, chonta palm, wild roses and grapes. Within the reserve are huge tracts of tropical rainforest and massive lakes including the Zancudococha.

Cayambe-Coca Ecological Reserve is approximately 100 kilometres (60 miles) from Quito and has an area of over 400,000 hectares (950,000 acres) and contains the snow-capped Cayambe Volcano and other smaller mountains including Cerro Sara Urco, Cerro Negro Rumi and Volcano Reventador. There are condors, hawks and caracaras. It includes the Cayapas, Santiago and Esmeraldas Rivers and Lake Cuicocha. North-east from Cayambe is Laguna San Marcos, which is naturally well-stocked with trout and because of this is a popular haunt of fishermen from all over the world. Nearby, closer to Caymbe it's possible to see the elusive mountain tapir and also in the same vicinity are deer, foxes and the Andean spectacled bear. You can find, although with difficulty, armadillos and without difficulty large numbers of rabbits. That's why the foxes are so happy. The primary forests and *páramos* provide support for the fauna and also the extensive vegetation. The Reserve contains the larger Laguna Puruhanta, also extremely popular with fishermen.

Chimborazo Fauna Production Reserve is approximately 175 kilometres (109 miles) from Quito and covers an area of 59, 000 hectares (145,000 acres). It naturally contains the tallest mountain, Chimborazo at 6,310 metres

(20,703 feet). There are now in operation important new llama and vicuna and alpaca breeding programmes. There are also sword-billed hummingbirds and condors. Also pumas, wolves, deer and rabbits as well as marsupial rats can be found, if you look hard enough but you probably want to give the rats a miss. The sacred plant of the Incas, Quinua, also grows in this region and is part of the staple diet of the local Indian tribes.

The Galapagos National Park and Marine Recreation Reserve is in the Archipelago and has absolutely the most astounding fauna and flora of all. It is 1,000 kilometres (622 miles) from the mainland and you can get there by ships, boats or planes or by any other means you can conceive. Just get there.

APPENDIX 4

ECUADOR'S MOUNTAINS

The Andean mountain range as it is now known was created at the beginning of the Pliocene period around five million years ago, which makes it relatively 'young' in geological terms. There is even an older rock history prior to the creation of the existing range which dates back a further 20 million years and forms a substrata. The Andes stretch the full length of the South American continent from Panama and Venezuela to Patagonia and Cape Horn, covering in total 7,250 kilometres (4,500 miles). They contain the highest mountains outside Asia. There are volcanoes, active and non-active, huge rock monoliths and ice-capped mountains, all testing rock and ice climbs, magnificent to view and experience on all levels.

Ecuador is divided north to south by its Andean Cordillera (Cordillera de Los Andes), so dividing the mainland of Ecuador into three major zones, the Andean and Sierra middle section itself, the Western coastal region and the Oriente (Eastern) jungle and rainforest region. The Galapagos Archipelago is considered the fourth region or zone of Ecuador but is of course set entirely apart from the three connected mainland regions. The Cordillera divides itself within the Loja Provinces and splits into the Cordillera Occidental on the west and the Cordillera Oriente to the east, the higher and wider parts. The two Cordillera mountain ranges flank within them a relatively narrow land region which was named by the explorer and traveller Humboldt in 1802 as 'The Avenue of the Volcanoes' and has ever since been referred to with that evocative description. The Highlands experience their rainy season mainly between November to April and the remaining months are 'dry' but the weather patterns throughout can be unpredictable, so it's necessary to go prepared.

Ecuador is a totally challenging country whether travelling in its valleys, across its plains or climbing on its high mountains. There are 280 volcanoes, 18 of which are potentially active and some 25 mountain peaks over 4,000 metres (14,000 feet), 10 over the snowline, 5,000 metres (16,000 feet), all of them difficult and tough, particularly because of the necessity to climb at altitude. Chimborazo at over 6,000 metres (over 20,000 feet) is higher than any point between Alaska and central Peru. I knew it would be an extreme testing of my resolve and fitness and I needed to climb at lower altitude first to have a chance of summiting 'the big one'. The valleys and rivers inside the Avenue of the Volcanoes (also known as the Highland Basins) promote some exceedingly rich flora and fauna, helped previously with their evolving because of the special mountain protection provided. No rivers run down the length of the Avenue of Volcanoes, most of them running to the East and the Amazonas, although a few run to the West and the coastal region. The Andean highlands and moorlands (the *páramos*) are covered with pillow-like grasses and all kinds of interesting vegetation. It is also a place to beware of bears and to be concerned of cougars. The mountain or woolly tapirs are also found there but will usually leave you alone, unless you try to remove their jumpers. They are cleverer than they look and you will find it hard to pull the wool over their eyes.

The Sierra region houses the Andean Cordillera and is probably regarded as the most dynamic of the three mainland regions, as its mountains have a collective powerful image which literally stands out in contrast to everything else. A mountain always has a spiritual element to its being and has invariably been worshipped or portrayed within most religions of whatever kind, as the place on which the words or messages of all the gods were created or where they could be found. The Ten Commandments brought down from Mount Sinai are probably the greatest influences that have shaped the behaviour of Mankind. The Andes are a set of jagged peaks which have not existed long enough to be rounded by erosion, so that their climbing is always difficult and is usually a painful though hopefully rewarding experience. Although it is said 'there's no gain without pain' sometimes there's just pain and the gain is illusory. Still it's the trying that's the most important, as in everything we do and attempting to climb a mountain personifies that act more than most things. Set your mind towards the mountain and you will be surprised what it has in store for you. I won't try to describe what that can be, a surprise is a surprise.

As the Earth in recent years has continued to get progressively warmer, one of the benefits (though there are more disadvantages) is that more vegetation grows on what was once barren scrubland and it's always a delight suddenly, climbing on the lower rock slopes, to come across some colourful mountain flowers. However, it also means the lower ice slopes are receding and where you might have only found snow and ice, stalactites and crevasses, there are just huge areas of scree and naked rock to cross. It is tougher on the feet and the legs, although possibly slightly safer but this can make the climbing more difficult and hazardous. In 1880 when Edward Whymper tried to climb El Altat he reached ice seracs in the Collanes Valley; Hans Meyer of Kilimanjaro fame sketched Altar showing huge glaciers; other mountaineers as recently as the 1970s practised ice climbing of the Antizana glacier; all the ice has now disappeared and only rock and scrubland exist there. There is an imperceptible but seemingly unstoppable upward advance of vegetation, also bringing with it a variety of insects, hummingbirds, bats and many other creatures. Even farmers have started planting their potatoes and other root crops at heights undreamed of only a few decades earlier. Where will it end? Will the last snow-caps continue to shrink and disappear altogether? The retreat of the glaciers changes the face of mountaineering and perhaps climbing will eventually be over rock and lava faces only? The repercussions for the planet as a whole are enormous and way beyond the challenges mountaineers may have to forego. Every time I climb I learn from my guides or fellow climbers, that this route has changed, this pass is now impassable or that this ice couloir has become a dangerous rock face instead. Of course the harm and devastation caused to the jungles and the mountains are inextricably linked and no where is that more apparent than in this country where both are continually at risk.

A number of volcanic eruptions have continued to occur amongst the Ecuadorian mountains, mostly minor but also one or two big ones, which can cause death and destruction to people as well as the extraordinary fauna and flora that is such an integral part of this country. Reventador (3,562 metres) in 2002 erupted with a fury that saw the nearby capital city of Quito completely engulfed in black smoke and ash. Quito had also suffered previously in 1999, when Guagua Pichincha (4,794 metres) sent eleven-kilometre clouds of ash spiralling skywards only for a large part to fall onto the city itself. In that same year Tungurahua (5,016 metres) also sent a stream of lava bubbling down its mighty flanks, forcing locals to flee and evacuate their homes. Sangay (5,230 metres), the most active of all the volcanoes, is likely to blow its top at any time and local guides themselves are always extremely reluctant to lead anyone more than onto the lower slopes. The lava spills and outcrops are black and red and all combinations of the two colours and cover the underlying rocks and terrain as if springing from a Martian-type other world. Nothing can live in the path of lava and the sulphur gases emitted from the volcanoes can suffocate all those unfortunate enough to be forced to breathe in their fumes.

All the mountains in Ecuador are high and the conditions on them, as with most other mountains throughout the world, are becoming more treacherous because of global warming. There are many new, exposed and extensive rock stretches visible amongst what used to be ice sections only, which can cause tremendous dangers even to the most experienced climbers and no one should ever climb here without experienced guides and back-up. The effect of global warming is a tragedy on so many levels and the rate is escalating at an enormous rate and may even now be too late to control. The rainforest similarly is also under threat from global warming and some consider this to be as terrible a danger as the threat from the voracious loggers, developers and prospectors.

A number of Ecuador's mountains are snow-capped but they are unfortunately reducing fast, as global warming wreaks its damaging effects on the mountains, as well as the rainforests, jungles and other natural habitats and on all their creatures, including of course mankind. As well as occurring at an alarming rate in the polar regions, where it is possible to find whole ice sections melting almost before your eyes, when you revisit any mountain you invariably now find you have to climb much higher to reach the snow line and then it really strikes home just what we have allowed to happen. If the mountain could speak what would it try to teach us and are we ever prepared to learn. Judging by our previous record it seems extremely unlikely. A volcanic mountain speaks in its own way and perhaps we will only finally understand the enormity of the situation when enough violent eruptions have taken place. It could be one of Nature's ways of trying to warn us of the terrible damage continually being caused by uncontrolled commercial acts of great folly. The destructive effects from El Niño on a more constant and harsher basis, the terrible consequences of the devastating tsunami of 2004, the re-occurring earthquakes which strike more often in various regions of the world, these are all signs. We ignore them at our peril.

Mountains are not static objects but move and react constantly. Ancient civilisations knew that and every mountaineer knows that as well. When you climb on a mountain you are there as a guest and at any time the mountain if it chooses can shake you off. When you hold onto a stone that seems to have been imbedded in the rock face for many thousands of years, it can suddenly come away in your hand and you may be looking into the void. When you step onto a bed of seemingly hard ice, it may give way beneath your feet and you can be plunging into a crevasse measuring several hundred metres in depth. A clear day can swiftly and without warning turn into a blinding, swirling snowstorm.

Mountains have played an integral part in most ancient religions, as being holy places and from where good or bad news has emanated. They have been given their own persona and character and have been treated with reverence because of their beauty and their majesty as well as their powers. The 'gods' were meant to reside in them and because of that it was not considered right to climb too high in order not to disturb them. Climbing to the actual summits is a relatively recent pursuit of the last hundred years or so, initially mostly by 'foreigners' and the mysteries of most of the mountains have gradually been uncovered, although many still remain hidden.

In Ecuador the mountains are known as 'Apus' and every Ecuadorian acknowledges their history is all important, stretching way back to ancient times and they must always be respected. Some of the mountains have affectionate nicknames and are considered to have had emotions and feelings that have influenced their behaviour in the past, one to another and also to the Ecuadorians. Chimborazo has as his 'wife' the mountain of Tungurahua and when he discovered that she was having a love affair with El Altar he unleashed his full fury on them both and attacked their cones, causing them to break. Carihuairazo tried to mediate and for his pains Chimborazo also broke his cone. Chimborazo won't allow anything of that kind to happen again and uses his great height to keep careful watch on Tungurahua, who every so often can't contain her pent-up frustration and sends her fiery smoke billowing into the sky. Imbabura always had an eye for the young 'girls' but eventually decided to marry the nearby maiden mountain, Maria de las Nieves Cotocachi (Maria of the Snows of Cotocachi). They had a son, Yanaurco de Piñan who is still playing and growing next to his mother. Young Ecuadorian girls falling pregnant often would blame it on Imbabura as being the *taita* (the father). There are many more clandestine relationships between mountains but they want them kept secret and we must respect their wishes if we want to climb there again.

The heights of the highest mountains over 4,500 metres are listed although some of the smaller ones are just as interesting and many are based within the National Parks and Reserves, forming part of the natural habitats of those regions.

ECUADOR'S MOUNTAINS

Location	Metres	Feet
Chimborazo	6,310	20,703
Cotopaxi	5,897	19,348
Cayambe	5,790	18,997
Antizana	5,752	18,891
El Altar	5,319	17,451
Iliniza South (Sur)	5,248	17,218
Sangay	5,230	17,159
Iliniza North (Norte)	5,126	16,818
Tungurahua	5,029	16,500
Carihuairazo	5,020	16,470
Cotacachi	4,944	16,220
Sincholagua	4,898	16,070
Quilindaña	4,877	16,000
Guagua Pichincha	4,794	15,729
El Corazon	4,788	15,709
Chiles	4,723	15,495
Rumiñahui	4,712	15,460
Quilimas	4,719	15,483
Soroche	4,694	15,400
Ruca Pichincha	4,698	15,413
Soroche	4,694	15,400
Sara Urco	4,675	15,340
Imbabura	4,630	15,190
Archipungo	4,629	15,186
Cerro Hermoso	4,571	14,997
Quispicacacha	4,537	14,884

BIBLIOGRAPHY

An Anthology of Modern Verse edited by A. Methuen.
Published by Methuen & Methuen in 1921

Andes of Ecuador by Jorge Anhalzer.
Published by Imprenta Mariscal in Quito in 2000

Animal Life of the Galapagos by Norman Hickin.
Published by Ferendune Books in London in 1979

Around the World in 80 Days by Jules Verne.
Published by Sampson Low, Marston in London in 1873

Climbing and Hiking in Ecuador by Rachowiecki, Thurber and Wagenhauser.
Published by Bradt Publications in England in 1984

Ecuador & Galapagos Insight Guide edited by Pam Barrett.
Published by Apa Publications Gmbh & Co in Singapore in 1991

Ecuador in Focus by Wilma Roos and Omer van Renterghem.
Published by Interlink Publishing Group Inc in New York in 1997

Journey to the Centre of the Earth by Jules Verne
Published by Griffith and Farran in London in 1872

Longitude by Dava Sobel.
Published by Fourth Estate Ltd in London in 1996

One River: Explorations and Discoveries in the Amazon Rain Forest by Wade Davis.
Published by Simon and Schuster in New York 1996

Sangay Survived by Richard Snailham.
Published by Hutchinson & Co. in England in 1978

South America Called Them by Victor Von Hagen.
Published by Robert Hale Limited in London in1949

Spectacular Galapagos by Tui De Roy.
Published by Visual Communications in Washington in 1990

The Explorers of South America by Edward Goodman.
Published by the University of Oklahoma Press in Oklahoma in 1972

The Next Horizon by Chris Bonington.
Published by Victor Gollancz Ltd, London in 1990

The Origin of Species by Charles Darwin.
Published in London in 1859

The Voyage Of The Beagle by Charles Darwin.
Published in London in 1839

Travels Amongst the Great Andes of the Equator
by Edward Whymper.
Published by Gibbs Smith Inc in Salt Lake City in 1987
(Original publication in London in 1892)

Zen Explorations In Remotest New Guinea
by Neville Shulman.
Published by Summersdale Publishers in England in 1997

Zen In The Art Of Climbing Mountains
by Neville Shulman. UK Edition.
Published in England by Element Books in 1992

Zen In The Art Of Climbing Mountains
by Neville Shulman. US Edition.
Published in Boston by Charles Tuttle Company in 1992

www.summersdale.com